Henry VIII

PROFILES IN POWER

General Editor: Keith Robbins

Henry VIII

A Study in Kingship

Michael A. R. Graves

London • New York • Toronto • Sydney • Tokyo • Singapore
Hong Kong • Cape Town • Madrid • Paris • Amsterdam • Munich • Milan

PEARSON EDUCATION LIMITED

Head Office:
Edinburgh Gate
Harlow CM20 2JE
Tel: +44 (0)1279 623623
Fax: +44 (0)1279 431059
Website: www.pearsoned.co.uk

First edition published in Great Britain in 2003

© Pearson Education Limited 2003

The right of Michael A. R. Graves to be identified as Author
of this Work has been asserted by him in accordance
with the Copyright, Designs and Patents Act 1988.

ISBN 0 582 38110 X

British Library Cataloguing in Publication Data
A CIP catalogue record for this book can be obtained from the British Library

Library of Congress Cataloging in Publication Data
A CIP catalog record for this book can be obtained from the Library of Congress

10 9 8 7 6 5 4 3 2 1

Set in 9.5/12pt Celeste by Graphicraft Limited, Hong Kong
Printed and bound in Malaysia

The Publishers' policy is to use paper manufactured from sustainable forests.

Contents

Abbreviations

BIHR	*Bulletin of the Institute of Historical Research*
Cal. SP Span.	*Calendar of Letters, Despatches, and State Papers, relating to the Negotiations between England and Spain*
Cal. SP Ven.	*Calendar of State Papers and Manuscripts, relating to English Affairs existing in the archives and collections of Venice, and other libraries of Northern Italy*
CHJ	*Cambridge Historical Journal*
Eccles. Mems	*Ecclesiastical Memorials*
Econ. HR	*Economic History Review*
EHR	*English Historical Review*
Eng. Hist. Docs	*English Historical Documents*
Hist. Today	*History Today*
HJ	*Historical Journal*
HLQ	*Huntington Library Quarterly*
HLRO, Orig. Acts	*House of Lords Record Office, Original Acts*
JEH	*Journal of Ecclesiastical History*
LP	*Letters and Papers, Foreign and Domestic, of the Reign of Henry VIII*
PER	*Parliaments, Estates and Representation*
Stats Realm	*Statutes of the Realm*
TRHS	*Transactions of the Royal Historical Society*

Chronology

1485	Henry Tudor defeated and killed King Richard III at Bosworth and succeeded him as King Henry VII
1486	Henry VII married Elizabeth, daughter of King Edward IV; Prince Arthur born
1487	Princess Margaret born
1491	Prince Henry born
1494	Prince Henry invested as duke of York
1496	Princess Mary born
1501	Marriage of Prince Arthur and Princess Catherine of Aragon
1502	Prince Arthur died; Prince Henry became heir-apparent and was created duke of Cornwall
1503	Prince Henry's mother died; Henry was created prince of Wales; Princess Margaret married King James IV of Scotland; Prince Henry and Princess Catherine of Aragon signed betrothal treaty; a papal dispensation, permitting them to marry, was sought
1504	The papal dispensation was granted
1509	King Henry VII died and Prince Henry succeeded him as King Henry VIII; Richard Empson and Edmund Dudley were imprisoned; marriage and coronation of Henry and Catherine of Aragon; Henry's grandmother Margaret Beaufort, countess of Richmond, died
1510	Empson and Dudley were convicted and executed for treason
1511	Henry joined the anti-French Holy League; his first son, Henry, was born but died within eight weeks
1512	An unsuccessful expedition to conquer Aquitaine; Westminster Palace fire; statute restricted benefit of clergy
1513	Edmund earl of Suffolk executed; Henry invaded northern France; 'Battle of the Spurs'; capture of Thérouanne and Tournai; Wolsey made bishop of Tournai; Scottish army routed at Flodden and King James IV killed
1514	Anglo-French peace; Mary Tudor married King Louis XII of France; Wolsey made archbishop of York; Charles Brandon

1532	Statute suspended payment of annates to Rome; house of commons' Supplication against clergy; convocation's Submission of the Clergy
1533	Henry married pregnant Anne Boleyn; Thomas Cranmer appointed archbishop of Canterbury; Act in Restraint of Appeals; Cranmer annulled Henry's first marriage and confirmed his second marriage; Anne crowned; Princess Elizabeth born
1534	Payment of annates to Rome ended; Act for First Fruits and Tenths; Submission of the Clergy confirmed; First Succession Act; Act of Supremacy; new Treasons Act; Elizabeth Barton executed
1534–6	Reorganization of council
1535	Bishop Fisher and Thomas More executed; Thomas Cromwell's visitation of monasteries; first royal visitation of universities
1535–6	*Valor Ecclesiasticus* compiled
1535–46	Intermittent negotiations with German Lutheran princes
1536	Smaller monasteries dissolved; the Ten Articles; Statute of Uses; Franchises Act; Statute for Wales; Anne Boleyn tried and executed for adultery and incest; Henry married Jane Seymour; Second Succession Act; Lincolnshire rebellion; Pilgrimage of Grace; Henry jousted for the last time; Henry Fitzroy died
1536–7	Irish Reformation Parliament
1536/8	Injunctions ordered destruction of relics and forbade pilgrimages
1537	Prince Edward born; Jane Seymour died; *The Institution of a Christian Man* (or Bishops' Book) produced; Henry acquired Oatlands Palace; earl of Kildare and five uncles executed
1538	Henry presided at the trial of John Lambert; building of Nonsuch Palace began
1539	Henry authorized vernacular Bible; Act of Six Articles; second Act of Dissolution
1540	Act concerning True Opinions; Henry married Anne of Cleves; Thomas Cromwell attainted and executed; Henry's marriage to Anne annulled and he married Catherine Howard; Henry established five regius professorships at Cambridge University; new executive privy council became operative
1541	Execution of countess of Salisbury; Henry's only visit to York
1542	Henry resumed war with Scots; battle of Solway Moss; Catherine Howard attainted by statute and executed for

adultery; Henry re-founded Magdalene College at Cambridge University

1543   Henry married Catherine Parr; *Necessary Doctrine and Erudition of a Christian Man* (or King's Book) published; war with the French resumed; Catholics' attempt to secure Cranmer's fall; Second Statute for Wales

1544   Third Succession Act; Henry invaded France and captured Boulogne

1544–6   Debasements of coinage

1545   Henry commanded defence of southern English coast against attempted French landing; *Mary Rose* sank at Portsmouth; Act empowering Henry to dissolve colleges and chantries

1546   Henry re-founded Wolsey's Cardinal College at Oxford University as Christ Church, and founded Trinity College at Cambridge; Anne Askew burned; England and France made peace; duke of Norfolk and earl of Surrey imprisoned in Tower

1546–7   Henry's will finalized and sealed

1547   Surrey tried and executed for treason; Norfolk attainted by statute; death of King Henry

Chapter 1

Henry Tudor, Duke, Prince and King:
The Formative Years, 1491–1509

It should be emphasized at the outset that the following work is neither yet one more biography of King Henry VIII nor another history of his reign. It is a study of the priorities, techniques and style of kingship of one early modern monarch in a rapidly and dramatically changing world. Of course, king and man cannot be separated, especially in a system of personal monarchy. Consequently, much attention has to be given to Henry's personal foibles, weaknesses and inconsistencies as well as to his considered policies and long-term goals as king. As environment, family and personal experiences during the formative years all help to mould the adult, these need prior consideration. So too do his education and training for kingship.

The new king, 1509

On 27 May 1509 William Lord Mountjoy wrote to the humanist Erasmus from Greenwich Palace on the River Thames:

O, my Erasmus, if you could see how the world here is rejoicing in the possession of so great a prince, how his life is all their desire, you could not contain yourself for joy. . . . The other day he said to me, 'I wish I were more learned than I am.' 'That is not what we expect of your Grace,' I replied, 'but that you should foster and encourage learned men.' 'Yea, surely,' said he, 'for without them we should scarcely exist at all.' What more splendid saying could fall from the lips of a prince?[1]

One such learned man, Thomas More, wrote to his new king in celebration of the coronation:

You, Sire, have the wisdom of your father, your mother's kindly strength, the intelligence of your paternal grand-mother and the noble heart of your mother's father. What wonder then if England rejoices since she has such a King as never before?[2]

Another Englishman, Edward Hall, described Henry Tudor as he observed him in the opening weeks of his reign in 1509:

The features of his body, his godly personage, his amiable vysage, princely countenaunce, with the noble qualities of his royall estate, to every man knowen, nedeth no rehersall, consideryng that, for lacke of cunnyng, I cannot express the giftes of grace and of nature, that God hath endowed hym with all.[3]

Such were the accolades heaped upon this careless, irresponsible seventeen-year-old prince, when he succeeded his father Henry VII as King Henry VIII in April 1509. Little if anything of significance could have been known about him abroad, in the courts and conclaves of Europe. Unlike privileged insiders, such as Mountjoy and More, who had court experience and contacts, the great mass of the new monarch's subjects can have had little knowledge or awareness of him. In 1509 he strode out from the royal seclusion in which he had been nurtured on to centre-stage, where he proceeded to dazzle a national audience. Although many of his subjects would never see him, his reputation, enhanced by his skill in image projection, spread throughout the kingdom.[4] Furthermore, he would soon become familiar to Europe's princes and popes by his diplomatic activity and military excursions: in brief, by his obsessive desire to 'cut a dash' and earn the plaudits of observers on both the national and international scenes.

The Yorkist threat

The commencement of Henry VIII's reign in 1509 marked the beginning of the *second* stage in the nation's recovery from a prolonged, divisive, sometimes bloody dynastic conflict, the so-called 'Wars of the Roses'. There was, of course, no guarantee that, when Henry Tudor of Lancaster defeated King Richard III of York at Bosworth in 1485, the conflict was over. In the same year parliament enacted that 'thenheretaunce of the Corounez of the Realmes of England and of Fraunce . . . rest, remayne and abyde in the most Royall person of oure nowe Soveraign Lord King Henry the [Seventh] and in the heires of his body laufully comyng'.[5] Nevertheless, rebellion, conspiracy and Yorkist pretenders to the crown characterized the first half of Henry VII's reign. National and dynastic stability strengthened with the passing of the years, but personal insecurity remained with the first of the Tudor kings. That sense of insecurity was reinforced by the poor breeding record of the Tudors and by the continuing threat posed by the de la Pole brothers, Edmund and Richard, who were genuine Yorkist claimants to the crown. Although Henry VII's Court and kingship were, in many ways, characteristic of the new-style, self-confident and even ebullient Renaissance monarchy, the long, dark shadows of late medieval English dynastic division and ambition were slow to recede.

It was in this uncertain, at times stressful, political and personal environment that the future Henry VIII grew up. The extent to which it affected his political attitudes and priorities as king must always be a matter of speculation. Sometimes, however, the cause–effect relationship is fairly clear. Edmund de la Pole, earl of Suffolk, who was arrested whilst travelling in the Low Countries, was handed over to Henry VII by King Philip of Castile in 1506. He lived out the first Tudor's reign in the Tower of London and was then exempted from the general pardon which Henry VIII issued on his accession. When, in 1513, the second Tudor prepared to invade France, he decided that it was too dangerous to leave a legitimate Yorkist claimant alive. Suffolk was duly executed. It was an early instance of the blood-letting which was to become such a familiar feature of Henry VIII's kingship. When Edward Stafford, duke of Buckingham, was brought to trial and executed in 1521, the official and legal justification was that he 'imagined and compassed traitorously and unnaturally the destruction of the most royal person of our said sovereign Lord', the king. The actual purpose, however, was to shed dangerous royal blood. As Buckingham's biographer concluded,

The duke threatened Henry VIII in only one way: as a potential claimant to the throne in the event that Henry left no male heir. . . . This dynastic consideration was the key to the king's decision to prosecute the duke for treason.[6]

The reign of King Henry VII: (1) 1491–1502

The *first* stage in England's recovery from the lengthy though intermittent conflict between Lancaster and York was the reign of the first Tudor, Henry VII (1485–1509). His marriage to Elizabeth of York was designed to secure the succession, partly as a healing and bonding alliance between the two houses and especially, of course, by the provision of heirs. Some of their children died in infancy, but four survived to marriageable age: Arthur (born in 1486), Margaret (in 1489), Mary (1496) and the future

Henry VIII, who was born at Greenwich Palace on 28 June 1491. Little is known about the first decade of Henry's life, apart from the fact that he was showered with honours and offices: warden of the Cinque Ports and constable of Dover Castle; earl marshal; lord lieutenant of Ireland; duke of York; knight of the Bath; Order of the Garter; and warden of the Scottish marches – all before he was five years old.

Much is known about his investiture as duke of York in October 1494. A surviving narrative record of the event parades an elaborate, colourful, sumptuous and spectacular sequence of dining, feasting and jousting. Whilst this event was unlikely to have had a significant impact on the three-year-old Henry, he was much more aware and, indeed, involved in the extraordinary celebrations which accompanied the marriage of Prince Arthur and Princess Catherine of Aragon in 1501. On 14 November he led Catherine's procession to St Paul's Cathedral and, after the wedding ceremony, he escorted her forth. Between the wedding day and 25 November a riotous succession of extravagant banquets, disguisings, 'divers and many goodly dances' and jousting entertained guests and, at the same time, attracted the attention of the greater world outside Westminster. Courtiers provided the support structure for this display of royal magnificence. So, on one occasion, twelve disguised nobles and a dozen ladies played lutes, harps, recorders, clavichords, dulcimers and other musical instruments on separate carnival floats. In another disguising a pageant car was drawn into the tournament arena by 'four great beasts': two lions, one gold and the other silver, a hart and an ibex. Each 'beast' concealed two men, 'oon in the fore parte, and another in the hynde parte'.[7] The ten-year-old duke also attracted much favourable attention during the celebrations when he tossed away his robe and danced in his jacket with his sister Margaret.

The focus of the wedding celebrations was a week of jousts and tiltings accompanied by chivalric imagery, all of which were observed by foreign ambassadors and dignitaries, London's governors and also the common people. Here was the point and purpose of the whole exercise. Despite Henry VII's longstanding reputation for meanness, he was very much the Renaissance prince. His Court was both dignified and, when occasion required, lavish, even spectacular. Henry was generous with hospitality and gifts for foreign visitors and ambassadors. He duly observed all the traditional festive occasions of the calendar year, and important family, State and diplomatic events were celebrated in style. In such ways he used the Court, the royal home, as a means to impress both his own subjects and foreign observers. There can be little doubt that it impressed the king's second son. As young Henry grew up he became an increasingly active participant in court festivities. When King Philip and Queen Joanna of Castile took refuge from a storm in 1506, they received extended hospitality from the English monarch. This included hunting and the usual sequence of feasts, jousts and disguisings. One highlight occurred at Windsor, when Philip was installed in the Order of the Garter and Prince Henry became a member of the Order of the Golden Fleece. This was the last outstanding entertainment of the reign. Under the second Tudor king, however, the entertainments and spectacles would become more frequent, elaborate and lavish. This was not only because he too used the Court as a political tool of kingship, but also because of his love of pleasure and pastime with good company.

The reign of King Henry VII: (2) 1502–1509

Little is recorded of Henry's early life, especially before 1502. Prince Arthur, as eldest son and heir of Henry VII, was the contemporary focus of attention. In April 1502, however, Arthur died and so Duke Henry became first in line, duke of Cornwall (1502) and prince of Wales (1503). This made little difference to the rigorous educational process which he experienced, first under the poet John Skelton (from the mid-1490s until 1502) and the French specialist Giles Dewes, and then under William Hone. In 1501 Skelton, who claimed to have taught his royal pupil 'his learning primordial', penned for him *Speculum Principis*. This was a heavy, virtue-drenched manual on how to be the perfect prince. It included the advice 'to pick out a wife for himself and love but her alone'.[8] How can a teacher ever be sure that he has a receptive audience?

Much less detail is known about Henry's education than about the instruction given to his brother. It is probable, however, that, like Arthur, Henry received a classical humanist training. In 1499 Erasmus accompanied Thomas More to Eltham Palace in Kent. There he met Henry, whose linguistic skill and style so impressed him that the future king and the great humanist began to correspond. Erasmus later referred to him as a genius, who had never neglected his academic studies. More was equally flattering and ambassadors wrote back letters of admiration to their masters. Lord Mountjoy, whose responsibility it was to instruct Henry in the requisite modes of aristocratic and courtly conduct, extolled his love for scholars. Here is another guide to the nature of Henry's style of kingship. His Court would be not only an irresistible stage of public spectacle, pageantry and entertainment. It would also be a cultural centre of scholarship and learning, presided over by a royal patron who was himself both scholar and theologian. And its artistic dimension was fostered by a monarch who had been given his first lute at the age of six, who also mastered the organ and harpsichord and who, as a ten-year-old on the dance floor, won the plaudits of onlookers and brought great pleasure to the king and queen. The fruits of his broad-ranging education could not be better summed up than by some of those whom his Court, and the public images which he projected, were intended to impress. On 3 May 1515 the Venetian ambassadors wrote home after dinner and a bout of jousting:

The King tilted against many, stoutly and valorously. According to their own observation and the report of others, King Henry was not only very expert in arms and of great valour, and most eminent for his personal endowments, but so gifted and adorned with mental accomplishments, that they believed him to have few equals in the world. He spoke English, French, and Latin, understood Italian well, played on almost every instrument, sang and composed fairly, was prudent, sage, and free from every vice. . . .

The ambassadors' letter draws attention to one aspect of Henry's training which, long before they wrote in 1515, had become and was to remain a lifelong passion: physical activity. In 1494 the duke, 'a child of iiij yer of Age or therabowte', had ridden 'vpon a Courser' through the City of London, down the Strand and into Westminster Palace. He became an accomplished horseman and an enthusiast for tennis and hawking, but above all jousting. Martial skills, however, were not just a source of pleasure to the future king. They were essential for the son of a Lancastrian monarch whose Yorkist rivals had not relinquished their claim to the crown. He was taught to engage in combat on both foot and horseback, and he was trained in a variety of weapons, including the sword, lance, spear, poleaxe and bow. So he was personally equipped and ready to defend his throne and kingdom. Henry also revelled in the chivalric game-playing of the tournament, which was to become a regular feature of the Court when he became king. It not only helped to satisfy his personal appetite for physical exercise, but it also enhanced the image of knightly, Renaissance prince and chivalric, heraldic court, at home and abroad. And it was, above all, in image projection that Henry VIII excelled.[9]

Prince Arthur's death in 1502 heralded a time of change and uncertainty for Henry. On 11 February 1503 his mother died, nine days after giving birth to a short-lived daughter. Four years later, in a letter to Erasmus, he wrote that he had heard 'with great unhappiness the report about the death of the king of Castile my deeply, deeply regretted brother.[10] For no less welcome news has ever come here since the death of my very dear mother.' In June of the same year Henry's sister Margaret left the court and travelled north to Edinburgh, where she wedded King James IV.[11] So in swift succession he was deprived of most of those closest to him.

There are varied, even contradictory, stories about Henry's lifestyle during the remaining years of his father's reign. For the first time, in the summer of 1504, the king took his son hunting with him on the royal estates. The Spanish ambassador Hernán duque de Estrada, who was with the hunting party at Windsor, reported that, in the past, the king had not taken his son with him, because he would not interrupt his education. It was wonderful, he observed, how devoted Henry VII was to his son. During the last years of the reign, however, Henry appears to have led a rather reclusive existence in the shadow of the ageing, perhaps ailing king. He was often with his father, especially in public, but, according to Gutier Gomez de Fuensalida, another Spanish ambassador writing in 1508, he was in such a state of subjection that he only spoke when spoken to by his father. In 1538 Henry Lord Montague reputedly reminisced that 'King Henry VII had no affection nor fancy' for his heir. Fuensalida described the prince of Wales as recluse and prisoner, shut up like a young woman in a room adjoining the king's bedchamber.[12] Communication with others was regulated by his guards, and his only exit was a secret door into a park where, under observation of the guards, he jousted with selected companions. Of course this strict royal control can be seen as a father's protection of his only surviving male heir. Henry VII revived Edward IV's council in the Welsh marches for Arthur, who went to live at Ludlow Castle with his new wife Catherine in 1501. Henry, however, was given no public responsibilities or duties and he was not employed in active royal service, even though he had been appointed to a range of offices in his infancy. Once again, this may have been paternal protection. Furthermore it is clear that Henry VII was not neglectful but gave much attention to the preparation of his heir for kingship: his education, especially oral skill in languages, his cultural accomplishments as instrumentalist and composer, and his military training.

In one respect the king was curiously and even dangerously dilatory. A secure, stable dynastic succession was a normal, natural royal priority, especially when the legitimacy of that succession was rejected by a rival family. Yet Henry VII appeared to lack any sense of urgency. It is true that the duke of Cornwall was only ten when his brother died and Henry

VII did move to secure his son's betrothal to Arthur's widow. However, a betrothal treaty was not signed until 23 June 1503 and, throughout the protracted negotiations, the king's chief concern was immediate payment of the outstanding portion of Catherine's dowry rather than the future, long-term provision of another generation of heirs. The betrothal treaty included a clause that, as it was forbidden by the law of God for a man to marry his brother's widow, a dispensation would have to be obtained from the pope. Once that had been done, the marriage could take place when Henry was fifteen. Although the dispensation was duly granted in 1504, changes in Spain's political circumstances made the marriage a much less attractive diplomatic proposition to the king. In June 1505 the prince of Wales was required by his father to read aloud and sign a statement that

Although I while of tender years ... contracted a de facto marriage with her most serene highness Catherine, daughter of the king of Spain; and although that contract, because of the impediment of my minority is in itself already invalid, imperfect, and of no effect or force; nevertheless because, with the onset of my year of manhood ... the contract might in itself be thought or seem to be clearly validated. ... [I] declare that I do not intend in any way to approve, validate or ratify that pretended contract.[13]

There followed negotiations for his marriage to the daughter of Philip of Castile.[14] Other options were tossed about – for example Margaret of Alençon or the daughter of the duke of Bavaria – but nothing eventuated. Four years later, when Henry VII died in April 1509, his sole male heir, now King Henry VIII, was still unmarried without his own heirs of the body.

Accession of King Henry VIII, 1509

Bachelorhood was not a secure state for a new monarch. This was particularly so for one who not only had rivals in the wings but who may have been discounted by some of his more powerful subjects, such as the duke of Buckingham. Only five years before, some unidentified 'grett personages' had considered Edmund de la Pole and Buckingham as possible alternative successors to Henry VII. When Henry VII died at night on 21 April 1509 his death was kept secret, even from Prince Henry, until the afternoon of the 23rd. Such secrecy indicates councillors' fears about an intended coup by some un-named Yorkists, ambitious nobles, royal servants fearful for their future or other notables.[15] So the new reign began in a climate of uncertainty and insecurity. Henry VIII's fear about insecurity and his responses to it would have an ongoing importance in his kingship.

How well equipped was Henry VIII to rule England, Wales and Ireland? As already observed, he must have been an unfamiliar figure and an unknown quantity to many of his subjects. He had received no formal training for kingship, which may explain why the preparation of his own son Edward was to be extensive and elaborate. Nevertheless, as we have seen, he brought with him many assets to the role and responsibilities of personal monarch: in particular his linguistic skills, which extended to Italian, French and some Greek as well as Latin and French, but also astronomy, mathematics, medicine and theology; courtly graces such as dancing and especially music; ability and versatility in weapon handling and horsemanship. There were also his passion for imagery and his talent for effective and popular image projection: the cultivated prince, the warrior-king, the chivalrous knight, the caring Christian and God's anointed lieutenant. He was aided in this image projection by the inestimable benefit of being a handsome prince of magnificent physique and a giant who stood six feet two inches tall. His appearance was, as already observed, admired by diplomats and reported back to the courts of Europe.

Comparisons were made, to Henry's advantage, in the competitive world of European monarchies:

He is much handsomer than any other Sovereign in Christendom – a great deal handsomer than the King of France. . . . Hearing that King Francis [of France] wore a beard, he allowed his own to grow, and as it was reddish, he had then got a beard which looked like gold.[16]

He was also admired in diplomatic circles for his talents and virtuosity. In his report, written on the completion of his service as Venetian ambassador in England in 1519, Sebastian Giustinian described Henry as 'a good musician' and 'a capital horseman' who, whenever he hunted, tired out eight or ten horses in a day.[17]

For the same reasons the new monarch enjoyed prestige and popularity amongst his subjects. Polydore Vergil recorded that, when the date of the coronation was announced, 'a vast multitude of persons at once hurried to London to see their monarch in the full bloom of his youth and high birth. . . . [E]verybody loved him. . . . [I]n general appearance, in greatness of mind and generosity', he was very like Edward IV, 'the most warmly thought of by the English people among all the English kings . . . and for that reason was the more acclaimed and approved of by all'. Vergil proceeded to recite a catalogue of strengths and virtues of this princely paragon:

his handsome bearing, his comely and manly features (in which one could discern as much authority as good will), his outstanding physical strength, remarkable memory, aptness at all the arts of both war and peace, skill at arms and on horseback, scholarship of no mean order, thorough knowledge of music, and his humanity, benevolence and self-control.[18]

Henry's first priority, however, was not popularity but security. When, on 23 April, the proclamation of the new king in London 'by the blast of a Trumpet' was received 'with muche gladnes and reioysyng of the people', he withdrew to the Tower. There he 'remayned closly and secrete with his counsayll, till the funeralles of his father were finished and ended'.[19] Once the majestic, sumptuous and solemn funeral obsequies and burial of his father were over, on 9–10 May, he could turn from the past to the future.

Within a few days Henry declared his intention to marry Catherine of Aragon. Whether he was responding to his father's deathbed wish, as he claimed, or he was acting on his own initiative is uncertain. What is clear – and significant – is that he set aside his earlier declaration of the invalid nature of such a marriage without hesitation or comment. It is an early example of his capacity to make fundamental shifts in position without defence, justification or apology. Catherine's years of isolation and financial hardship, since Henry's renunciation of 1505, came to a sudden end as events moved rapidly. King Ferdinand of Spain ordered confirmation of the betrothal treaty on 11 May;[20] the outstanding instalment of her dowry was paid by her father (16 June); she renounced any claim to her dowry in favour of Henry VIII (7 June) and was granted jointure on 10 June.[21] According to Edward Hall, not every one of the king's subjects was happy with the prospect of Catherine as his wife.

This mariage of the brother's wyfe was muche murmured agaynst in the beginnyng and ever more and more searched out by learning and scripture, so that, at the laste, by the determinacion of the best universities of Christendom it was adiudged detestable, and plain contrary to Goddes law.[22]

However, Hall may have been writing from hindsight. He lived through the late 1520s, when Henry VIII consulted the universities because it then suited him to repudiate his marriage on the grounds of invalidity.

In 1509 Archbishop Warham of Canterbury reputedly expressed his disapproval of the intended marriage, because he questioned the validity of the pope's dispensation. Even the young king experienced a brief flutter of uncertainty. Thereafter, however, he exhibited no signs of doubt or second thoughts. In a letter to Catherine his prospective father-in-law Ferdinand expressed joy at his decision to marry her. Furthermore, the marriage, solemnized at Greenwich on 11 June, inaugurated the honeymoon period of Henry's reign. He had already gained widespread popularity when, on 23 April, the very day on which he was proclaimed king, he issued a general pardon to all offenders, except those charged with treason, murder and felony. The pardon, which was a modified version of that issued by his father shortly before his death, also specifically exempted by name seventy-seven offenders, including two of his father's closest advisers, Richard Empson and Edmund Dudley.[23] On the same day they were arrested. Recorded contemporary opinion is consistent about the reputation of these two lawyers. Vergil wrote that 'the people everywhere cursed [them] . . . with being the most savage extortioners who eagerly plundered all secular and ecclesiastical wealth'. They were accused of calling many before them 'for many surmised causes, of the which none escaped without paying of fines. . . . [A]ll was done in the king's name and yet the most profit came to their coffers.' In the service of the first Tudor, Empson and Dudley had become notorious figures, 'whom the people esteemed as his horse-leeches and shearers' and who 'turned law and justice into wormwood rapine'.[24] Whether or not the two lawyers were guilty of the widespread accusations is of less concern here than the fact that the government responded to public hostility. Henry, we are told, 'consulted his counsellors on the matter',[25] and it remains unclear who initiated the move to arrest them. Hall hinted that their downfall may have been 'procured by malice of theim that with their authoritie in the late kynge's daies were offended'[26] – in other words, malicious infighting. Whatever the explanation, the king was clearly the beneficiary. When the two lawyers were convicted and executed on trumped-up treason charges in 1510, 'everyone was grateful to the monarch'.[27] It was an early royal bid for popularity and the first of many.

Henry's coronation and 'the beginning of joy'

Henry's first image to his people was that of the just king. That, however, was speedily overshadowed by other images in the festivities which accompanied the wedding and coronation and which occurred repeatedly in the following years. These were times of celebration, in which the new king's virtues were extolled and which Henry exploited to the full.

> Ryght myghty prynce our good souerayne lorde
> To god enclynynge be hardy and gladde
> Of you and your realme he wyll se concorde
> Though other nacyons be therfore full sadde
> Agaynst you murmurynge with theyr werkes badde
> Yet drede ye nothynge for god with his myght
> Wyll be alwaye redy to defende the ryght

Stephen Hawes' 'A ioyfull meditacyon to all Englonde of the coronacyon of our moost naturall souerayne lorde kynge Henry the eyght' may be of questionable quality, but it expressed the mood of the moment. So did the verses of Henry VIII's ex-tutor, John Skelton:

> Adonis of freshe colour
> Of yowthe the godely flour
>
> . . . .
>
> Our king, our emperour,
> Our Priamus of Troy,
> Our welth, our worldly joy,
>
> Upon us he doth reigne
> That makith our hartis glad,
> As king moost sovereine
> That ever Englond had;
>
> . . . .
>
> God save him in his right[28]

Henry was imbued with chivalric ideals and the image of the knight errant. The costs of Henry VII's funeral included the painting of many 'scochyns', coats of arms and banners. Only eight days later, at Greenwich, the new king held a chapter of the Order of the Garter, at which Lords Darcy and Dudley were nominated and chosen to fill the vacant stalls.[29] On 22 June he created twenty-six new knights of the Order of the Bath after their ritual baths and night-long vigils. Nothing, however, could match the coronation for magnificence, symbolism and image projection. Hall recalled 'what payn, labour and diligence the Taylers, Embrouderers and Golde Smithes tooke, both to make and devise garmentes for Lordes, Ladies, knightes and Esquiers, and also for deckyng, trappyng and adornyng of Coursers, Jennets and Palfries. . . . [F]or a suretie, more riche, nor more straunge, nor more curious workes hath not ben seen then wer prepared agaynst this coronacion', which took place on 24 June, Midsummer Day.[30] The focus of attention throughout the festive occasion was, of course, the young Goliath. When, on the 23rd, he rode from the Tower to

Westminster Palace he wore a crimson velvet robe edged with ermine, a golden coat, a 'placard [a garment worn beneath the coat] embrowdered with Diamonds, Rubies, [Emeralds], great Pearles and other riche stones' and a baldric [a traverse or cross belt to support a sword] decorated with rubies. Before him rode two richly attired gentlemen bearing robes, one of the duchy of Guienne and the other of the duchy of Normandy. The royal procession also included 'the nyne children of honor, upon greate coursers, appareled on their bodies in Blewe Velvet, poudered with [fleur de lys of gold], . . . every one of their horses trapped with a trapper of the kyng's title [as of England and France, Gascony, Guienne, Normandy, Anjou, Cornwall, Wales, Ireland] &c wrought upon Velvette, with embrouderie and Gold Smithes' work'.[31] So colour, magnificence, symbolism and images were all present, projecting the crown's wealth, power and territorial claims.

After the solemn ritual of the coronation in Westminster Abbey, a banquet was held in Westminster Hall. It consisted not only of 'sumptuous, fine and delicate meats' but also of many delicacies which, typically, included heraldic devices and mottos.[32] The fact that, during the 'long and royal' feast, '[a]t the kynge's fete, under the table, wer certain gentlemen [a]nd in likewise with the quene' was a public statement of the majesty of monarchy.[33] There followed days of 'tournaments and many sorts of games'.[34] To accommodate the royal couple and guests as they watched the tournaments, a pavilion, covered with tapestries and rich Arras cloth, was erected in the tiltyard. Nearby 'a curious fountain' was erected and over it a castle. Throughout the festivities red and white wine and claret flowed out of the mouths of gargoyles on the castle. More extravagance! On top was 'a greate Croun imperial' and the battlements were decorated with gilded roses and pomegranates, a theme repeated in the green and white lozenges which decorated the castle walls. More symbolism: the imperial concept; Tudor colours (green and white); the union of Tudor king (a rose) and his queen from Aragon (a pomegranate).[35]

Sombre reality intervened to end the celebrations. On 28 June Henry attained his majority, but on the following day – less than a week after the coronation – his grandmother, Margaret Beaufort, countess of Richmond, died. That, however, could neither overshadow for long the festive atmosphere of the Court, stifle the natural ebullience of the king, nor affect his glowing reputation and the current air of optimism. This was exemplified by the celebratory spirit with which Thomas More greeted the coronation: 'This day is the end of our slavery, the fount of our liberty; the end of sadness, the beginning of joy.'[36] His friend Lord

Mountjoy joyfully (if rather naïvely) welcomed, as a gift from God, the new king who opened up a new age: 'Heaven smiles and earth rejoices; all is milk and honey and nectar. . . . Generosity scatters wealth with an unstinting hand. Our king's heart is not set upon gold or jewels or mines of ore, but upon virtue, reputation and eternal renown.' In his *The Tree of Commonwealth*, written in the Tower of London, even the condemned Edmund Dudley pronounced, 'But now Englishmen, . . . Ye haue a prince and king in whome was neuer spott or bleamysshe of vntroth knowne or found.' He also proclaimed Henry as the prince who would revive the decayed commonwealth. However, as one who protested his innocence and perhaps hoped for a reprieve, Dudley can hardly be regarded as an impartial commentator.[37]

A year later a foreign observer, Andrea Badoer the Venetian ambassador, described Henry as 'a courageous and worthy sovereign, very robust and nineteen years old'.[38] He was describing a young man who was martial, athletic, obsessively fond of jousts and tourneys and who, in Anglo's words, 'exulted in the display of his physical prowess to friends, subjects, and visitors from abroad'.[39] Henry VIII's passion for military games had a political benefit. The English Court acquired an international reputation for martial prowess, especially when the tournaments were embellished with the romantic, allegoric and chivalric settings and rituals adopted from the Burgundian Court. Henry always figured prominently, dressing up on various occasions as Hercules, Saint George and other heroic figures. On 29 May 1510 the Spanish ambassador, Luis Caroz de Villaragut, informed King Ferdinand that two days a week were devoted to an ongoing tournament, which would continue until the feast of St John. It 'is instituted in imitation of Amadis and Lanzilote, and other knights of olden times, of whom so much is written in books'. He added that Henry 'amuses himself almost every day of the week with running the ring and with jousts and tournaments on foot'. Whilst there were many young men who excelled in this 'kind of warfare', the king was 'the most conspicuous amongst them all, the most assiduous, and the most interested'.[40] Some of the king's councillors, however, were less impressed. They knew and feared that he could be injured, maimed, even killed. Their fears were understandable and justified. Serious injuries did occur and later the king came near to death. Henry responded to council pressure when he had hollow lances made. These reduced impact on the body of the person who was struck. Nevertheless, tournaments were a constant risk. It is true that, as a much-admired exemplar of martial prowess, Henry added to the prestige of the English monarchy. However, even when allowance is made for such contemporary macho priorities, his constant combat was a foolhardy danger when, for so many years, there were no legitimate male heirs of the body.

In this, as in so many other ways, Henry VIII was a stark, dramatic contrast to his father. In one vital respect the contrast would grow with the passing of the years. The second Tudor king's reign would be beneficial to some in his realms. It would, however, bring burdens, anguish, spiritual confusion and loss, deprivation and murderous cruelty to many, as he rode his ego in pursuit of self-fulfilment, glory and the delusion of personal greatness. He was a ruler of both great personal strength and abundant weakness. One strength, however, makes him a constant source of fascination: like his daughter Elizabeth he had public relations skills and a talent for image projection which would have allowed no place or need for the spin-doctors of modern politics.

Notes

1 R. A. B. Mynors, D. F. S. Thomson and W. K. Ferguson, eds, *The Correspondence of Erasmus*, 11 vols, Toronto, 1974, 2, pp. 147–8; G. Mattingley, *Catherine of Aragon*, New York, 1960, p. 127; J. Gairdner and R. H. Brodie, eds, *Letters and Papers, Foreign and Domestic, of the Reign of Henry VIII*, Her Majesty's Stationery Office, London, 1920, 1 (1), no. 51 (hereafter *LP*).

2 E. E. Reynolds, *Thomas More and Erasmus*, London, 1965, p. 65. The royal relatives, to whom More was referring, were King Henry VII, Queen Elizabeth of York, Lady Margaret Beaufort and King Edward IV.

3 E. Hall, *The Union of the two noble and illustre famelies of Lancastre and Yorke*, London, 1550, fol. 2v.

4 When I use the term 'image projection' I refer (1) to the ways in which Henry chose to project himself to the world by his actions, interests and activities – martial, majestic, artistic, scholarly, theological, chivalrous, and so on – and (2) to the creation of a magnificent stage on which to perform. At this point I am not concerned with discussion about the revolution in royal iconography (e.g. as in S. Thurley and C. Lloyd, *Henry VIII: Images of a Tudor King*, Oxford, 1990, and G. Walker, *Persuasive Fictions: Faction, Faith and Political Culture in the Reign of Henry VIII*, Aldershot, 1996).

5 A. Luders, T. E. Tomlins et al., eds, *Statutes of the Realm*, 11 vols, London, 1810–28, II, p. 499 (hereafter *Stats Realm*).

6 B. J. Harris, *Edward Stafford, Third Duke of Buckingham, 1478–1521*, Stanford, 1986, p. 206.

7 A herald's description in S. Anglo, *Spectacle, Pageantry and Early Tudor Policy*, Oxford, 1969, pp. 101–2.

8 'Coniugem tibi delige quam unice semper dilige' (fol. 20), F. M. Salter, ed., 'Skelton's "Speculum principis", *Speculum*, 9 (1) (Jan. 1934), 35.

9 R. Brown, ed., *Calendar of State Papers and Manuscripts, relating to English Affairs in the archives and collections of Venice and other libraries of Northern Italy*, 2, London, 1867, no. 614 (hereafter Cal. SP Ven.); C. L. Kingsford, ed., *Chronicles of London*, Dursley, Gloucs, 1977, p. 201.

10 Archduke Philip, husband of Joanna, who was daughter and heiress of the late Isabella, queen of Castile.

11 Mynors et al., eds, *Correspondence of Erasmus*, 2, pp. 126, 128–9; P. Buchanan, *Margaret Tudor, Queen of Scots*, Edinburgh, 1985, pp. 15–23.

12 C. Erickson, *Great Harry*, New York, 1980, p. 51, cit. *Correspondencia de Gutierre Gomez de Fuensalida, embajador en Alemania, Flandes e Inglaterra (1485–1509)*, Madrid, 1907, p. 449; *LP*, 13 (2), no. 804 (p. 318).

13 M. L. Bruce, *The Making of Henry VIII*, London, 1977, pp. 164–5.

14 Kingsford, ed., *Chronicles*, p. 231.

15 S. J. Gunn, 'The Accession of Henry VIII', *Historical Research*, 64 (1991), 279–80.

16 *Cal. SP Ven.*, 12, no. 1287 (p. 559).

17 Ibid.

18 D. Hay, ed., *The Anglica Historia of Polydore Vergil, 1485–1537*, Camden Series no. 3, 74 (1950), p. 151.

19 Hall, fol. 1.

20 *LP*, 1 (1), no. 24.

21 G. A. Bergenroth, ed., *Calendar of Letters, Despatches, and State Papers, relating to the Negotiations between England and Spain*, 2, London, 1866, nos 14, 18 (hereafter *Cal. SP Span.*); *LP*, VIII, 1 (1), nos 60 and 94 (35).

22 Hall, fol. 2.

23 *LP*, 1 (1), nos 2, 8, 11 (1, 10).

24 *Anglica Historia*, p. 151; C. H. Williams, ed., *English Historical Documents, 1485–1558*, London, 1971, V, pp. 400–1 and n. 1.

25 *Anglica Historia*, p. 151.

26 Hall, fol. 1.

27 *Anglica Historia*, pp. 151, 153.

28 B. Lüsse, 'Panegyric Poetry on the Coronation of King Henry VIII: The King's Praise and the Poet's Self-Presentation', in U. Baumann, ed., *Henry VIII in History, Historiography and Literature*, Frankfurt, 1992, pp. 69, 73; J. Scattergood, ed., *John Skelton, The Complete English Poems*, New Haven, 1983, pp. 111–12.

29 *LP*, 1 (1), no. 37.

30 Hall, fol. 2–2v.

31 Ibid., fols 2v–3.

32 Ibid., fols 3v–4v.

33 Hall, fol. 3v.

34 *Anglica Historia*, p. 151.

35 Hall, fol. 4v.

36 D. Starkey, *The Reign of Henry VIII: Personalities and Politics*, London, 1985, p. 37.

37 Mynors et al., eds, *Correspondence of Erasmus*, 2, no. 215 (pp. 147–8); D. M. Brodie, ed., Edmund Dudley, *The Tree of Commonwealth*, Cambridge, 1948, p. 39.

38 *Cal. SP Ven.*, 2, no. 63.

39 Anglo, *Spectacle*, p. 110.

40 *Cal. SP Span.*, 2, no. 45.

Chapter 2

The Reign of Henry VIII, 1509–1547

The young king's priority was to reactivate the longstanding English enmity towards France. He needed allies, but it was not until November 1511, when he joined the anti-French Holy League of Pope Julius II, Spain, Venice and Emperor Maximilian I, that he found them. By then he and Queen Catherine had already experienced the first of a series of misfortunes: a son, born on 1 January 1511, sparked joyous celebrations but he died on 22 February. Henry turned to war: in 1512, after Julius II had divested the French king of his title and kingdom and bestowed them on Henry, an Anglo-Spanish force was supposed to conquer the French province of Aquitaine for him. When the English arrived at the agreed rallying point near San Sebastian, the Spanish did not co-operate and four months later the demoralized English returned home. Henry then decided on a cross-Channel assault on northern France, which he personally led in June 1513. During his successful siege of Thérouanne, in alliance with Emperor Maximilian, his cavalry drove away a French relieving force. It was a brief foray, afterwards puffed up into the glorious 'Battle of the Spurs'. He then besieged and captured Tournai, before returning to England in October, after several weeks of feasting, partying and tourneying. During his absence the Scots, France's traditional ally, had predictably invaded England. On 9 September an English army, under the earl of Surrey, destroyed the Scottish force at Flodden. Then, in a policy *volte-face*, Henry made peace with France in August 1514, and his unfortunate sister, Mary, was married to the aged, worn-out King Louis XII.

These years saw the rise of Thomas Wolsey, cleric, royal chaplain and almoner. He rose through royal favour to prominence and power because of his commissariat skills in organizing the supply of Henry's war machine. He became adviser and chief minister and, in appreciation of his services, the king made him lord chancellor (1515). Henry also secured Wolsey's appointment as bishop of Tournai (1513) and Lincoln (1514), archbishop of York (1514), cardinal (1515) and legate *a latere* (1518).

Wolsey was also obliged to play a prominent part in a protracted and serious controversy between Church and State. The refusal of a London merchant, Richard Hunne, to pay a mortuary fee for the burial of his baby son in 1511 eventually led to suits against the clergy in the king's courts, heresy proceedings against Hunne, his arrest and, in 1514, his mysterious death by hanging in a prison cell. There was widespread belief that churchmen had murdered him. Henry Standish's declaration in convocation (1514) that clergy could be tried in secular courts and his summons on suspicion of heresy by convocation (1515) turned the longstanding question into an urgent issue. Henry responded by calling a meeting of parliament, his councillors and judges at Baynard's Castle in London. He rejected the bishops' claim that it was against God's law to try clergy in his courts. Wolsey defused the issue by abandoning clerical claims and ending moves against Standish.

In 1515 Francis I became king of France, and in 1516 Ferdinand's grandson, Charles, succeeded him as king of Spain. Henry helped to fund Maximilian's military campaigns against the new French king in northern Italy. In 1518, however, Wolsey negotiated with France the treaty of London, a collective security pact which became 'the universal peace' when Charles and Maximilian also signed. In a separate treaty Henry also agreed to restore Tournai to France in return for 600,000 crowns. For several years he played the peacemaker. When Maximilian died in 1519 Henry made an unsuccessful bid to be elected Holy Roman Emperor, but he pursued his peace policy with the new emperor, Charles V (Habsburg), already king of Spain. They met in England for three days of entertainment and discussion in May 1520. Then Henry and Francis I met for more than two weeks of tournament and festivity at the lavish Renaissance extravaganza, the Field of the Cloth of Gold.[1] It can be seen as a mutual bid by two Princes to outdo each other or as an attempt to overcome traditional enmities. '[I]t was hoped that, through friendly competition in sport, true friendship would grow and peace be nurtured.'[2]

It did not last. When Henry met Charles again in July, he resisted imperial attempts to forge an anti-French alliance. But next year they signed a secret anti-French pact, in May–July 1522 Emperor Charles made an extended visit to Henry, and England declared war on France. With typical inconsistency Henry switched from 'the peacemaker' to 'the warrior king'. In 1523 an English army besieged Boulogne unsuccessfully and gave up its march on Paris when only fifty miles away. When, two years later, Francis I became the emperor's prisoner at the battle of Pavia in northern Italy, Henry saw the opportunity to regain French provinces once held by the English. But Charles would not assist. In August 1525 an angry, aggrieved Henry ended hostilities with France; in 1526 he helped to organize the anti-Habsburg league of the liberated Francis, Italian States and the papacy; and in 1528 an Anglo-French alliance was formed. A year later, however, the peace treaty of Cambrai was signed.

By then foreign affairs had become entangled with Henry's domestic problems. In his earlier years the king handled domestic crises with a mixture of firmness, flexibility, aplomb and an acute sense of what was popular. After destructive riots, which erupted against foreign merchant communities in London on May Day 1517, many penitent rioters were graciously pardoned by Henry. 'It was a very fine spectacle and well-arranged, and the crowd of people present was innumerable.'[3] In response to the collective complaint of his council in 1519, he removed some objectionable young courtiers, his 'minions', and for a while played the role of princely reformer;[4] in 1521 his distrust of the 'overmighty' duke of Buckingham led to the noble's arrest, trial and execution.[5] In the same year, in response to the threat of heresy and at Wolsey's prompting, the devout Roman Catholic king completed writing (with assistance) and published *Assertio Septem Sacramentorum*. Although its theology was flawed, this royal assault on the German heretic Martin Luther was a polemic very accessible to a wide readership and 'something of a best seller'.[6] It did not, however, stop Henry from making war on other Catholic princes. From 1522 repeated financial demands culminated in the misnamed 'Amicable Grant', which was required to fund the military annexation of French provinces after Pavia in 1525. It provoked widespread disturbances and resistance. King and minister, acting realistically, withdrew it 'in a stage-managed display of "clemency"'[7] and made peace with France. So the king's appropriate responses usually resolved or at least defused domestic problems.

At about the same time, however, a problem of longer duration became both more pressing and more complex. Henry had various liaisons during his first marriage, one of which, with Elizabeth Blount, produced a son, Henry Fitzroy, in 1519. By 1525, when he was created duke of Richmond, the king was clearly grooming him as male heir.[8] By then Henry VIII's marriage to Catherine had produced one surviving child, not a son but Princess Mary, who was born in 1516. It was also in 1525 (or early in 1526) that he became attracted to Anne Boleyn. He persuaded himself that lack of sons was divine punishment for marrying his brother's widow, despite a papal dispensation allowing him to do so. He sought papal annulment of his marriage but, unfortunately for him, in 1527 the emperor's soldiers sacked Rome and took the pope prisoner. Charles V, who was Queen Catherine's nephew, would not allow annulment proceedings to succeed. Wolsey, whose future depended on Henry ending his first marriage, secured from Pope Clement VII a commission to establish the facts and reach a decision. He and Cardinal Campeggio heard the case at Blackfriars, London, in the summer of 1529, but on 31 July Campeggio adjourned it. Wolsey was dismissed and exiled to York. In December 1530 he died on his way south to stand trial.

In 1529 Henry summoned what became known as the 'Reformation Parliament' and the Canterbury convocation met concurrently. It is not clear why he called parliament. In its first session (1529) it legislated against clerical abuses, cancelled Henry's obligation to repay past loans and discussed Wolsey's misconduct and excesses. But nothing was presented or considered about the king's divorce. Meanwhile Henry had been canvassing the opinion of European universities and reformers about his predicament. At the same time he was developing ideas about his own authority, especially that, within his realm, he owed allegiance to no superior. In 1530 a handful of churchmen were charged with *praemunire* (or invasions of royal authority) and early in the following year the entire clergy of England were similarly indicted. Their specific offence was simply that they had exercised their spiritual jurisdiction. The convocations of Canterbury and York duly submitted, paid fines of £100,000 and £18,000 respectively for the royal pardon and acknowledged Henry as 'singular protector, supreme lord and even, *so far as the law of Christ allows*,[9] supreme head of the English Church and clergy'.[10]

In 1532 Henry applied pressure on the papacy through parliament. An act empowered the king, after one year, to suspend the payment of annates, the larger part of one year's income due to the pope from newly appointed upper clergy. It was an exercise in political blackmail. More pressure was also mounted against the clergy. The house of commons' Supplication against the Ordinaries (petition against the clergy) was presented to a king in uncompromising mood. Convocation surrendered. In the Submission of the Clergy it accepted that the king alone could summon it and that his approval was necessary for new ecclesiastical laws. This was a denial of papal authority. In May Henry accepted the resignation of Sir Thomas More, Wolsey's replacement as lord chancellor. The king's business was increasingly in the hands of the cardinal's successor as chief minister, Thomas Cromwell. Change accelerated. Henry secretly married the pregnant Anne Boleyn in January 1533. Two months later Thomas Cranmer, Henry's chosen successor of Archbishop Warham of Canterbury, who had died in the previous August, was consecrated with papal approval. Parliament enacted the statute in Restraint of Appeals. It denied the pope's right to judge 'causes of matrymonye', including the validity of Henry's marriages, and it generally prohibited appeals to Rome on temporal causes.[11] Cranmer could now annul Henry's first marriage and declare his second lawful, which he did in May. Anne was crowned queen in June and gave birth to Elizabeth in September.

The pope, however, responded to developments by ordering Henry back to Catherine on pain of excommunication. Henry countered by enforcing the Annates Act and, in the January–March session of 1534, parliament enacted the end of such payments. It also empowered Canterbury instead of the pope to issue dispensations, confirmed the 1532 Submission and enacted the first Succession Act, which recognized the succession through the children of Henry's second marriage and imposed an oath to uphold the statute. There was no clear declaration of untrammelled independence until, on 23 March, the pope judged Henry's marriage to Catherine to be lawful. In the second parliamentary session of 1534 the Act of Supremacy recognized the king and his heirs as supreme head of the Church of England. The Act for First Fruits and Tenths gave the king the first year's income of anyone appointed to Church office and ten per cent annually afterwards. Finally a new Treasons Act was enacted. Its purpose was to to destroy opponents of these changes by making denial of the royal supremacy a capital offence. It reaped a rapid harvest of victims in 1535, including Carthusian monks, parish clergy, Bishop Fisher of Rochester and, on 6 July, Thomas More.

It was the beginning rather than the end of change. In 1535 Cromwell, now vicegerent in spirituals, supervised the royal visitation of the monasteries. This, like First Fruits and Tenths, was part of a concerted plan by the government to plunder the Church. In 1536 a statute dissolved the smaller monasteries, which were characterized by 'manifest sin, vicious, carnal and abominable living', and their property and chattels were transferred to the crown. Another act established the royal court of augmentations, which was to administer this wealth.[12] In the following years the larger houses were persuaded by Cromwell's agents, by their 'own free and voluntary minds', to surrender their houses and wealth to the crown. The process was confirmed by the second Dissolution Act of 1540. Cromwell, Cranmer and their evangelical supporters also conducted a campaign against shrines and relics, including (with Henry's wholehearted support) the destruction of Thomas à Becket's Canterbury tomb in 1538.[13] The Ten Articles, a scrappy Catholic–Lutheran compromise, which discussed only three sacraments, was devised in 1536. The first officially authorized English vernacular Bible appeared in 1539 There were even on-and-off negotiations with German Lutheran princes in 1535 and 1536. But, amidst all these developments, in 1536 Queen Anne, patron of evangelicals, fell from grace. Henry accepted convenient accusations of adultery against her; she was duly tried and, in May, executed. He promptly married Jane Seymour, who gave him his male heir, Edward, before dying after childbirth in October 1537.

By then the king was troubled by widespread expressions of discontent and resistance. These ranged widely in their nature and danger to royal authority. There were the attacks by Elizabeth Barton, the 'Nun of Kent', on Henry's divorce (from 1528 until her execution in 1534); regular clergy and even some parish priests preached against Henry's religious policies; and locals physically assaulted royal employees when they were expelling monks and nuns or destroying relics, images, shrines and rood screens. More dangerous, in late 1536, were the Lincolnshire rebellion and the most serious uprising of the reign, the Yorkshire-based Pilgrimage of Grace under Robert Aske. They were unsuccessful, but they were alarm signals to Henry. Gradually, albeit inconsistently, he moved back to a more conservative position. He was critical of the rather Lutheran consideration of justification in the so-called Bishops' Book, a new statement of doctrine by a Cranmer–Cromwell-chaired committee in 1537. In November 1538 he publicly debated with John Lambert at his trial for heresy and issued a proclamation against heretics: public signals of his return to a more orthodox position. Yet Cromwell was still influential. Henry feared papal ability to raise a European Catholic coalition for the invasion of the schismatic kingdom. He targeted the Yorkist family and friends of the pope's agent and his enemy Reginald Cardinal Pole. So his minister secured the conviction and death for treason of the marquess of Exeter and Lord Montague in 1538, and a year later the attainder of the countess of Salisbury (who, however, was not executed until 1541). In 1539 parliament enacted the Six Articles, a Catholic orthodox religious statement which now made life difficult for the reformers. Cromwell's life was further complicated by the marriage which he negotiated between Henry and Anne, the daughter of the duke of Cleves. Although the king married her in January 1540, he found her distasteful and the marriage was not consummated. Cromwell's favour with the king was declining because of his religious position; it was weakened by the failed marriage; and it was undermined when the conservative Howard interest focused Henry's attention on the duke of Norfolk's desirable fifteen-year-old niece Catherine Howard. Cromwell was imprisoned, attainted by parliament and executed on 28 June 1540. Henry's marriage was annulled on 9 July and he married Catherine on the 28th.

Thereafter, until the last months of his reign, his rule was dominated by two characteristics. First, he displayed a revitalized orthodoxy and preference for the conservatives. Heretics were regularly burned – from Robert Barnes and others (in 1540) to Anne Askew (in 1546). And there appeared in 1543 the King's Book, a formulary which was less influenced by Protestantism than was its predecessor, the Bishops' Book. Secondly, the warrior king, albeit an obese and aged one, re-emerged. Henry resumed war with Scotland (from 1542) and France (from 1543). In 1542 the Scots were defeated at Solway Moss. In 1544 Henry led an invasion of France and captured Boulogne. But next year he defended the southern English coast against an attempted French invasion. In 1546 the two kingdoms made peace.

In 1541/2 the conservatives' recent triumph over Cromwell was to some extent undermined by Queen Catherine's revealed adultery, for which she died in 1542. Henry married once more: Catherine Parr in July 1543. She had evangelical interests and the prominent conservative Bishop Gardiner fell out of favour when he conspired, unsuccessfully, to remove her for harbouring heresy in her household. Then, in December 1546, Norfolk and his son Surrey were arrested for treason. Surrey was tried and executed and Norfolk was attainted by statute, both within days of Henry's death on 27 January 1547. So the king bequeathed his son's government to the earl of Hertford and other reformers. The extent to which he knew of their religious position, however, is not clear.

Notes

1 See below, Chap. 4, p. 71.

2 D. Starkey, ed., *Henry VIII: A European Court in England*, London, 1991, p. 51.

3 R. Brown, ed., *Four Years at the Court of Henry VIII, 1515–1519*, 2 vols, London, 1854, 2, p. 75; see below, Chap. 3, p. 32.

4 See below, Chap. 3, pp. 34–6.

5 See above, Chap. 1, p. 3 and below, Chap. 5, p. 91.

6 J. J. Scarisbrick, *Henry VIII*, London, 1970, pp. 110–13.

7 J. Guy, 'Thomas Wolsey, Thomas Cromwell and the Reform of Henrician Government', in D. MacCulloch, ed., *The Reign of Henry VIII: Politics, Policy and Piety*, London, 1995, p. 46.

8 See below, Chapter 7, pp. 131–2.

9 The clergy could argue that this qualification meant 'no change'.

10 S. E. Lehmberg, *The Reformation Parliament, 1529–1536*, Cambridge, 1970, pp. 112–15; Scarisbrick, *Henry VIII*, pp. 273–5.

11 C. Haigh, *English Reformations*, Oxford, 1993, p. 116; Lehmberg, *Reformation Parliament*, pp. 163–9.

12 27 Henry VIII, c. 27, *Stats Realm*, III, pp. 569–74.

13 D. MacCulloch, *Thomas Cranmer*, New Haven, 1996, pp. 227–8.

Chapter 3

Henry VIII's Kingship:
Images and Reputation

In government by personal monarchy the king's personality, his conception of kingship and the ways in which he tried to implement it were all crucial to the effectiveness and success (or otherwise) of his rule. Early modern monarchs, however, were active image projectors and those images often obscured or distorted the truth. This, together with the nature of the surviving evidence, has contributed to the diverse interpretations and assessments of Henry VIII and his government. In 1985 David Starkey also ascribed the differing views of historians to the complexity of Henry's character, illustrated, for example, in his 'wilfully complicated' position in religion.[1]

Of course contemporary chroniclers, writing in the lifetime of Henry or his children, focused on what they perceived to be the qualities of a great king. To have done otherwise would have been harmful, even fatal, to future prospects. In 1545 John Leland extolled Henry's qualities and glorious feats.[2] During the reign of Henry's daughter, Elizabeth, Richard Reynoldes's *Chronicle of all the noble Emperours of the Romaines* described the late king as worthy of 'perpetuall fame of memorye' for his martial feats.[3] And Polydore Vergil dedicated his *Anglica Historia* to King Henry, in gratitude for his bounty and out of professed respect. This may explain why he glossed over the controversial process of Henrician schism and Reformation in less than a page: it enabled him to avoid expression of his criticism and disapproval.[4]

Other Tudor chroniclers were glowing in their eulogies of Henry. William Thomas, for example, wrote a stout defence of his Catholic king against accusations of tyranny. He consistently praised his royal virtues of '*temperantia, prudentia, iustitia*, and *fortitudo*'.[5] In his *Union*, first printed in 1548, Edward Hall wrote about the scrupulous king who 'ever labored to know the trueth [about his first marriage] for discharge of his conscience'.[6] Ulpian Fulwell's *The Flower of Fame* (1575) dwelt in fulsome fashion upon 'the bright Renowne and moste fortunate raigne of King Henry the VIII' – understandable, as he dedicated the book to Lord Burghley, chief minister of Henry's daughter. Two years later the *Chronicles* of Raphael Holinshed, drawing extensively on Hall, were intended to demonstrate the glories and great achievements of Henry's reign. Holinshed summed up the king as a terror to his enemies, yet a king who desired peace and one whose majesty was 'tempered with humanitie'.[7]

Not all, however, were united in their praise of Henry, especially once the Tudors had ceased to rule. In his *Annales* of Queen Elizabeth I's reign (1615 and 1627) William Camden offered a more realistic, balanced assessment:

A magnanimous Prince, but I know not what confused temper of spirit he had: great virtues he had; and no lesse vices.[8]

Sir Walter Ralegh, writing at the same time, had nothing good to say about him:

[I]f all the pictures and Patternes of a mercilesse Prince were lost in the World, they might all againe be painted to the life, out of the story of this King. For how many seruants . . . gaue hee aboundant flowers from whence to gather hony, and in the end of Harvest burnt them in the Hiue? How many wiues did hee cut off, and cast off, as his fancy and affection changed?

Ralegh also condemned Henry for his 'vaine enterprises abroade' into which he poured 'more Treasure, than all our victorious Kings did in their seuerall Conquests'.[9]

In 1649, the year in which another king was executed, Edward Lord Herbert's *The Life and Raigne of King Henry the Eighth* was published. During and after the seventeenth century it was accepted as the pre-eminent study of him. He acknowledged that Henry had strengths: for example, 'that none of his predecessours understood the temper of Parliaments better than himself' and that he could display a 'generous disposition'. On the other hand he deserved his reputation, at home and abroad, as Henry the 'Cruell'. Herbert argued that 'With all his crimes yet, he was one of the most glorious Princes of his time.' This 'glorious' reputation, however, did not long outlive him and 'reasons of State' were no longer accepted as an excuse for his conduct. 'To conclude,' Herbert wrote, 'I wish I could leave him in his grave.'[10]

Henry VIII has remained a subject of seemingly endless fascination for historians and others. There is, however, no consensus of opinion about him. Studies of his life, reign, persona, moral and political conduct have been diverse in their approach, treatment and conclusions.

I. C. Flugel put him on the psychoanalyst's couch and established – to his satisfaction – that the young Henry early developed 'a powerful Oedipus complex', which was then transferred on to his sister-in-law Catherine. When marriage to her failed to produce male heirs, 'the idea of sterility as a punishment for incest' was an 'all-important factor' in terminating it. And so on.[11] The title of Clement Wood's biography, *King Henry the Rake*, indicates a very different approach, though still a lusty sexual focus:

A man who hungered and thirsted, and who in consequence ate and drank; a man who lusted and in consequence bedded whom he willed. . . .[12]

Henry also received treatment from a medical historian, Sir Arthur MacNalty. He too dealt with Henry's love life, or rather the possible consequences thereof, refuting the earlier belief that that his leg ulcer was syphilitic. MacNalty argued convincingly that it was a varicose ulcer.[13]

One undramatic yet unmistakable development in the historiography of Henry VIII is prominent historians' increasingly harsh criticism of both the man and his kingship. J. A. Froude, writing in the 1880s, was a notable exception. As G. R. Elton later wrote, he 'came to the study of the reign with every ingrained prejudice against that bloodstained monster . . . ; he left it with an ardent admiration for the king'.[14] Certainly Froude acknowledged that Henry had 'great . . . personal faults' as well as sharing in 'the errors of his age'. He concludes, however, that 'far deeper blemishes would be but as scars upon the features' of a king who 'in trying times' nobly upheld England's honour and guided it 'securely through the hardest crisis in its history'.[15] A. F. Pollard too was remarkably tolerant. In his biography (1902), a formidable work which mined the rich historical lode of the *Letters and Papers*, he acknowledged the 'terrible contradiction' between morals and politics during Henry's rule. However, he downplayed it as something 'inherent in all forms of human society'. He argued that the second Tudor's career must be explained by a study of his environment rather than of his character. Henry still emerges as the hero:

Surrounded by faint hearts and fearful minds, Henry VIII neither faltered nor failed. He ruled in a ruthless age with a ruthless hand, he dealt with a violent crisis by methods of blood and iron, and his measures were crowned with whatever sanction worldly success can give.

Pollard added, seemingly as words of praise, 'He is Machiavelli's *Prince* in action'. And he concluded on a favourable note, that for England's peace and material comfort it was well that she had as her King, in her hour of need, a man, and a man who counted the cost, who faced the risk, and who did with his might whatsoever his hand found to do.[16]

G. R. Elton, who was critical of Pollard, represented a shift to a harsher judgement of the king:

[W]e are no longer quite so likely to accept Henry's egomania with indulgence merely because it somehow helped to advance the cause of Protestant England.

He added that now we are also less willing to 'submerge the nastiness of the man in approval of the achievement'.[17] Six years later J. J. Scarisbrick's major biography of Henry VIII was published. It was, in many respects, a damning indictment of man and king. Despite all the glittering image projection, charm, good humour, camaraderie, warmth and affection, 'it is difficult to think of any truly generous or selfless action performed by him'. Furthermore, 'rarely, if ever, have the un-awareness and irresponsibility of a king proved more costly of material benefit to his people'.[18]

Not all are equally critical. Greg Walker, for example, cannot accept either of the juxtaposed images of the king as 'an unapproachable tyrant who would brook no contradiction' or 'a weak and malleable figure, prone to manipulation'. He acknowledges the repression and cruelty of the reign and Henry's active, personal involvement in it. At the same time, however, he emphasizes the various ways in which dissent, 'even on matters of high policy', could be openly expressed at the Court and even to Henry's face.[19] Nevertheless, historians have increasingly focused on the impressive and depressive array of personal weaknesses. They will crop up repeatedly. One example must suffice here: David Starkey's description of 'Henry's suspiciousness ... [which] turned into a huge distorting glass through which he viewed the world'. It could transform 'the most trivial incident' or 'the lightest word' into a capital offence.[20] Starkey's studies of the king, however, also illustrate one consistent feature both of early modern chronicles and of the regnal studies and biographies from Edward Lord Herbert onwards: Henry's ability to project powerful, lasting images. He was that mighty man of 'hardy prowess and great strength' (Hall), 'a special pattern of clemency and moderation' (Fulwell), 'one of the most glorious Princes of his time' (Herbert), a 'handsome giant with his bright and penetrating eye' (Elton) and 'To all appearances the very model of a strong king' (Starkey).

How Henry wanted the world to see him

Whether or not the Holbein paintings and the other images of the king, especially during the revolutionary decades of the 1530s and 1540s, amounted to conscious and deliberate royal propaganda is not clear. Greg Walker, for example, sees such artistic imagery as simply normal, traditional exercises in royal portraiture.[21] One cannot ignore or deny the power of the iconography to be found in Henry's palaces, which were stages as well as royal homes. Holbein's portraits, especially his fresco in the privy chamber in Whitehall, were powerful images of the personal dominance of Henry and the might of monarchy. Furthermore, the king also used imagery and emblems to project his imperial aspirations. The arched or closed crown imperial, already employed as an image in his father's reign,[22] figured throughout his coronation, the following celebrations, and at the tourney to mark the birth of his son in 1511. In 1533 Henry's newly proclaimed imperial authority was stated in Anne Boleyn's coronation pageants, again by the use of the closed crown.[23] For most of the time, however, the artistic images of the king were in places where only a minute fraction of his subjects could see them. Henry's image projection focused much more on the grandeur and newsworthy activity of his Court and on his personal conduct and exploits than on less accessible portraiture and iconography. He projected himself in person rather than in artistic image, especially within the context of his stately homes.

This accounts for the frenetic building, extension and renovation of royal homes which characterized much of Henry VIII's reign. He was not satisfied with those which he inherited. Westminster, for example, was uncomfortable, the home of the common law courts and chancery as well as the house of lords' venue whenever parliament met; then, in April 1512, much of the palace was destroyed by fire. His London residences were no better: the stone White Tower, within the Tower of London, was cold and inappropriately small for one of Henry's grand vision; and Baynard's Castle nearby could not be expanded. Richmond up-river and Greenwich downstream were more regal and palatial, but, although Henry was attached to the latter, both were outside the focus of monarchy in Westminster and the City. Henry proceeded to acquire or build new royal homes: Bridewell on the Thames was completed in 1523; Beaulieu in Essex was purchased and from 1516 converted to royal needs; St George's Chapel at Windsor, begun by Edward IV, was completed in 1519; and a new chapel was added at Eltham in 1519–22. There was also the wasteful and extravagant temporary palace, erected in 1520, at the

Field of Cloth of Gold and with fountains free-flowing with wine as the English and French kings competed in the projection of images of power, wealth, honour and glory.

Discounting the temporary folly of 1520, these were the most important improvements during the first twenty years of the reign. They amounted to a relatively modest addition to royal residences. Furthermore, Thomas Wolsey, not Henry, was the driving force managing these projects. However, as Simon Thurley has shown, Wolsey's fall from royal favour and from his position as chief minister resulted in a dramatic transformation. Henry became actively involved in the acquisition and extension of properties and their elaborate, impressive refurbishment, in order to provide regal settings fitting for a great Prince.[24] From Wolsey he obtained five properties, most notably Hampton Court and York Place, renamed Whitehall, just up the road from Westminster Palace. Many other properties came to him by exchange, forfeiture, purchase or as a consequence of the dissolution of the monasteries.

This spate of acquisitions was accompanied by – perhaps it triggered – the king's active interest in desirable architectural developments. Hampton Court and Whitehall were transformed into magnificent settings in which he could strut before an admiring English elite and the ambassadors of Europe. Together with other royal dwellings, such as Beaulieu, Greenwich, Richmond, Windsor and Woodstock (in Oxfordshire), they could accommodate and provision both the king and his Court. To these Henry added Oatlands (in Surrey) which he acquired in 1537. There were also the 'lesser houses', such as urban St James's (started in 1531), and the rural hunting lodges to which he could withdraw with hunting companions but without the full Court. His last building venture, commencing in 1538, fell into this category. 'Nonsuch' was 'the ultimate expression of Henry VIII's quest for privacy'.[25] It was, at the same time, lavishly decorated and architecturally ostentatious: a public statement to the world about a prince and a palace nonpareil and at the same time a bid to outdazzle Francis I's Chateau de Chambord. The venture involved the entire destruction of the village of Cuddington and, in order to provide the necessary building stone, the demolition of Merton Priory.

Henry's role in the royal building process after 1529 was a typically flamboyant as well as active one. When he added apartments and a study and renovated the great hall at Eltham, he decided that the view from his new study at Eltham was impaired by a hill. He issued an order that workmen were to remove the obstruction. During the many building operations in his reign he would require to see plans or send modified ones. Speed was of the essence and he was intolerant of delays. His impatience and frequent interference resulted in ceaseless work by day and candle-lit night, costly overtime payments, injuries and deaths among the workmen, often shoddy workmanship, and a palace at Whitehall which consisted largely of a hastily thrown-up string of buildings.[26] Despite such shortcomings the building achievements of his reign added to his contemporary and posthumous reputation. William Harrison, writing in Elizabeth I's reign, exclaimed, 'Certes masonrie did neuer better flourish in England than in his time.' He described the late king as 'nothing inferiour in this trade to Adrian the emperour and Justinian the lawgiuer'.[27] Simon Thurley, writing in Elizabeth II's reign, endorsed Harrison's opinion: 'Henry VIII was certainly the most prolific, talented, and innovative builder to sit on the English throne.'[28]

The palaces were the stages on which Henry acted out roles and projected images for native and foreign audiences to applaud. In theatrical set-pieces, incorporating verse, music and dance, he would play the chivalrous lover seeking against the odds to win the hand of a virtuous, unblemished beauty. In one such piece, staged for the delectation of the imperial ambassador in 1522, 'Ardent Desire' (played by Henry) and his friends launched a barrage of oranges and dates against a castle in which eight beautiful women were imprisoned. The warrior heroes triumphed and all concluded with much dancing. We may find it trite or frivolous now, but it was acted out with allegorical solemnity then. And it had a curious portent, because one of those maidenly innocents who was rescued was Anne Boleyn.[29]

It was within the Court structure, physically most evident in the king's 'greater houses' or palaces, that Henry was able to play out most effectively his various idealized public roles. Some of his constructive roles were carried out continuously, without the public fanfare and focus which we might come to expect of such an arrogant king. For example, there was the 'caring' Prince: Henry's privy purse expenses included regular payments to 'poor people', a hermit and others, as well as charitable gifts to 'a poor man that had thirteen children, for their relief', to a 'frantick man', to 'three sick women at Greenwich', to 'a blind woman being a harper' and to many others. No doubt the distribution of alms during royal progresses cultivated the public image of the loving Prince. In October 1532, for example, money was paid to 'Thomas foteman to dispose in Almesse by the way towards Shepey' and other sums to poor women, some of whom had brought chickens, quinces, apples and pears to the king.[30] Such acts, however, were carried out without public ceremony or fanfare, nor were they confined to progresses. Daily alms were distributed when Henry was in residence: for example, the household books in 1529 recorded this when he was staying at Hampton Court, Greenwich and Bridewell.[31] Two years later an impressed Venetian ambassador reported that 'He gives many alms, relieving paupers, orphans, widows and cripples, his almoner disbursing annually ten thousand golden ducats for this purpose.'[32]

Royal generosity also extended to scholars at Cambridge and Oxford. Some received occasional gifts. Others were king's scholars whose exhibitions at the two English universities and also at Paris were financed by Henry. Amongst the king's scholars in Paris was an Oxford MA, John Mason, who afterwards entered royal service and, in 1552, became chancellor of his old university. In contrast, Henry's exhibitioners also included Reginald Pole, who became in the 1530s an ardent papist and enemy of the king. Other exhibitioners are less well known to us. It all adds up to a genuine royal interest in educational patronage. As already noted, Lord Mountjoy wrote in 1509 of Henry's warm attachment to men of letters.[33] It was no mere image projection but an expression of the king's love of learning, about which there can be no serious doubt. It also manifested itself in his endowments at the universities of Cambridge and Oxford.[34] Henry's educational patronage was extremely modest when considered in relation to the enormous assets which he received from the dissolution of the monasteries. Nevertheless, that patronage contributed favourably to his contemporary reputation and anything which fed his insatiable ego was personally gratifying.

Other images were more clearly cultivated for public plaudits: that he was, for example, a merciful monarch. On 'Evil May Day' 1517 crowds of Londoners ran amok in anti-foreign riots. The ring-leaders were executed and several hundreds were imprisoned. In response to a personal appeal, made on bended knees by Queen Catherine, her husband agreed to pardon them. This was then done in a public showpiece:

the kynge satte in Westmyster halle, and there was commandyd the citte to come in their clothynge, and the rest of them that was pardent to come with halters abowte their neckes and to aske pardone, and soo a generall pardone was gevyne unto theme alle that came that tyme.[35]

Henry showed little interest in one form of image projection, that of the British connexion. This is surprising, especially because of the Tudors' Welsh origins and Henry's imperial ambitions. It would have been consistent for a king who sought French conquests, claimed the crowns of France and Scotland and aspired to the office of Holy Roman Emperor to present himself as a ruler of British descent. Yet an early interest in the British origins of the Tudors declined in Henry VII's reign, and his son made no serious attempt to claim a pedigree as ancient and prestigious as any European monarchy. It is particularly surprising that Henry VIII did not exploit the Arthurian legend for propaganda purposes. After all, King Arthur asserted his authority over England and Scotland, defeated the Irish and the Vikings of Denmark, Iceland, Norway and Sweden – and he seized Gaul. Furthermore, Henry's elder brother was born in 1486 at Winchester, where King Arthur's round table was preserved, and he was christened Arthur. These events triggered a revival of interest amongst Court poets, but it was not cultivated by the Tudors and the revival was a brief one. Henry had the round table repaired and painted in 1516. Nevertheless, King Arthur rarely figured in his Court pageants, the last occasion being in 1522,[36] during the visit of Emperor Charles V, when eight pageants were staged in his honour. The fourth pageant depicted the 'victorious emprowr' King Arthur, enthroned 'with a crowne imperiall' and flanked by all the 'prynces thatt were under his obeisaunce'.[37] It was, however, a representation designed to flatter and please the imperial visitor rather than a statement about the English king. Two years before, a statue of Arthur was prominent in the entertainment Henry provided for Charles at Calais. This was not just 'an international figure of chivalry', nor did it proclaim Henry's British pedigree. Rather, it has been persuasively argued, the statue symbolized England and Henry.[38] One other British symbol was the red dragon, reputedly of Welsh descent and associated with the last British king. It certainly figured prominently in Tudor heraldry, as supporter and other forms of decoration. It does not seem, however, that it was consciously used to indicate a royal pedigree of British or specifically Welsh origin. The red dragon 'symbolized the Tudor dynasty rather than the Tudor descent'.[39]

In contrast Henry revelled in the image of the Godly King, an image expressed partly through the significance of religious rituals in the routines and calendar of his Court. Twelve of the most important Court days, such as Michaelmas, Christmas, Twelfth Day and Easter, were lifted straight out of the Christian calendar.[40] Henry developed the use of the processional canopy (similar to that used in Corpus Christi Day processions in the Catholic Church), his courtiers used the triple bow (with its Holy Trinity association), and he had a pulpit constructed in Whitehall's chapel court for the delivery of Lenten sermons. In all of these ways Henry presented himself as the Lord's chosen and anointed lieutenant. When Archbishop Thomas Cranmer and Thomas Cromwell tried to persuade a reluctant Henry to authorize an English Bible, they supported the publication of Miles Coverdale's translation (1535). Holbein's title page was clearly designed to secure the king's approval, because it depicted him 'like a little god, handing the Bible down to the prelates and lords'.[41] Henry, however, did not endorse the Coverdale Bible. The first authorized English translation was the Great Bible of 1539. Its frontispiece presented a simple royal image. It depicted the enthroned king not only as the Godly monarch, ensuring that his subjects received *Verbum Dei* (the Word of God), but also as a Godlike figure. So the spiritual and temporal counsellors and various social ranks are shown saying '*vivat rex*' and 'God save the King', not 'Praise the Lord'.[42] Few images would have been likely to circulate as widely within Henry's dominions as this one.

Of course Henry's supposed semi-divinity was not the product of some personal quirk. Throughout Christian Europe monarchy was a sacred institution. The king's sacrosanct quality was confirmed at his coronation when he was anointed and the symbols of his power – his regalia – were blessed. English and French kings were also supposedly endowed with the miraculous power to cure scrofula (tuberculosis of the lymph glands) by laying hands upon the affected parts. Another popular use of the English monarch's miraculous power was to protect people against epilepsy by touching gold and silver cramp rings. David Starkey identifies another significant expression of the sacred quality of English kingship: that the monarch had an aura which made it extremely difficult for many men to face him. This was clearly particularly true of Henry VIII. Late in his reign John Hale described the reverence, fear, even reluctance of his subjects to come into his presence, such was the majesty and 'divine estate' of a king. In this case, however, one has to add into the equation the huge, formidable bulk and the powerful presence of this moody, inconstant Tudor.[43]

Henry's strong religious convictions and his theological skills are considered elsewhere.[44] Of more immediate concern, as discussed above, is the imagery of the Godly Prince, which was how he wished the world to see him, especially once he had received statutory recognition as 'supreme head of the Church of England' in 1534. Alongside godliness, and not unrelated to it, was another essential quality of kingship: honour. Defence of royal honour was a driving force and 'one of the motivating principles' in Henry's life.[45] This was demonstrated in the disgrace of his most intimate boon companions, the 'minions', in 1519. During the previous year he had created a new position in his household, that of Gentlemen of the Privy Chamber, presumably to give official status to some of those closest to him. Disapproval or downright hostility was widely expressed. The Venetian ambassador, Sebastian Giustinian, reported that the minions, some of whom had been his intimates since 1513, had been responsible for the king's 'incessant

gambling, which has made him lose of late a treasure of gold'.[46] Furthermore, whilst on a diplomatic mission to France late in 1518, 'they with
the frenche kynge roade daily disguysed through Parys, throwyng egges,
stones and other foolishe trifles at the people' – a diplomatic embarrass-
ment for Henry. Worse still, when they returned to England, his boon
companions

were all frenche, in eatyng, drynkyng and apparell, yea and in frenche vices and
bragges, so that all the estates of Englande were by them laughed at. . . . [They]
so highly praised the frenche kyng and his courte, that in a maner they thought
litle of the [English] kyng and his court, in comparison of the other.[47]

The council now intervened and approached Henry, because of its
concern that these young men, 'not regardyng [the king's] estate nor degree,
were so familier and homely with hym, and plaied such light touches
with hym, that they forgat themselves'. The council then authorized the
removal of four of the minions – Francis Bryan, Nicholas Carew, William
Collin and Edward Neville – together with some other courtiers, from
their positions and from the Court. At about the same time, proposals for
reform of the royal household and financial administration were drawn
up. They were drafted in Henry's name and involved his active role.
Then, after the minions' fall, they were implemented. In particular, they
transformed the privy chamber into a large, organized, autonomous
department at the centre of the royal household and therefore 'of the
king's private life'.[48] It has been variously argued that the instigator of
these events was Cardinal Wolsey, who was jealous and fearful of political rivals, a group of councillors who were offended by the minions'
dishonourable conduct, or Henry himself.[49] One cannot be certain who
initiated the expulsion of the minions and the subsequent reforms. However, the surviving evidence makes the cardinal the least likely. Hall's
account is the fullest available one and this certainly points to the king.
According to Hall, the reason why the council approached him was its
belief that the 'minions' behaviour was 'not mete to be suffred for the
kynges honor'. This brings us back to Henry's concern about his honour.
So he told his councillors 'that he had chosen them [to be] of his counsaill,
both for the maintenaunce of his honor, and for the defence of all thyng
that might blemishe the same.' Therefore, he committed the matter to
them for 'their reformacion'. Hall's identification of Henry as the chief
mover, in response to his councillors, is reinforced by Giustinian. The
king's lord treasurer, the duke of Norfolk, had informed him 'that on
coming to himself, and resolving to lead a new life, he, of his own accord,
removed these companions of his excesses'.[50] Norfolk would not have

dared to pass on such intimate detail and food for gossip without royal authorization.

The 'minions' episode illustrates the lifelong importance of honour to Henry VIII. The political culture of honour had traditionally been pluralistic, resting upon lordship. The king was 'the greatest of lords and his court the exemplar, as well as the largest, richest and most brilliant of all honour communities'.[51] At the same time, kingship was only one of many lordships. This, however, changed under Henry, who, in the words of Mervyn James, carried through 'a "nationalization" of the honour system. . . . [T]he kingship launched a powerful initiative to establish itself as "the fount of honour", the source not only of "dignity" and office within the crown's gift, but also of gentility itself.' Increasingly, honourable status could be conferred or confirmed only by heraldic visitations authorized or approved by the crown. This enlarged the role and importance of the heralds, incorporated by the crown in the college of arms in 1484. Then, in 1530, Henry asserted more direct royal control. During a jurisdictional conflict between two heralds, he informed the disputants and the other heralds who were present that the power of 'giving of arms and the cognizances of arms to ennoble any person . . . belongeth to his prerogative'. Future visitations were carried out by royal commission.[52]

Another expression of the importance of honour was the creation of new chivalric orders or the reactivation of old ones in the Courts of Europe. In England, for example, the Order of the Garter had gone into decline during the long reign of Henry VI, but it was revived by Edward IV and the first two Tudors. To be elected one of the twenty-six knights of the Garter was one of the greatest honours which a king could bestow, especially in Henry VIII's reign, when it 'attained a greater height than at any time before'.[53] Its annual grand feast was celebrated in St George's Chapel and Hall at Windsor Castle with solemn grandeur and elaborate ceremonies on St George's Day, the anniversary of England's patron saint. The drafting of the largest body of statutes, compiled in Latin and dealing with the proceedings, conduct of members and the collar of the Order, was undertaken in 1519–22 'by that munificent increaser of the splendor of this most Noble Order, King Henry the Eighth; chiefly in regard some of the former Statutes were obscure, doubtful, and needed further explication; others wanted reducing and contraction'.[54] His devotion to the Garter was understandable. The Order's founder, Edward III, had spent much of his energy, resources and reign 'for the recovery of his right to the Kingdom of France'. The constant goal of Henry too was the French crown and kingdom.[55] Furthermore, the Order was founded 'to honor military Virtue with some glorious favours and rewards; that so true Nobility ... after long and hazardous adventures, should not enviously be deprived of that honor which it hath really deserved'.[56]

The Order of the Garter illustrates how one of the most important images inseparable from the Henrician ideals of honour and chivalry was that of the warrior. This was expressed in two ways: disporting himself on the Continent as the great general and, at home, in tournaments involving feats of arms and also chivalric theatrical entertainments.[57] Tournaments were designed to entertain the Court and, at the same time, to project to the world images of England's chivalrous and honourable king.[58] Henry certainly had a favourable impact on subjects and foreigners alike. When Tournai surrendered in 1513, he staged a tournament after an excellent exhibition of personal horsemanship and before a sumptuous banquet. He duly impressed Margaret of Savoy and many foreign nobles. According to John Taylor, clerk of the parliaments, Henry excelled every one 'as much in agility and in breaking spears, as in nobleness of stature'. In fact the king lost the first match, against de Walhain, he and a Spanish captain, Arriere, both broke their lances and, at the end, Roberet Macquereau awarded the day to Henry's opponents. Diplomats and English observers simply glossed over this and praised the king's dashing performance.[59] In 1515 it was the turn of the Venetian ambassadors to be dazzled and in 1517 of Flemish representatives.[60] The image of the royal warrior could not be separated from the sensitive royal honour. Politicians learned that and attempted to exploit Henry's honour to their own ends. In 1542 Imperial ambassador Chapuys was endeavouring to persuade him to ally with Charles V in order, as he put it, to prevent the destruction of Christendom by France and the Ottoman Turks:

[In] respecte that God hath ordened his Majestie to be soo gret a prince, soo rich a prince, with such excellent wisedom, his Majestie shuld not let Christendom perish in his tyme, but use his gretnesse, his riches, and his wisedome to the pacification and repose of Christendom.

Thereby, Chapuys concluded, Henry would enjoy 'the good wyl, gret renowne, and fame of al the worlde, ... deserve rewarde of God ... [and also have] so moch honnour as never prince had'.[61] Three years later Bishop Gardiner of Winchester, writing to Secretary Paget, lamented the costly war being waged against France and regarded peace as both necessary and urgent, not only because of the expense and suffering but also because of Henry's declining physical condition. What stood in the way? Not Henry's honour, according to Gardiner.

Youe wyl saye the Kinges Majestie ... canne digeste the displeasour and ... willingly contempne his owne honnour for the wealth and preservation of the realme; or elles ... understand that to be most honnorable that is most expedient for the realme. I thinke noo prince in Christendom coulde excede his Highnes in thiese considerations.

The bishop's lengthy and troubled letter, however, makes these words ring hollow. He told Paget that 'we be in a labyrinth' and his letter reads like an attempt to work through it; in particular, to muster arguments for peace and to meet Henry's probable objections, including the matter of honour.[62]

Finally, Henry was, and sought to be recognized as, the cultivated king *sans pareil*. Music was his particular passion. He was not only an able performer on the flute, harp, keyboard, lute, recorder and virginals, but he also sang well and composed. His generous patronage attracted accomplished musicians from all over the Continent, but also poets, painters, architects, sculptors, gilders and carvers. As a consequence his Court became a European cultural capital.[63]

How the world chose to see Henry

Public opinion about Henry VIII changed in some respects over the course of years. This was partly the consequence of hostile religious positions produced by the Reformation, whether the voices were Catholic, Protestant or papist. It was partly due to partisan political positions: whether, for example, when Henry plunged into war, those expressing opinions about him were pro- or anti-Habsburg, Francophile or Francophobe. His transformation from the young Apollo to the bloated spectre of his later years, the jettisoning of wives and ministers, the long list of State killings and religious martyrs, all contributed to changing perceptions. Furthermore, it is not always possible to be sure of the sincerity of praise offered up by his favour-hunting, self-interested, ingratiating or simply vulnerable subjects. Edmund Dudley wrote glowing words about the newly crowned king, who

hath fullie determynid hym selfe not only to reforme all suche thinges as in tymes past haue ben disorderid and abusyd within this his realme, But also to his greatest merite to restore his subjiectes from diuers wronges and iniuries, and as an obedient child ... to see the will of his said father and king to be truly performid, to his mervelous grete ... honour.[64]

A desire for clemency, however, rather than sincerity, may have prompted such praise.

The young king's tutors too extolled his virtues. In a letter to Erasmus, just a month after Henry's accession, William Lord Mountjoy told him that, if only he knew 'how courageously and wisely he is now acting, and what a passion he has for justice and honesty . . . with or without wings you would fly to us here to look at the new and lucky star'. He proceeded to wax lyrical about the joyous time. Erasmus 'would be bound to weep for joy' if only he was there to see 'how all are congratulating themselves on their prince's greatness' and praying for his long life. He went on to laud the way in which '[o]ur king's heart is set . . . upon virtue, reputation and eternal renown'.[65] Henry's old tutor may have believed all that he wrote. On the other hand, it was potentially hazardous to put critical pen to paper about the king. In the fast communication network of a watchful, gossip-hungry Court it was common practice and common-sense to favour discretion at the expense of honest confession.

Another tutor, the poet John Skelton, wrote in frequent praise of his royal master, whom, in 'The Douty Duke of Albany', he compared to Hercules, Solomon, Absalom, Hector and Scipio. He confessed in verse that Henry's virtues were so many and diverse that his 'Lernyng is too small/For to recount them all'. Yet he became increasingly and even bitterly hostile to Thomas Cardinal Wolsey, whom Henry promoted, patronized and to whom, for so long, he delegated much power and authority. 'Why Come Ye Nat to Court?', 'Colyn Cloute' and 'Speake Parrot', all written in 1521–2, were outspoken attacks upon the king's chief minister. In his play *Magnyficence*, which is concerned with the ways in which 'a corrupted king and his corrupters abuse a commonwealth', Henry, his minister and his minions all figure.[66] In his earlier *Speculum Principis* (1511), written for his royal ex-pupil and presented to him, Skelton advised Henry: 'Bind yourself to a spouse and bind yourself to her indissolubly. . . . Do not believe everyone easily. Hear the other side. Be affable. . . . Restrain anger. . . . Cherish the constant. . . . Deliberate slowly. . . . Do not consider only yourself. . . . [Be] always pious, always gracious, always gentle, clement and humble.' His advice fell on deaf ears, as he must have realized when he wrote *Magnyficence* in 1516.[67] This illustrates the way in which early purveyors of panegeyrics about Henry could become more critical in the course of time. Skelton's extravagant praise of Henry in that much later composition, 'The Douty Duke of Albany', would seem to contradict this. It may be explained, however, either as a bid to safeguard his personal security after the attacks on Wolsey, or as a contrast with the 'lousy lothsumnesse' of the 'rude ranke Scottes' whom Skelton detested.[68]

Skelton was not alone in his comparison of King Henry with King Solomon. In about 1535 Holbein portrayed him as that prince of 'unparalleled wisdom and prudence', receiving gifts from a kneeling queen of Sheba.[69] More frequent, when the schism with Rome occurred, were the comparisons with Darius, who proclaimed the God of Daniel as 'the living God'; with Moses the lawgiver and (as Catherine Parr described him) the deliverer of his people from bondage; with Paul, the spiritual counsellor of his people; and, above all, with David, reputed author of the psalms and the liberator who vanquished Goliath.[70]

Panygerics by prominent men were a common feature of the reign. Erasmus, for example, lavished praise upon this royal devotee of learning and the arts. In 1513 he sent greetings 'To the invincible king of England', describing him as 'of all kings the most illustrious' and avowing the continuation of the same loyalty and devotion which he had promised 'long ago when you were a boy full of promise'.[71] John Leland was commissioned by Thomas Treffry of Fowey to adorn the newly built St Mawes Castle with a suitable Latin inscription in honour of Henry. Translated it reads,

Henry VIII, King of England, France and Ireland, the most invincible, placed me here as protection for the state. . . . Submit your sails, O ships, to the authority of Henry. Your glory and fame, Henry, will endure for ever. . . .[72]

In Thomas Starkey's *Dialogue between Pole and Lupset,* written probably between 1529 and 1532, the fictional Thomas Lupset states that 'we have so nobul a prynce, whome we are sure no thyng to haveso prynted in hys brest as the cure of hys commyn wele, both day & nyght remembryng the same . . . '. Later, Reginald Pole concurs with Lupset, recalling that 'as we sayd in our fyrst days communycatyon, . . . we have now . . . by the provydence of god such a prynce & of such wysedome that he may ryght wel & justely be subyecte to no law, whose prudence & wysedome ys lyvely law & true pollycy . . .'[73]

It is ironic that Starkey put such words of praise into the mouth of one who was to become one of the king's fiercest and enduring opponents. Nevertheless it is understandable that such men as Erasmus, Leland and Starkey sang Henry's praises. Erasmus was unabashed in his fulsome flattery of the great and the wealthy who might be beneficial to him. The king was Leland's patron, whilst Starkey presented the *Dialogue* to him in the hope of advancement.

A much more significant and impressive testimony to Henry's skilful projection of public images, through his personal skills paraded in the context of a lavish theatrical Court, was the response of diplomatic representatives, who were often bedazzled by their first encounter with him. For example, in 1515 Piero Pasqualigo, Venetian Ambassador Extraordinary, and Ambassador Badoer were taken by river from London to Richmond, where, on St George's Day, the king celebrated the institution of the Order of the Garter. On arrival they were fed and then escorted 'through sundry chambers all hung with most beautiful tapestry'. Pasqualigo recounted how they passed down the ranks of three hundred halbardiers in silver breast-plates 'and, by God, they were all as big as giants, so that the display was very grand'. Finally they reached Henry, who sat under a canopy of Florentine cloth of gold, 'the most costly thing I ever witnessed'. He was magnificently attired in crimson velvet hat, white and crimson satin doublet, scarlet hose and mantle of purple velvet. He was also adorned with a gold collar, 'from which there hung a round cut diamond, the size of the largest walnut I ever saw, . . . a pendent St George, entirely of diamonds' over his mantle, and on his left shoulder the Garter, whilst 'his fingers were one mass of jewelled rings'.

Pasqualigo's detailed description illustrates the importance of magnificent royal dress and its visual impact. Edward Hall was equally attentive to Henry's clothes in his *Chronicle*. The king clearly appreciated the importance of clothing in impressing onlookers, though furs, ornate buttons and dress jewellery were re-used and some of his old clothes were recycled, for example as cushion covers. Henry also armed himself with sumptuary laws in order to regulate dress. This enabled his personal control of the dress of those around him in Court in order 'to reflect his favour – or lack of it – and to promote himself'.[74]

Not only Pasqualigo but all the Venetians were in awe of Henry's presence, appearance and talents. Ambassador Guistinian, writing three days after Pasqualigo, reported that he is 'most excellent in his personal endowments, but is likewise so gifted and adorned with mental accomplishments of every sort that we believe him to have few equals in the world'. Guistinian (and Pasqualigo too) praised his linguistic skills, and his musical virtuosity: he 'plays well on the lute and harpsichord, [indeed] almost on every instrument; sings and composes fairly . . . [and] sings from book at sight'. The Venetian diplomats were also lyrical about Henry's beauty, 'which is indeed very great'. Pasqualigo described him as 'the handsomest potentate I ever set eyes on; above the usual height, with an extremely fine calf to his leg, his complexion very fair and bright, with auburn hair combed straight and short, in the French fashion, and a round face so very beautiful, that it would become a pretty woman . . . '. Guistinian thought it 'the prettiest thing in the world' to watch him play tennis, 'his fair skin glowing through a shirt of the finest texture'.

Of course Henry made sure that the diplomatic corps was also aware of his martial prowess, and, if the Venetian reports are an accurate gauge, he was successful in this. Giustinian reported that 'from what we have seen of him and in conformity, moreover, with the report made to us by others, this most serene King is . . . very expert in arms, and of great valour'. Giustinian's secretary, Nicolò Sagudino, described the three hours of jousting which they watched, 'the King excelling all the others, shivering many lances, and unhorsing one of his opponents; so that the show was most beautiful'. Sagudino, however, was not beguiled. He understood the purpose of Henry's display:

[O]n this occasion, his Majesty exerted himself to the utmost, for the sake of the ambassadors, and more particularly on account of Pasqualigo (who is returning to France to-day), that he may be able to tell King Francis what he has seen in England, and especially with regard to his Majesty's own prowess.

Nevertheless Henry's demonstration of personal excellence, wealth and power was persuasive. French diplomats admired his respect for *les savants* whilst one Venetian described him as generous to 'men of science, whom he is never weary of obliging'. Francisco Chieregato, the papal nuncio, appreciated the 'very elegant manners, extreme decorum and great politeness' of the Court. But his warmest praise was reserved for 'the invincible king, whose acquirements and qualities are so many and excellent that I consider him to excel all who ever wore a crown'. Guistinian wrote home that Henry had paid them such great honour, 'both in public and private, that were we to attempt narrating them in detail, we should not know how to do it in becoming terms'. So 'we exhort and remind your Highness to write him a letter of thanks . . . for it would prove not a little to your advantage'. In such ways did the king's skilful image projection win and retain allies.[75]

In 1531 Henry Tudor was forty and no longer the young athlete of twenty years earlier, yet he still managed to project images of youth, virtue and talent. He enjoyed one inestimable advantage, that he possessed in abundance the physical, mental and cultural attributes and sense of majesty which made such image projection effective. This is clear in the report made to the senate of Venice by its ambassador, Lodovico Falier, in November 1531:

In this eighth Henry, God combined such corporal and mental beauty, as not merely to surprise but to astound all men. Who could fail to be struck with admiration on perceiving the lofty position of so glorious a Prince to be in such accordance with his stature, giving manifest proof of that intrinsic mental superiority which is inherent in him?

In his forty-first year the king's physical appearance was still striking:

His face is angelic rather than handsome; his head imperial and bald, and he wears a beard, contrary to English custom. Who would not be amazed when contemplating such singular corporal beauty . . . adapting itself with the greatest ease to every manly exercise.

Falier then described Henry's skill as horseman, jouster and archer, adding that he 'plays at tennis most dextrously'. Thus far the ambassador reported back with the usual glowing words of the diplomats about the host-king. He was, however, also aware of Henry's deliberate image cultivation:

[N]ature having endowed him in youth with such gifts, he was not slow to enhance, preserve and augment them with all industry and labour. It seeming to him monstrous for a Prince not to cultivate moral and intellectual excellence, so from childhood he applied himself to grammatical studies, and then to philosophy and holy writ, thus obtaining the reputation of a lettered and excellent Prince.[76]

Henry was no poseur. He had a genuine love of letters and learning and a passion for the arts. But at the same time he wanted, in A. G. Dickens' words, 'to show off and earn himself a reputation that would put his contemporary fellow-sovereigns in the shade'.[77]

Time passed and the glorious physical images of youth faded. Not only did Henry grow older but his public persona changed. In 1531 Falier reflected on the way that he had 'allowed himself to be so allured by his pleasures that, accustomed to ease', he had left the business of government to Wolsey. After the cardinal's fall, however, he had taken 'such delight in his own rule, that from liberal he became avaricious'. The diplomat regretted the change from those days when anyone taking their leave received generous gifts, 'so now all quit his presence dissatisfied'.[78] Writing a decade later, French ambassador Marillac painted a gloomier picture of a Prince who 'seems tainted, among other vices, with three which, in a King, may be called plagues'. He itemized them as greed, 'distrust and fear' and 'lightness and inconstancy. . . . The first is that he is so covetous that all the riches in the world would not satisfy him' – hence the dissolution of the monasteries and 'the accusation of so many rich men who, whether condemned or acquitted, are always plucked. . . .

Everything is good prize', and the king gave no thought to the fact either that he had impoverished his people in order to make himself rich or that his material gains were less than his loss of reputation. Secondly, he trusted no-one and feared everyone, because of the many changes, 'tragedies and scandals' which he had caused. The third 'plague ... has perverted the rights of religion, marriage, faith and promise, as softened wax can be altered to any form'. Ambassadorial reports always have to be treated with caution, especially those of diplomats of the competitive Habsburg and Valois dynasties. Marillac in particular was very biased, unreliable and often inaccurate, although in this case it is difficult to quarrel with his assessment.[79]

Such criticisms were aired confidentially in diplomatic correspondence. Naturally it was potentially much more dangerous for the king's subjects to express critical opinions. It is well known how under James I, a much more lenient king than Henry VIII, Sir Anthony Weldon destroyed his own career prospects when he carelessly left lying around an essay highly critical of the Scots. Nevertheless, adverse opinions were expressed by a wide range of Henry's subjects, both during and after his reign. Some, such as the following, had obvious axes to grind.

George Cavendish, Cardinal Wolsey's servant, looked back from Mary I's reign on the career and fall of his master. He explained Wolsey's rise as a consequence of Henry's disposition 'all to mirth and pleasure and to follow his desire and appetite, nothing minding to travail in the busy affairs of this realm'. Wolsey held the key to personal success: he understood 'the King's natural inclination, and so fast as the other counsellors advised the King to leave his pleasure and to attend to the affairs of his realm, so busily did [Wolsey] persuade him to the contrary'. This, Cavendish tells us, 'delighted [Henry] much and caused him to have the greater affection and love to [him]'.[80] It is an insight into the early reign of a young, wayward, irresponsible Prince.

Sir Thomas More, who succeeded to the office of lord chancellor on Wolsey's fall, had no illusions about Henry. More's conversation with his son-in-law William Roper, oft-quoted to the point of tedium, nonetheless has its place here. Roper described the king's familiarity with Sir Thomas: how he would visit him at his Chelsea home, dine and 'be merry with him'. On one occasion after dinner, Henry walked for an hour in the garden with More, 'his arm about his neck'. Later, when Roper expressed his delight at the king's warmth, his father-in-law replied,

I find his grace my very good lord indeed; and I believe he doth as singularly favour me as any subject within this realm. Howbeit, son Roper, . . . if my head could win him a castle in France (for then there was war between us) it should not fail to go.[81]

Thomas Elyot was embittered by his dismissal, first from the position of clerk to the council in 1530 and then from the ambassadorship to Charles V in 1532. His anger was expressed in his disputation, *Of the Knowledge which Maketh a Wise Man.* In this dialogue between Dionysius and Plato, Alistair Fox saw implied parallels with Henry VIII and Elyot. If the description of Dionysius is to be read also as one of Henry, then it is a damning portrait of the Tudor: 'wonderfull, sensuall, vnstable & wandring in sondrye affections. Delytinge sometyme in voluptuous pleasures, [at other times] in gatheryng of great tresure and rychesse', and frequently given to 'a bestly rage and vengeable crueltie'. Elyot's description of his priorities recalls Cavendish's observations:

Aboute the publicke weale of his countraye alway remysse, in his owne desyres studious and diligent.[82]

His 'crueltie' and brutality were condemned, openly by Reginald Pole for the execution of More and Bishop Fisher and privately by Starkey, who, after the rebellion of 1536–7, cited the prophet Ezekiel's prediction of 'punishment for those who kill citizens without mercy'.[83] Such men as Cavendish, More, Elyot and Starkey were in and around the Court. They could pay a high price for criticism or opposition, as More certainly did.

During the turbulent years of the 1530s public discontent with Henrician policies and hostility to the king were frequently voiced and publicly expressed in many parts of the country. Images of the godly, virtuous Prince cut no ice there. Christopher Haigh has demonstrated this for Lancashire. There monks avowed to choose their own abbots, declared that 'there should be no lay knave head of the Church' and even denied that Henry was rightful king, because 'his father came in by no true line but by the sword'.[84] Many northern regular and secular clergy supported the Pilgrimage of Grace in 1536–7. The Pilgrims revealed a wide-ranging and deep discontent:[85] over Henry's 'divorce', the doubtful reputation and religion of Anne Boleyn, the break with Rome, the assault on the monasteries and the influence of such councillors as Thomas Audley, Richard Rich, Archbishop Cranmer and especially Thomas Cromwell.[86] One man petitioned the Pilgrims that it was necessary 'that vertuus men that luffythe the communwelthe schulde be of his [council]'. If the king would not oblige, then there should be a council of the commonwealth because princes should appoint 'vertus men as woylde regarde the communwelthe abuffe their princys lo[ve]'. He went on to recite precedents for the deposition of monarchs who would not take sound advice.[87] The stance of loyalist critic and petitioner, assumed by the rebel leader Robert Aske,[88] cannot detract from the threat posed by such discontent.

Furthermore, discontent was wide-ranging not only in issues but also in geography. The king's unpopularity, amongst the commons as well as the clergy, was evident in the widespread critical, abusive, even condemnatory reports, not only from the north but also across southern England: Henry was 'knave', 'heretic', 'adulterer', even the cause of the 'troublous and unstable' weather. A Sussex yeoman reported that the king had recently fallen and broken a rib, and 'it were pity but he should break his neck'. In Buckinghamshire one local declared that, 'I set not by the King's crown, and, if I had it here, I would play at football with it.'[89] The frequency and 'enormous popularity' of prophecies, circulating not only but 'most widely among the relatively humble orders of society' and 'not just in London but also in the provinces', were further indicators of common fears. Prophecies assumed a common form: darkness followed by light or, more precisely, division and conflict preceding recovery and renewal. They could and, especially during the 1530s, did focus on Henry VIII, sometimes as the cause of darkness and division.[90] The prophesiers were many and varied: monks, secular clergy such as John Dobson, men outside the elite, and women too, such as Elizabeth Barton. Dobson's prophecy, that Henry would lose two-thirds of his kingdom and that the pope would restore 'the right feithe againe', illustrates their danger. In prophecies, 'those like Dobson who resisted the political and religious revolutions of the King could not only find comfort for their fears but justification for their resistance'.[91]

Religious change was one of the most serious causes of discontent. Henry VIII's images of the Godly Prince were ineffective where either Protestants or papists were concerned. From Germany Luther led the Protestant assault in his response to the king's defence of the Catholic sacraments, *Assertio Septem Sacramentorum*, released in 1521.[92] He dismissed Henry as a 'deaf adder', warning him that if he deliberately 'forges lies against the majesty of my King in heaven', it was Luther's right 'to spatter his Anglican royal highness with his own mud and filth'. He proceeded to dismiss Henry as a 'wretched scribbler, suffering from lack of matter', and as someone who 'with his lies acts the part of a comic jester rather than that of a king'.[93] Images of the Godly King had no place either in the convictions of English Protestants who took refuge in exile. Indeed, quite the reverse: Richard Hilles, writing from Strassburg to Henry Bullinger in September 1543, informed him that 'Our king has within these two months ... burnt three godly men in one day. For in the month of July he married the widow[94] of a certain nobleman, of the name of Latimer; and he is always wont to celebrate his nuptials by some wickedness of this kind.'[95]

Not all Protestants, however, condemned Henry. In the early 1540s, when Thomas Becon was twice obliged to recant, he wrote *The Policy of War*. The sincerity of his sentiments expressed there may be questioned, but it cannot be disproved. Becon stressed the duty of every Prince to 'conserve and keep his realm in safe estate' and free from invasion. He then proceeded to praise 'our most puissant and redoubted king' for the way he had

fortressed this his most flourishing monarchy, empire, and kingdom, with all things that any man can invent for the prosperous conservation of a common-weal! Never was there prince that took like pains for the safeguard of his commonalty. . . . [He] is a very right and true father to this our country of England, as his most godly acts and virtuous enterprises do manifestly shew every day more and more.

Becon's priorities explain the praise: Henry had fortified England against the deadly enemy, popery. Furthermore, as his text reveals, he had accepted Henry's assertion of *imperium*.[96]

Whereas even Luther moderated his hostile position of the early 1520s, there was no real room for manoeuvre or compromise between the Henrician and papal positions. This placed English papists in a perilous position. The clear, inflexible terms of statutory treason in the Succession Acts and the Treason Act of 1534 made overt criticism or opposition to changes a dangerous, even suicidal, practice during the 1530s and 1540s. It could be argued that such laws were necessary to protect and preserve both Henry and his patrimony. But C. S. L. Davies argues with reason that 'the treason law was sometimes used . . . as an everyday weapon of politics . . . [which] in turn depended as much on the king's whim, as on any consideration of the public good'.[97] There were victims aplenty. Henry Pole Lord Montague, for example, incurred the ultimate penalty in 1538, solely on his brother Geoffrey's evidence. Montague reputedly said that Lord Darcy, one of the Pilgrims' leaders in 1536, 'played the fool; he went about to p[luck away the] Council. He should first have begun with [the head].' So once again we have reputed talk of the desirability of Henry's death or removal.[98] Meanwhile, the third brother, Reginald, a cardinal in exile at Rome, waited like other English papists for a better day. That came, albeit briefly, in 1553 with the accession of Henry VIII's Roman Catholic daughter, Mary. During her reign Nicholas Harpsfield wrote a treatise on the late king's termination of his first marriage. It was a classic indictment of both the king and his mistress: 'Oh what a strange and unlucky thing was this for the King to put away such a noble, virtuous lady . . . and his true, most loving, chaste, tender wife, for such an incestuous woman [Anne Boleyn]', with whom, Sir Thomas Wyatt told him, he had had his 'carnal pleasure'. After 'this divorce' the king was

wonderfully changed and altered to the worse:

1, that is in fleshly and sensual carnality;
2, in schism and heresy;
3, in cruelty; and
4, in covetousness.[99]

The Roman Catholic Scottish bishop and chronicler John Leslie was similarly hostile to a schismatic king who also displayed brutality, dishonesty, a disregard for justice, vanity and gullibility, tyranny, brutality and inhumanity and a joy in blood-letting. His fellow countryman and chronicler, George Buchanan, was not as harsh in his judgement. As a Protestant, he approved of Henry's break with Rome. Yet he too portrays him as a seriously flawed king. He was 'short-tempered, childishly proud, and not a great thinker – out go temperance and wisdom – and he may be cruel'. Leslie and Buchanan laboured under no illusions about their aggressive southern neighbour and their unfavourable perception of him was reinforced by fear of his designs upon Scotland. Certainly they saw the harsh reality behind the Tudor's attempts at image projection. Indeed one image, that of Henry the warrior, could have served only to strengthen their distrust and distaste.[100]

Conclusion

The supposed importance, even existence, of State-sponsored image-making has been persuasively questioned by Sydney Anglo. He recognized that a variety of opportunities were available for a monarchy to make statements about kingship, for example through preaching, pictures and printed texts and, especially, in the symbols and emblems to be seen on State occasions, royal buildings, works of art and the coinage. Few of those who observed such emblems, however, would have been capable of interpreting their meaning and grasping their significance.[101]

If an important purpose of major royal ceremonial occasion was to make public statements about the monarchy, then the changes in royal aspirations and in religion during the sixteenth century would have affected rituals and ceremonies. Yet the two most important State occasions, the coronation and royal funeral, retained their traditional character and forms. Royal progresses were more frequent events, when royalty displayed itself publicly. However, apart from Henry VIII's visit to York in 1541, his progresses 'normally did not go very far'. In any case, as Anglo points out, the normal purpose of the progress was recreational not political and only a tiny percentage of his subjects ever witnessed the monarch 'on the road'. When Renaissance Princes entered their cities they were greeted with elaborate, often extravagant, civic pageantry, full of historical, Scriptural and classical symbolism. These spectacles, however, were staged by city governors and citizens, not by monarchs, and they projected civic aspirations and loyalties rather than royal images. Tournaments, which Henry loved, and annual ceremonies of the Order of the Garter, to which he attached great importance, provided further opportunities for the public to view him and his Court. Some members of the public were admitted to the viewing stands around the tiltyard and to the Garter Chapel, but they amounted to a miniscule, certainly insignificant, proportion of the national population.

Anglo justifiably concludes that 'There is little evidence to support the view that the English monarchy employed a propaganda machine other than sporadically.' He also dismisses the 'modern, academic invention' of 'a carefully-thought-out systematic sales promotion of recondite imagery to the nation at large'.[102]

Nevertheless, Henry VIII enjoyed the projection of personal images to the world wherever he moved. It was a personal characteristic of his particular style of government. His subjects did not have to comprehend the heraldic niceties and subtle symbolism which adorned royal palaces and State occasions. The imposing figure of their king, parading in a setting of richness, pomp and grandeur, was enough to impress them. Image projection also had a political importance on the diplomatic scene. The contemporary reports from the Field of the Cloth of Gold, from Henry's meetings with Emperor Charles V and from ambassadors resident at the Tudor Court all attest to that. One last word: the situation was not static. The European Reformation, Henry's break with Rome and his brutality towards opponents caused instability and conflict. As Sharon Jansen writes, 'Those at both the highest and lowest social levels actively and strongly challenged the government's new order.'[103] Renewed war also hardened diplomatic positions. Image-making could have little effect in such circumstances, yet it remains a characteristic of Henry's kingship.

Notes

1 Starkey, *Personalities and Politics*, pp. 15–16.

2 See below, p. 40; Baumann, 'The Virtuous Prince', in idem, ed., pp. 168–9.

3 Ibid., pp. 170–1.

4 *Anglica Historia*, pp. xxviii–xxx, 333, 335.

5 Baumann, 'The Virtuous Prince', pp. 171–3, 187.

6 Hall, fol. 180–180v.

7 Jürgen Beer, 'The Image of a King', in Baumann, ed., pp. 147–8, 190.

8 W. Camden, *Annales: The True and Royall history of the famous Empresse Elizabeth*, London, 1627, fols 3v–4.

9 C. A. Patrides, ed., Sir Walter Ralegh, *The History of the World*, London, 1971, pp. 56–7.

10 Edward, Baron Herbert of Cherbury, *The life and raigne of King Henry the Eighth*, London, 1649, pp. 176, 571, 574.

11 I. C. Flugel, 'Of the Character and Married Life of Henry VIII', *International Journal of Psychoanalysis*, 6 (1920), 26–9, 33–4.

12 C. Wood, *King Henry the Rake [Henry VIII and His Women]*, Boston, Mass., 1929, pp. 322–3.

13 A. S. MacNalty, *Henry VIII: A Difficult Patient*, London, 1952, pp. 159–61. But see also MacNalty's views on the possibility of osteomyelitis in Scarisbrick, *Henry VIII*, p. 485 and n. 2.

14 G. R. Elton, *Henry VIII: An Essay in Revision*, London, 1962, p. 4.

15 J. A. Froude, *The Reign of Henry the Eighth*, 3 vols, London, 1908, 3, p. 426.

16 A. F. Pollard, *Henry VIII*, London, 1966, pp. 351, 353.

17 Elton, *Henry VIII*, p. 5.

18 Scarisbrick, *Henry VIII*, pp. 506–7, 526.

19 Walker, *Persuasive Fictions*, pp. 14–17.

20 Starkey, *Personalities and Politics*, p. 126.

21 Walker, *Persuasive Fictions*, pp. 72–95.

22 G. Kipling, *The Triumph of Honour: Burgundian Origins of the Elizabethan Renaissance*, Leiden, 1977, p. 71.

23 D. Hoak, 'The Iconography of the Crown Imperial', in idem, ed., *Tudor Political Culture*, Cambridge, 1995, pp. 54–5, 77–9.

24 Simon Thurley, *The Royal Palaces of Tudor England*, New Haven and London, 1993, pp. 41–8.

25 Ibid., p. 63.

26 Ibid., pp. 39–40.

27 F. J. Furnivall, ed., William Harrison, *Description of England*, London, 1877, pp. 267–8.

28 Thurley, *Royal Palaces*, p. 39.

29 Anglo, *Spectacle*, pp. 120–1.

30 N. H. Nicolas, ed., *The Privy Purse Expences of King Henry the Eighth*, London, 1827, pp. xxx–xxxi, 264–6.

31 J. P. Collier, ed., *Trevelyan Papers prior to 1558*, Camden Society, Series no. 1, 67 (1857), vol. 1, pp. 136–7.

32 *Cal. SP Ven.*, 4, no. 694 (p. 293).

33 See above, Chap. 1, p. 1.

34 See below, Chap. 4, p. 68; *Privy Purse Expences*, pp. 8, 46, 71, 82, 90, 119, 157, 165, 190, 207, 224, 243, 263; *Trevelyan Papers*, 1, pp. 148, 153, 156–7, 160, 170; Scarisbrick, *Henry VIII*, p. 518.

35 J. G. Nichols, ed., *Chronicle of the Grey Friars of London*, Camden Society, Series no. 1, 53 (1852), p. 30.

36 M. Biddle, ed., *King Arthur's Round Table*, Woodbridge, Suffolk, 2000, pp. 54–5, 427, 432.

37 Ibid., p. 427.

38 Ibid., pp. 456–61.

39 S. Anglo, 'The *British History* in Early Tudor Propaganda', *Bulletin of the John Rylands Library*, 44 (1961), 18–20, 25–40.

40 J. Adamson, *The Princely Courts of Europe, 1500–1750*, London, 2000, p. 102.

41 See below, Chap. 8, p. 165; John N. King, *Tudor Royal Iconography Literature and Art in an Age of Religious Crisis*, Princeton, 1989, pp. 57–60.

42 Walker, *Persuasive Fictions*, p. 92; see below, Chap. 8, p. 165.

43 D. Starkey, 'Representation Through Intimacy: A Study in the Symbolism of Monarchy and Court Office in Early Modern England', in J. Guy, ed., *The Tudor Monarchy*, London, 1997, pp. 47–9.

44 See below, Chap. 8.

45 G. Walker, 'The "Expulsion of the Minions" of 1519 Reconsidered', *HJ*, 32 (1989), 10.

46 *Four Years at the Court of Henry VIII*, 2, p. 271.

47 Hall, fols 67–68v.

48 *LP*, 3 (1), no. 576; D. R. Starkey, 'The King's Privy Chamber, 1485–1547', Cambridge University PhD Thesis, 1973, p. 121; idem, 'Court and Government', in C. Coleman and D. R. Starkey, eds, *Revolution Reassessed. Revisions in the History of Tudor Government and Administration*, Oxford, 1986, pp. 39–40; Scarisbrick, *Henry VIII*, pp. 118–19.

49 *LP*, 3 (1), no. 246; Starkey, *Personalities and Politics*, pp. 75–81; idem, 'King's Privy Chamber', p. 112, n. 1; idem, 'Court and Government', in Coleman and Starkey, eds, *Revolution Reassessed*, p. 40; G. R. Elton, *Reform and Reformation*, London, 1977, pp. 79–80; Walker, *Persuasive Fictions*, pp. 36–42; *Four Years at the Court of Henry VIII*, 2, pp. 271–2.

50 Hall, fol. 68–68v; *Four Years at the Court of Henry VIII*, 2, p. 271.

51 M. James, *Society, Politics and Culture. Studies in Early Modern England*, Cambridge, 1986, pp. 327–8.

52 Ibid., pp. 327–9, 335–6.

53 Elias Ashmole, *The Institution, Laws and Ceremonies of the Most Noble Order of the Garter*, London, 1672, p. 471.

54 Ibid., pp. 192–3.

55 Ibid., p. 182.

56 Ibid.

57 For the expenditure on his navy and his military campaigns, see below, Chap 9.

58 See below, Chap. 4, pp. 60–2.

59 C. G. Cruickshank, 'Henry VIII at Tournai', *Hist. Today*, 21 (Jan. 1971), 9–13; *LP*, 1 (2), no. 2391 (p. 1061).

60 Anglo, *Spectacle*, p. 114.

61 J. A. Muller, ed., *The Letters of Stephen Gardiner*, Cambridge, 1933, pp. 97–9.

62 Ibid., pp. 187–90.

63 For a more detailed consideration of Henry the artist and patron of the arts, see below, Chap. 4, pp. 64–6.

64 Brodie, ed., Dudley, *Tree of Commonwealth*, pp. 23–4; see above Chap. 1, p. 14.

65 Mynors et al., eds, *Correspondence of Erasmus*, 2, pp. 147–8.

66 A. R. Heiserman, *Skelton and Satire*, Chicago, 1961, pp. 119, 193. 'Colyn Cloute', however, also struck beyond Wolsey at the clergy in general. Ibid., pp. 193–8.

67 E. Sterling, *The Movement Towards Subversion: The English History Play from Skelton to Shakespeare*, Lanham, Maryland, 1996, pp. 67–8; Heiserman, p. 74.

68 Ibid., pp. 272–7.

69 J. N. King, 'Henry VIII as David: The King's Image and Reformation Politics', in P. C. Herman, ed., *Rethinking the Henrician Era. Essays on Early Tudor Texts and Contexts*, Urbana and Chicago, 1994, pp. 87–9.

70 Ibid., pp. 79–87; P. Tudor-Craig, 'Henry VIII and King David', in D. Williams, ed., *Early Tudor England*, Woodbridge, Suffolk, 1989, pp. 191–3.

71 Mynors et al., eds, *Correspondence of Erasmus*, 2, pp. 250–2.

72 J. Chandler, *John Leland's Itinerary. Travels in Tudor England*, Stroud, 1993, pp. 61, 89.

73 T. F. Mayer, ed., Thomas Starkey, *A Dialogue between Pole and Lupset*, Camden Society, Series no. 4, 37 (1989), pp. 17, 111.

74 *Four Years at the Court of Henry VIII*, 1, pp. 85–6; M. Hayward, 'Luxury or Magnificence? Dress at the Court of Henry VIII', *Costume*, 30 (1996), 37, 40, 42, 44–5.

75 *Four Years at the Court of Henry VIII*, 1, pp. 27, 76, 81, 86; *Cal. SP Ven.*, 4, no. 694 (p. 293); *LP*, 2 (1), no. 395.

76 *Cal. SP Ven.*, 4, no. 694 (pp. 292–3).

77 N. Williams, 'The Tudors: Three Contrasts in Personality', in A. G. Dickens, ed., *The Courts of Europe: Politics, Patronage and Royalty, 1400–1800*, London, 1977, p. 154.

78 *Cal. SP Ven.*, 4, no. 694 (p. 293).

79 *LP*, 15, no. 954.

80 R. S. Sylvester and D. P. Harding, eds, George Cavendish's *The Life and Death of Cardinal Wolsey*, in *Two Early Tudor Lives*, New Haven and London, 1962, pp. 12–13.

81 Idem, eds, William Roper's *The Life of Sir Thomas More*, in ibid., p. 208.

82 A. Fox and J. Guy, *Reassessing the Henrician Age: Humanism, Politics and Reform, 1500–1550*, Oxford, 1986, pp. 54–6, 58–61, 70–1.

83 T. F. Mayer, *Thomas Starkey and the Commonweal*, Cambridge, 1989, p. 256.

84 C. Haigh, *Reformation and Resistance in Tudor Lancashire*, Cambridge, 1975, p. 112.

85 See, for example, below, Chap. 5, p. 93 and Chap. 8, pp. 153–4.

86 R. W. Hoyle, *The Pilgrimage of Grace and the Politics of the 1530s*, Oxford, 2001, pp. 452, 461–2.

87 *LP*, 11, no. 1244 (p. 504).

88 M. Bush, *The Pilgrimage of Grace: A Study of the Rebel Armies of October 1536*, Manchester, 1996, pp. 8–11, 103–5.

89 *LP*, 8, no. 278; ibid., 13 (2), no. 307; M. H. and R. Dodds, *The Pilgrimage of Grace, 1536–1537*, 2 vols, London, 1971, I, pp. 69–71.

90 A. Fox, 'Prophecies and Politics in the Reign of Henry VIII', in Fox and Guy, *Reassessing the Henrician Age*, pp. 89–94.

91 S. L. Jansen, *Dangerous Talk and Strange Behaviour: Women and Popular Resistance to the Reforms of Henry VIII*, London, 1996, pp. 45–52; idem, *Political Protest and Prophecy under Henry VIII*, Woodbridge, Suffolk, 1991, pp. 1–4, 148–9, 153.

92 Thereafter, however, Luther's attitude softened, as in 1525 and 1535–6, when he believed that Henry was becoming more receptive to his position. N. S. Tjernagel, *Henry VIII and the Lutherans: A Study in Anglo-Lutheran Relations, 1521–1547*, Saint Louis, 1965, pp. 26–8,148–9; Scarisbrick, *Henry VIII*, pp. 113–14.

93 Tjernagel, pp. 18–19.

94 Catherine Parr.

95 H. Robinson, ed., *Original Letters Relative to the English Reformation*, 2 vols, Cambridge, 1846–7, 1, pp. 241–2.

96 J. Ayre, ed., *The Early Works of Thomas Becon*, Parker Society, Cambridge, 1843, p. 245.

97 C. S. L. Davies, *Peace, Print and Protestantism, 1450–1558*, London, 1976, pp. 236–7.

98 *LP*, 13 (2), no. 804.

99 N. Pocock, ed., *Nicholas Harpsfield, A Treatise on the Pretended Divorce between Henry VIII and Catherine of Aragon*, Camden Society, Series no. 2, 21 (1878), pp. 253, 255, 285.

100 Ulrike Moret and Sonja Vathjunker, 'Henry VIII in Sixteenth-Century Scottish Chronicles', in Baumann, ed., pp. 157–64.

101 S. Anglo, 'Image-Making: The Means and the Limitations', in Guy, ed., *The Tudor Monarchy*, pp. 16–17.

102 Ibid., pp. 17–27, 38–9.

103 Jansen, *Political Protest and Prophecy*, p. 150; G. R. Elton, *Policy and Police*, Cambridge, 1972, Chap. 3.

Chapter 4

The King in His Court

This chapter is less about novelty than individuality. As Greg Walker persuasively argues, those features of the second Tudor's Court which historians tend to regard as Henrician innovations were common to both medieval and Renaissance Courts in Europe. Exploitation of the Court as the political heart and seat of power, the fierce rivalry, intrigue and corruption which characterized it, the importance of regular access to the king, transformation of great nobles into obsequious courtiers, and the deferential elevation of the king: all are cited inappropriately as novelties of Henry's Court. What was new in 1509 was a new king whose personality, a marked contrast to that of his father, was reflected in his lifestyle and that of his Court. Even then one must see his culture of magnificence or *maiestas* as characteristic of the time rather than as something uniquely personal. The Tudor *maiestas* 'was a necessary ingredient of order and discipline in an age when the coercive machinery of the state was primitive and ineffectual'.[1]

Undoubtedly there were changes in the Court, notably in location and organization. Westminster was the official royal residence for much of each year until an extensive fire early in the reign in 1512. When, in 1529, Henry acquired York Place, renamed Whitehall, it became his most frequent residence. Wherever the Court was located, the development within it of the privy chamber was a significant organizational change. It was established by Henry VII to service the king's private needs. In 1518 Henry VIII, imitating the French king, introduced a new set of posts, the gentlemen of the privy chamber. From the 1520s on it was a fully developed department, headed by the groom of the stool, who, together with his subordinates, had direct and daily contact with the king. In terms of influencing Henry and procuring royal favours they enjoyed an obvious advantage over others. However, the politicization of the privy chamber and its effects can be exaggerated. Unlike his father, who valued distance, Henry VIII was companiable, convivial and public, in frequent even daily contact with so many: men and women, politicians and bureaucrats, churchmen, generals and diplomats, nobles and gentlemen. Intimates and those in his confidence were not confined to the privy chamber, before or after the 'expulsion of the Minions'.[2] Nevertheless a degree of politicization did occur, if only because of Henry's personal priorities. He enjoyed his privacy. The privy chamber was the instrument whereby he sought to achieve that end. But, at the same time, he used it as a means to maintain his freedom of action. Yet it was the very same instrument with which Wolsey and Cromwell, in David Starkey's words, 'sought to bridle their ever-changeable master by packing [it] with their creatures'.[3]

Purposes and functions of the Court

The original and oldest function of the Court, indeed its *raison d'être*, was to provide the monarch with a provisioned and serviced home. This simple domestic purpose could not in practice, however, be separated from the needs of kingship and royal government. The Court was physically structured to serve these various purposes: a 'Downstairs' of servicing departments and an 'Upstairs' divided between the public reception areas and the monarch's privy chamber and personal apartments. It was, at the same time, a public statement about the greatness of the Tudor State, its wealth and its power to crush enemies within and without the kingdom. Henry's Court certainly succeeded in impressing foreigners such as the Venetian ambassadors. In 1517 Francesco Chieregato, papal nuncio in England, bedazzled by Henry's two-week-long reception of the Spanish king's embassy, wrote: 'In short, the wealth and civilization of the world are here; and those who call the English barbarians appear to me to render themselves such.' The sixteenth-century Court was a setting for Renaissance kingship, a Prince's Mirror reflecting his cultural and other talents, as we shall shortly see.[4] Because the Court was the monarch's place of residence it was the seat of government too. Until the Westminster fire of 1512 and after Henry's occupation of Whitehall, the treasury, other departments of State and the law-courts, which were all housed in and around Westminster, were physically close to that seat of government. Furthermore, as policy decisions resided with the king, ministers and others who wished to influence policy had to be resident at Court or, as in the case of Wolsey, had to have access to him in his Court and to enjoy his confidence.[5]

The Court also reflected the Prince's piety, religious devotion and, from 1534, his place as supreme head of the Church of England. Private chaplains personally attended the king in the royal closet, whilst the Chapel Royal ministered to the needs of the Court. A reduced Chapel staff travelled with Henry on his progresses, but when the Court was lodged in the great royal houses and palaces over the winter months the full complement of dean and forty chaplains, lay clerks and choristers was present. He regularly attended mass in the Chapel Royal, but on these public occasions he did not participate. This does not mean, however, that he was not devoutly religious. Henry heard mass and other offices in his personal closet. In his early years he regularly went on pilgrimage: for example, to Southwick (as in 1510), Our Lady of Walsingham (e.g. in 1522 and 1530), Thomas à Becket's tomb at Canterbury, Edward the Confessor at Westminster, St Bridget of Syon, and when, on 10 June 1530, he made 'offring to King Henry [VI] of Wyndesore, Saint George, and at the high auter'. He wrote in defence of the Church against Martin Luther. And, as late as 1539, a correspondent of Lord Lisle informed him that 'upon Good Friday last past the King's Grace crept to the Cross from the chapel door upward, devoutly, and so served the priest to mass that same day, his own person, kneeling on his Grace his knees'.[6] In contrast, Henry's appearances in the Chapel Royal were primarily intended as demonstrations of magnificent monarchy. When, for example, the Spanish ambassadors accompanied him to mass in 1517, he 'wore royal robes down to the ground, of gold brocade lined with ermine, and another different collar of very great value, and his train was carried. All the rest of the court glittered with jewels and gold and silver, the pomp being unprecedented.'[7]

Henry VIII's Court performed two other important functions. The royal fount of patronage could be tapped only by contact with the king (either personally or through a proxy) and with his consent. Each suitor for an office, estates (by grant or generous lease terms), a pension, economic benefits or some other royal favour had succeeded only when he obtained a bill bearing the sign manual, the king's signature. This had to be achieved in the Court where the king lived. Those in search of favours became clients of patrons – especially a Wolsey or Cromwell, a favourite such as the duke of Suffolk, a trusted member of the privy chamber such as Nicholas Carew and Henry Norris, or the hypochondriac Henry's physician, William Butts. Such men could advance their causes with the king. Each suitor, however, was rivalled in his quest by many other favour-seekers. So the Court was a competitive arena in which a legion of clients hotly contested for *douceurs* from the ultimate patron, the personal monarch. The generous-natured king's acquisition of enormous Church wealth opened up unparalleled new opportunities for enrichment, especially to favoured friends, household officials, councillors and magnates: for example, grants and opportunities to purchase to the dukes of Suffolk (in Lincolnshire) and Norfolk (in East Anglia), Henry's master of the horse Sir Anthony Browne (in Surrey), the household treasurer Sir Thomas Cheyney (in Kent), John Lord Russell (in Devon, especially Tavistock Abbey), Lord Chancellor Wriothesley (in Hampshire and seven other counties), John Dudley (in London and Hereford, Kent, Shropshire, Staffordshire and Warwickshire) and Edward Seymour (in Wiltshire). Many other families, active in their localities rather than in the Court, also benefited from the king's generosity and, in the process, they became members of landed county elites or rose to prominence within them. Such royal generosity, often calculated, naturally strengthened their loyalty to the crown.[8]

The lure of royal favour played its part in the fulfilment of another function of the Court: as a point of contact between the king and his subjects. It had an important role in the continuous process of managing the men who mattered in regional and local government.[9] It was also the vehicle which enabled Henry to show himself to the great mass of his subjects, both rural and urban. Such points of contact could be achieved only by a mobile Court – and Henry VIII was a very peripatetic Prince. The royal progress, facilitated by his acquisition of so many great houses and hunting lodges, both projected the divine sanction, wealth and power of monarchy and reinforced its authority.

Not all of Henry's journeys can be termed progresses, especially during winter and spring, when they were simply movements of the Court from one residence to another. Even such necessary journeys, however, were undertaken in style. Often Henry travelled on water[10] between his Thameside palaces. For example, between January and the beginning of his progress in July 1531 he moved in style in his splendid great barge from Westminster to Bridewell (in March), to Greenwich and York Place (in April), Greenwich and Hampton Court (in May–June) and in July to York Place and Windsor.[11] The summer progresses were different in purpose. They were deliberate summertime displays, planned in stages known as *giests*, and with specific political purposes.[12] In 1526, for example, Henry's progress covered seven counties. Then, as always, 'the emphasis was upon meeting the prominent men of the locality, staying with noblemen on the way and generally "making good cheer"'.[13] A royal visit to a nobleman's house or an episcopal palace was an obvious mark of favour. Entertaining the king and his Court was very expensive for the host, but the value was considered to outweigh the cost.

As in so many other ways, Henry's youth was reflected in the nature, bustling activity and duration of his earlier progresses. During his first, in 1510, he

[exercised] hym self daily in shotyng, singing, daunsyng, wrastelyng . . . playing at the recorders, flute, virginals, and in setting of songes, making of balettes, [and] dyd set ii. goodly masses. . . . And whan he came to Okyng, there were kept bothe [J]ustes and Turneys; the rest of thys progresse was spent in huntyng, hawkyng and shotyng.[14]

Visits to cities and towns also featured prominently in his earlier progresses, but, from the later 1520s, they focused increasingly on nobles, other prominent locals and the shire homes of royal servants. Throughout the reign, however, hunting remained the key activity. As Samman explains, it served several purposes: 'the king was entertained and met members of the local elites, liberally rewarding them with the spoils of the day's kill'. During the 1515 progress, for example, Sir Philip Draycot reported

[I]n the meads under Chertsey was killing of stags, holden in for the purpose, one after another all the afternoon . . . and they were not only coursed with some greyhounds, but also with horsemen, with darts and spurs and many so slain, the most princely sport that hath been seen.

The roasted carcasses would bring pleasure to many who dined at the boards of local nobles and gentry.[15]

So the regular purposes of the royal progress were contact, pleasure and, at the same time, the use of ostentation, extravagance and spectacular entertainment to demonstrate royal magnificence. Sometimes, however, it was undertaken to serve an additional, specific and important political end.

First, in 1522 the visit of Emperor Charles V gave Henry the opportunity to fête his guest with a progress of extraordinary extravagance: before entering the City of London on 6 June the two princes changed into identical cloth-of-gold outfits embroidered with silver; they were treated to pageants galore, the theme of which was their 'friendship, equality, and shared power'; in the following weeks they wined, dined, jousted and hunted their way to the Thames palaces of Richmond, Wolsey's Hampton Court and Windsor; thence to Winchester before Charles sailed in early July. The real purpose of this itinerant rhapsody of mutual love and respect was fulfilled on 16 June when they concluded a military alliance against France.[16]

Secondly, in 1535 the long summer progress[17] took Henry and his Court westwards through Oxfordshire, Gloucestershire, Wiltshire and Hampshire. It was a step in the enforcement of the recent breach with Rome and of his authority as supreme head. Thomas Cromwell, whom he had empowered to visit all monasteries, accompanied him for two months, in order to supervise personally the visitation of religious houses in the western counties.[18]

Thirdly, just as Henry VIII's father went to York in 1486 'in order to keep in obedience the folk of the North, savage and more eager than others for upheavals', so did he progress there in 1541, five years after the most serious rebellion of his reign. It was simultaneously an exercise in contact with local elites and an assertion of his authority over 'this barbarous and mutinous people', whom Marillac described as looking 'like men of greater "execution" than the rest of his subjects'.[19]

The value of progresses was, in practice, limited by the king's personal preferences and priorities. Most of his progresses, with the significant exception of 1541, were confined to the home counties. Henry was also hyper-sensitive about personal security and safety. He always took with him a smith with special locks and bolts for the doors of his personal apartments, wherever he stayed.[20] A specially significant concern was disease, which could influence, even determine, the itinerary and duration of the royal summer 'rideabout'. Giests were shaped to take into account current epidemics, and searchers were sent out to ascertain the presence of disease on the planned itinerary. Thomas Cromwell's son Gregory, for example, warned his father from Lewes, which was on the current giest, that the plague there 'is not as yet all whole extincte and quenched'.[21] Outbreaks of sweating sickness and plague triggered prompt and even dramatic royal responses. Giests would be modified suddenly and significantly and Henry would alter course or retreat: for example in 1517 (when through summer, autumn, even into winter, flight from a sweating sickness epidemic in London took priority over business), 1518, 1526 (when two died of plague in Woodstock and the king altered his giest to dally in Winchester), 1529, August 1533 (when he avoided even Windsor in his giest) and 1539. Indeed giests might be scrapped and sometimes a fearful king would retreat into isolation: in 1518 he and his Court celebrated Easter shut up in Abingdon Abbey for three weeks; and in November 1522 plague in Greenwich and Richmond and around London led him to hide away in Hertford Castle.[22]

These were no doubt sensible precautions. Henry's chronic hypochondria, however, resulted in an obsessional concern, constant vigilance and possibly excessive precautions. On one occasion he intended to visit

Wolsey 'at the More' until, as Gardiner informed the cardinal, he was advised that 'townes aboute the More . . . have had the Swet; the oonly name and voyce wherof is soo terrible and fearful in his Highnes eeres that he dare in noowise approch vnto the place where it is noysed to have been'. When the king intended to visit Calais in summer 1534 the lord deputy was instructed that

the town etc. may be made as clean and as sweet as is possible. If any should chance to be sick that ye should mistrust to be the plague, then immediately they should be conveyed out of the town unto the outermost part of the English pale, and the doors shut up after them.[23]

Given the annual visitations of sweating sickness, plague, smallpox, measles or a combination thereof, the king's activities and especially attention to business frequently took second place to fearful self-preservation. He was even careful to remain apart from his 'good sweetheart' and 'own darling' Anne Boleyn, when she was taken ill with the sweating sickness in 1528.[24]

Self-indulgence and the pursuit of pleasure: the martial arts

The Court was an obvious propaganda stage for the projection of appropriate royal images.[25] Behind its glittering façade of order, formality and splendour, however, was a real, simmering, sometimes seething, cauldron of ambition, rivalry and even ruthless strike and counter-strike.[26] The nature of the Court was influenced less in Henry's case by politically calculated or high-minded symbolism and image projections. These were certainly there and of considerable importance, especially in relation to his honour. More conscious priorities, however, were the self-indulgent pursuit of the good life, surrounding himself with opulence, ensuring the means to indulge in his personal pleasures and passions and creating a stage on which the royal ego could strut to the plaudits of an adoring audience. Enter, for example, the warrior king.

The Tudor Court was greatly influenced by the extravagant and spectacular Burgundian tradition, especially in martial entertainments. These were lavishly funded: the tournament of 1511, for example, cost £4,000. The extravagance and cost of tournaments and the promotion of chivalry might have been justified as preparation for war.[27] After all, the tournaments were genuine contests in which combatants engaged in tilting on horseback with lances or combat on foot with short spears, swords or axes. In the earlier years of Henry VIII's reign, however, they were also interwoven with the romanticism and allegoric traditions of the Burgundian Court. So combat took place within the context of lengthy romantic and heroic speeches, disguisings, elaborate pageant cars and scenic devices. The first, held to celebrate his coronation, began with the entry of a wheeled mountain pulled by a 'lyon made of Glyteryng gold'. Lurking in the mountain were two Challengers. They rode out to await the Answerers, whose leader appeared in a mobile castle. It was adorned with a Saint George vane and a 'cunnyngly' wrought pomegranate tree, the respective emblems of the English king and his Spanish wife. The entertainment was accompanied by speeches, trumpets, 'yong galantes & noble menne gorgeously appareled' displaying riding skills, and Lady Pallas in a castle adorned with pomegranates and English roses and carried in by 'strength of menne and other prouision'. More play-acting and speeches followed before the jousting began.[28]

Such pageants and accompanying disguisings were a major courtly preoccupation of the young king. The centrepiece of the Westminster tournament in February 1511, celebrating the birth of a son to Henry and Catherine, was an enormous pageant car. Drawn 'by strength of twoo great beastes . . . florished all ouer with Damaske golde [and] syluer of Damaske', it resembled a forest 'with rockes, hylles and dales, with diuers sundrie trees, floures, hathornes, ferne and grasse . . . [and i]n the middes of this forrest was a castell standing, made of golde'. When the pageant car stopped, foresters blew horns and four Challengers rode forth. The first, named *Cure Loial*, was Henry. In the jousting which followed, the king, who was naturally in the limelight, outshone every-one else.[29] On another occasion, 1 January 1512, *Fortresse Dangerus* was 'garnished with artilerie and weapon[s] after the most warlike fashion'. Nevertheless, the king and five lords assaulted it so effectively that the ladies inside surrendered and danced with the victors. In the Epiphany revels of that year Henry starred in a disguising 'after the manner of Italy, called a mask, a thing not seen afore in England'. The predominant cultural influence, however, remained Burgundian, reinforced by the pageants devised by William Cornish from 1501 onwards.[30]

After the first war with France (1512–14) such elaborate pageantry, characterized by disguisings, fantastic pageant cars and speeches, was rarely staged. This seems to have been a simple change of fashion due to the development of indoor pageants. In any case there was one constant feature: until 1527 Henry was Chief Challenger in every tournament, except in 1524, when he was Chief Answerer. Everyone who viewed him in action was full of admiration: amongst them Margaret of Savoy and Imperial, Milanese, papal and Venetian ambassadors. In 1517 Guistinian

wrote home that 'a most stately joust was kept . . . that I doubt the performance of a finer or more sumptuous spectacle for many years past.
The King jousted with his brother-in-law, the Duke of Suffolk, and they
bore themselves like Hector and Achilles.'[31] Their military prowess was
one of the most important bonds between Charles Brandon (Suffolk) and
Henry. Together they challenged alone in the jousts between 1512 and
1514. From 1517 until 1524 they led the opposing teams in all the jousts
at Court.[32] Ironically it was the king's close friend who nearly killed him
in March 1524. Henry, trying out a new suit of armour of his own design,
failed to lower his visor and so, when his helmet was struck by Suffolk's
lance, it filled with splinters. From the late 1520s, jousting declined in
importance as a royal pleasure. No doubt age had a hand in this. Then,
whilst competing at Greenwich in January 1536, the forty-four-year-old
king was unseated by his opponent, crashed in full armour onto the turf
under his mailed horse and was unconscious for two hours.

It was the end of Henry's jousting career but not of his military pastimes. He had always been an outstanding archer and, as late as 1542,
he had a wheeled frame built for an archery butt in the 300-feet-long
gallery at The More, a property acquired from Cardinal Wolsey. He also
exercised with firearms: not only handguns, which, after his accident in
1536, he fired from a special platform or 'standing', but also, it would
seem, artillery, because he managed to demolish the roof of Henry Norris's
house in Greenwich Park.[33] Such activities were doubtless the conscious
embodiment of a chivalric ideal and a warrior king's necessary maintenance of his personal military skills. But they were also and especially
amongst his greatest pleasures.

The royal athlete

As in so many other ways, so in sporting activity the Court of Burgundy
provided a model for early modern princes to follow. Burgundian palaces
included sports complexes which accommodated not just the military
activities, like tilting and archery, but also indoor sports such as bowls,
tennis and cockfighting. The latter were also social pastimes, because
they were spectator sports and conducive to the courtly predilection for
wagering, amongst both contestants and onlookers. Here was a sign of
the changing significance of sporting activity. In 1527 Castiglione summed
up and reinforced that change in the *Book of the Courtier*. He still
believed that the 'true profession of a Courtier ought to bee in feates of
armes', but he argued that he should also have 'the arte of swimming, to

leape, to runne, to caste the stone . . . whereby hee getteth him a reputation, especially among the multitude'. He also recommended that

it is a noble exercise, and meete for one living in Court to play at Tenise, where the disposition of the bodie, the quicknes and nimblenesse of everie member is much perceived. . . . Also they play at tenise always in open sight, and this is one of the common games, which the multitude with their presence much set forth.

Such activities were now increasingly regarded as social graces and courtly skills, or simply as a way of improving health and keeping fit rather than as means to equip a man for the battlefield.[34]

Henry was an obsessive participant in physical activities and in his earlier years he focused on martial skills, building tiltyards in his palaces to facilitate such pursuits. In addition, as Prince he had been taught not only archery and hunting skills but tennis too. He was certainly aware of its value as a spectator sport, as illustrated in the Venetian ambassador's complimentary words.[35]

Henry also played bowls and he was the first king to build cockpits. Tennis, bowling and cockfighting all enabled him to indulge another pleasure: gambling. When age and injury ended his jousting career, he focused more on such pastimes, especially indoor tennis. In 1527 accident-prone Henry managed to injure himself during a game. Shortly afterwards, at a court entertainment the dancers were masked,

and all wearing black velvet slippers on their feet, this being done, lest the King should be distinguished from the others, as from the hurt which he received lately on his left foot when playing at tennis he wears a black velvet slipper.[36]

Henry did not, however, withdraw from outdoor pastimes. Thurley states that hawking had not appealed to him as a young man, perhaps because he 'found it too sedentary'.[37] Yet Henry's experience in 1525 suggests that, because the hunters followed their hawks on foot, it was physically exacting and, because he was impulsive, it was even dangerous. He was pole-vaulting over a ditch when the pole snapped and he landed head-first in mud. If a footman had not pulled out his head, which was stuck fast in the clay, he would have drowned. Generally, however, hawking was less arduous than tourneys, and sometimes in the early 1530s his second queen accompanied him. Age and corpulence made it increasingly acceptable. Fishing, however, never managed to excite his interest. Despite the payments made, for example, 'for two Angelyng Roddes' in 1530 and another in 1532, it is difficult to imagine this physically impulsive king waiting patiently for a fish to bite.[38]

In contrast, there is no doubt about his continuing and unquestionable appetite for the hunt. Indeed it would be no great exaggeration to say that hunting often dictated his life. He enlarged, acquired or created many new emparkments and he increased the number of royal hunting lodges. In 1520 he 'rises daily, except on holy days, at 4 or 5 o'clock, and hunts till 9 or 10 at night'. In Richard Pace's words, 'He spares no pains to convert the sport of hunting into a martyrdom.'[39] Any royal enthusiasm, however, was popular among favour-seeking courtiers. As the Eltham Ordinances observed in 1526, whenever the king went walking, hunting or hawking, most of the nobles and gentry of the Court went with him, leaving the Court deserted and getting in his way. It was Wolsey, not Henry, who remedied matters. Thenceforth only a small band of hunting companions would go with him.[40] As jousting declined, hunting increased, even into the 1540s. It could disrupt or delay business. On 17 September 1540, for example, Marillac wrote that there was nothing to report, 'the King being, with a small company, hunting, about twenty miles from [here] . . . until Michaelmas, when the Court will re-assemble here'; in December 1542 Chapuys was frustrated in his attempts to make contact as Henry was 'moving about hunting'; in August 1543 he was having difficulty in engaging the king because he was 'hunting, 33 miles hence, without sojourning in any place'.[41] The thrill of the chase seemed to be less rewarding than the scale of the slaughter. In August 1541 Marillac, accompanying the king and his Court north towards York, informed Francis I that a few days before,

was a chase made at Hatfeil, where there are ponds and marshes, when, with boats on the water and arbalists and bows on land, were slain in one day 200 stags and does, and next day, two miles off, was scarcely less slaughter.[42]

This, however, was Henry's idea of enjoyment. In his last years the mounting blocks at Greenwich Park were raised, so that he could mount and dismount easily. Eventually he needed to be hoisted onto his horse. Yet, to the very end, Henry was driven by the pursuit of such pleasures.[43]

The cultivated king

There was much more to Henry than the warrior and the athlete. He epitomized the Burgundian ideal of learned chivalry.[44] His Court reflected his diversity of activities, cultural, intellectual, religious and academic. The king's energy, curiosity and range of interests provided the dynamic which made the Court an exciting, exhilarating magnet for all kinds of artists and scholars, technicians and craftsmen, specialists and pioneers – and always Henry was personally involved. His patronage recruited many,[45] especially painters. Best known is Hans Holbein the Younger, decorative artist – especially at Greenwich – and Court portrait painter. But there were also a growing number of other foreign artists, especially Italians, who were chiefly employed in the decoration of the royal palaces with wall-paintings.[46] The Florentine sculptor Pietro Torrigiano and glaziers such as the Fleming Galyon Hone were engaged in the king's service. Distinguished artists, among them Antonio Toto (who became Henry's serjeant painter), Hans Eworth and Guillim Scrots, were enticed to England and settled there.

In the same way, foreign instrumentalists were brought to England by a talented king, for whom music was more than mere image projection.[47] Castiglione stressed its importance for the courtier, and Henry was certainly a role model: a virtuoso king who sang well and an accomplished musician. Assessments of his ability as a composer and the compositions which are ascribed to him do vary.[48] However, even if 'Pastime with good company' may not be ascribed solely to Henry, its high moral tone suggests his authorship:

> Company with honesty
> Is virtue – vices all to flee
> . . . .
> My mind shall be
> Virtue to use,
> Vice to refuse.
> Thus shall I use me.[49]

Particularly important, as so often with Henry, was his patronage: both of English musicians, such as William Cornish, Robert Fayrefax and Thomas Tallis, and of others from Flanders, Germany and Italy, especially Dionisio Memo, the organist from St Mark's in Venice. Most important, as a projection of the cultivated Tudor Court, were the composers and choir of the Chapel Royal. When he became convinced that Wolsey's chapel choir was superior to his own, Henry was prepared to poach men and children from it. Royal attention and money paid dividends. As early as 1515 the Venetian ambassador's secretary attended mass in the Chapel Royal:

[I]t was sung by his Majesty's choristers, whose voices are really rather divine than human; they did not chaunt, but sang like angels, and as for the counter-bass voices, I don't think they have their equals in the world.[50]

The musician was also the poet, as shown in the lyrics of 'Pastime'. What is evident in Henry's verse, as in his music, dance and (as we shall see) use of the theatre, is the projection of *public* images and messages. They were all for public consumption. Some of his poems, expressing the love, devotion and especially fidelity of the ardent lover, simply fail to convince. In fact they amount to a convergence, even coalescence, of the unquestionable male dominance and royal authority which he paraded and trumpeted throughout his rule. Even as 'Lusty Youth' he has a message for stuffy councillors:

> For they would have him his liberty refrain,
> And all merry company for to disdain.
> But I will not do whatsoever they say.[51]

The message was clear: royal Henry was in charge, as he spelt out elsewhere:

> Though some say that youth rules me,
>   I trust in age to tarry.
> *God and my right,*[52] and my duty,
>   From them I shall never vary.[53]

Drama too had its place in the grand theatre of the Court. Henry was served by the gentlemen and children of the Chapel Royal and the Old and New King's Players. Each member of his family, including Henry Fitzroy, had players. Theatre was used not only to entertain the Court and foreign ambassadors but also, especially by Henry and Wolsey, to deliver political propaganda.[54] With typical insensitivity, Henry, 'supping with several ladies' in May 1536, 'manifested incredible joy at the arrest of Anne [Boleyn]' and told his host, the bishop of Carlisle, that he had long predicted 'the end of this affair, so much so that I have written a tragedy'.[55]

The arts were both a pleasure and a political tool for Henry. He did much to change the common European opinion of the English, as summed up by Benvenuto Cellini in one word, 'beasts'. Witness the praises sung by the papal nuncio Chieregato about the mannered, courteous, elegant English and their talented king.[56] In a few years Henry had created a cultivated Court admired across Europe.[57]

This was not the consequence simply of his artistic patronage. He was also a patron of humanists, who focused on an approach to the Christian faith and moral questions through both religious and pagan sources, notably the scriptures, patristic writings and the classics. Erasmus and the young Henry, as prince and king, were mutually attracted and impressed.

They corresponded and the great humanist visited the Court, where he observed the gathering of 'excellent scholars'. Amongst them was Thomas More, who was particularly influential when he became a councillor attendant. William Roper recalled how the king would send for More and 'sometimes in matters of astronomy, geometry, divinity, and such other faculties . . . sit and confer with him'.[58] English humanists came rapidly and increasingly to the fore at Henry's Court, amongst them not only More but also Thomas Linacre (who became Princess Mary's Latin tutor), Erasmus's friend Lord Mountjoy, the antiquary John Leland (who became keeper of the king's books in the 1530s), Dean Colet of Saint Paul's and Cuthbert Tunstal. Also, in Henry's last years, there was his trusted councillor Sir Anthony Denny, who advanced two great scholars and teachers, Roger Ascham and John Cheke. Leland and the other later recipients of royal favour, together with writers such as Richard Morison who were active in Henry's interest, are evidence that the events of the 1530s neither caused a royal rejection of humanism nor resulted in some kind of lapse in humanistic activity in England.[59]

This is understandable because of Henry's love of scholarship and the range of his interests, not only academic but also technical. Nicolaus Kratzer, an accomplished mathematician, became the king's astronomer. Henry's interest was recognized by Roper, who recorded that he used to have Thomas More 'up into his leads, there to consider with him the diversities, courses, motions and operations of the stars and planets'. But Henry also employed Kratzer to practical ends: for example, to survey the profitable royal tin mines in Cornwall in 1529.[60] Kratzer probably aroused Henry's interest in cartography and its practical application in the production of utilitarian 'plats'. Most important, commencing in 1538–9, was the production of survey maps of England's coastlines as a basis for planning national defences. The king ordered and financed a catographic survey of England's shorelines and he imported foreigners, such as Jean Rotz from Dieppe, to map them. Peter Barber concludes that in two decades 'and in large part in response to [Henry's] wishes, maps had become an indispensable tool of English government'.[61]

Henry's wide-ranging interests are reflected in his libraries: the largest collection of books at Whitehall, another 329 at Greenwich and other libraries at Richmond and Hampton Court. The number of reference works increased significantly under Henry, and although John Bale justifiably lamented the loss of the monastic libraries at the dissolution – 'a most horrible infamy' – manuscripts from them were collected for Henry. Furthermore his books were not bought for mere show, as his innumerable annotations bear witness. And from her study of the contents and 'originators' of Henry's personal books, Janet Backhouse concludes that they 'underline the extremely international flavour' of the Court and 'the many scholarly and cultural currents that mingled there'.[62] In particular, as a 1535 inventory of the Royal Library collection reveals, Henry had the same active appreciation and enjoyment of fashionable Burgundian books as his father.[63] He was encouraged in this by his Royal Librarian and ex-tutor, the Fleming Gilles Duwes, who brought famous illuminators, including the Horenbout family, into royal service. The result was the establishment of a flourishing Flemish artists' school at the Court.[64]

The king was writer as well as reader: not only the *Assertio*, but also, for example, *Glasse of the Truthe*.[65] The latter reveals his views on sovereignty as early as 1531: the law of God places the king alongside God, whereas the pope 'is but a man, and subjects must obey God rather than man'.[66] Henry's appetite for scholarship was also reflected in his educational patronage, not only of teachers such as Skelton, Ascham and Cheke, but also in the foundation of new colleges and professorships at Cambridge and Oxford. Most of this, however, had to wait until his last years, prior to which he seemed to show little interest in the state of England's only two universities. When Wolsey fell in 1529, Henry separated his Oxford foundation, Cardinal College, from the university and reorganized it as an ecclesiastical college. Then, in 1535, he authorized the first royal visitation of the universities. When the royal visitors left the two universities, 'the curriculum had been changed, the school of canon law closed down, books destroyed and the universities compelled to accept the royal supremacy over the Church'. So, through State agents, Henry and Thomas Cromwell dictated to Cambridge and Oxford 'what must be taught and what must not be taught, who must be read and who must not be read'.[67] The universities were deprived of their monastic halls of residence and student numbers fell.[68] Only in 1546 did Henry refound Wolsey's creation as Christ Church and handsomely endow it as a university college (and its chapel as the diocesan cathedral). A few days later he founded Trinity College in Cambridge, where, in 1540, he had also established five regius professorships,[69] and in 1542 he refounded Buckingham College as Magdalene College. However, he was acting less on his own initiative than in response to the pleas of two Cambridge humanists, Cheke and Thomas Smith, and their sympathetic queen, Catherine Parr. She assured them that she had already 'attempted' the king, who, 'being such a patron to good learning', promised them that he would 'advance new learning and erect new occasion thereof, than to confound those godly institutions'.[70] Better late than never.

Education could not be separated from politics. Nor, in the national political heart – Henry VIII's Court – could the arts be excluded, as we have seen in the case of the royal image. John Heywood, playwright and musician, exemplifies the connection. He used drama to question and express his lack of support for the changes of the 1530s and 1540s. Although he was condemned in 1543 for denying the royal supremacy, he survived and continued to benefit from his presence at Court.[71] Certainly artistic talent did not spare courtiers from the king's vengeance if he believed or was persuaded that they had betrayed him in any way. The poet Thomas Wyatt was twice imprisoned: when Anne Boleyn's supposed infidelities were 'revealed' in 1536 and when Thomas Cromwell fell in 1540. He was fortunate and survived. When he died of natural causes in 1542, fellow-poet Henry earl of Surrey penned an epitaph to a devoted, loyal servant of the State. Five years later, Surrey, the warrior-nobleman, who was regarded at Court and the universities as 'England's greatest living poet' and who was obsessed with honour, admired by the French Court and lavishly praised by Emperor Charles V, was executed for treason.[72] Such men were victims of a vicious, suspicious and susceptible king in a Court which was a warren of intrigue and a poisonous whispering gallery. But it remained, at the same time, a centre of the arts under a cultivated king. Credit must be given also to some of his consorts. Catherine of Aragon commissioned a book on matrimony from Erasmus. She was also was the patron of the Spanish humanist, Juan Luis Vives, who produced humanist handbooks for her daughter's instruction. Anne Boleyn, fluent in French, was, like Catherine, a patron of the universities. She discussed scripture with Henry and his chaplains and had books dedicated to her by French evangelical humanists. She was also actively involved with planning and building extensions to Hampton Court, Whitehall and royal apartments in the Tower of London. Another humanist queen, Catherine Parr, was one of few Tudor women to have works published and her household was praised for its learning and piety. She also protected the best interests of the universities.[73]

The courtly calendar and royal 'spectaculars'

The Court had a regular annual timetable of staged events, most but not all of which celebrated dates in the Christian calendar. Christmas was a favourite. At Greenwich in 1524/5 a mock attack was carried out against a prefabricated fortress, *Castle Loyal*, designed by Henry. Into the arena came 'twoo ancient knightes, with beardes of siluer [and] in robes of purple damask'. When they cast off their robes, 'it was knowen that it was the Kyng and the Duke of Suffolk. . . . [E]very man ran eight courses' and Scottish diplomats present 'preised and marveiled at the kynges strength'.[74] In 1531, however, the divorce proceedings dominated all:

This yere the kynge kepte his Christemas at Grenewyche wyth great solempnitie, but all men sayde that there was no myrthe . . . because the Queene and the Ladies were absent.[75]

New Year was an occasion for more military assaults, as in 1512, when, as we have seen, Henry and five lords successfully assaulted *Fortresse Dangerus*.[76] Twelfth Night ended the Christmas season: in 1513 with masked dancers; two years later with a stout defence of six more elegant ladies by knights who triumphed over wild men with 'terrible vysages' and covered in green moss; and in 1516 yet another mock castle, defended by knights before they danced with the queen and her ladies.[77]

Spring too was a festive season. Easter and Holy Thursday (or Ascension Day) on 15 May were solemn Christian celebrations and public displays of the piety of king and Court. On the eve of Holy Thursday there was a lighter touch: in 1539 Henry took barge at Whitehall and 'had his drums and fifes playing, and rowed up and down the Thames for an hour after evensong'.[78] Furthermore May Day, a fortnight before, was always an occasion for extravagant, light-hearted spring jollity. Even in 1511, not long after the death of Henry's infant male heir on 23 February, a 'shippe under sayle' fired a broadside of guns and sailed until it reached the tiltyard, where its arrival signalled the commencement of a tournament.[79] Four years later, Sagudino, secretary of the Venetian ambassador, described the Robin Hood-style May Day extravaganza which took place in a wood outside Greenwich. In a displaced Sherwood forest were Henry and his guards, all clad in green and armed with bows, and one hundred 'noblemen on horseback, all gorgeously arrayed'. All around were bowers of singing birds, and musicians on organ, lute and flutes. King and courtiers banqueted in a decorated arbour in the woods and then proceeded in great state to Greenwich, watched by a crowd which Sagudino estimated at 25,000. It was on this occasion that Henry, ever the performer, questioned Ambassador Pasqualigo about the French King's physique and, opening his doublet, showed off his thigh and calf.[80]

During the 1520s and 1530s the scale of such regular calendar entertainments diminished. On the other hand, lavish and magnificent spectaculars were staged throughout the reign to celebrate great occasions, many of which charted the political history of Henry's kingship. The opening act of his long theatrical rule was, of course, the coronation, a grand, solemn occasion, followed by prolonged festivities.[81] On 13 August 1514 the proxy marriage of Henry's sister Mary to King Louis XII of France was followed by high mass, a banquet and a ball. Nor was this the only occasion on which Court spectaculars were used as means to diplomatic ends. Between 7 and 24 June 1520 the celebrated seventeen-day 'summit' between the kings of England and France took place at the Field of Cloth of Gold, between Guines and Ardres. This was the most extravagant spectacular of them all.[82] Elaborate preparations began in February. They included accommodation, supplies, security and tournament facilities. Although a strict control on the numbers attending was imposed, Francis I asked the English ambassador if Henry would mind relaxing the rules, so far as the French ladies of the Court were concerned. The ambassador passed this on to his royal master, adding that he had told the French king, 'I never saw your highness . . . find default with over great press of ladies.'[83]

In June, Henry's retinue numbered more than 5,000. It resided in a township of tents, fountains flowing with wine and, as centrepiece, Henry's palace, a brick, wood and canvas fantasy, built by 560 imported English craftsmen and adorned with cloth of gold and silver. The French contingent had a temporary township of over 300 tents, of which the grandest, 120 feet tall and richly decorated, was naturally the king's.[84] After the meeting of Francis and Henry serious negotiations were left to their officials. Athletics and wrestling, jousting and tilting, wining and dining, masquing and mummeries, song and dance were the order of each day. Amidst the glamour, gold and gilt there would have been a dark moment if the tale that Henry had been wrestled to the ground by Francis was true, but the story is probably apocryphal.[85] In the end what was achieved? There was no Anglo-French treaty. And Knecht is realistic when he writes that no lasting peace was possible between the two kings, though the meeting 'did not, it seems, exacerbate their rivalry'. Dickens sums it up as 'a glorious excuse for the two courts to show off', nothing more.[86] Some, however, are less dismissive. To Scarisbrick it was possibly part of Wolsey's 'policy of imbalance', using England's power to tilt the Valois–Habsburg rivalry whichever way it chose. It may have been a genuine attempt at an Anglo-French *rapprochement*, in response to the rapid rise of Charles Habsburg, elected Holy Roman Emperor in 1519.[87] Or Wolsey could have seen it as a genuine step to lasting European peace, using the occasion to give substance to his personal triumph, the treaty of London or 'universal peace' of 1518.[88]

Shortly afterwards, on 10–14 July 1520, the king and Emperor Charles V came together in a cordial and less competitive atmosphere.[89] And two years later Charles visited England. This was a classic example of the way Henry used royal magnificence and lavish hospitality to political ends. He conveyed to his own subjects and to European Princes – especially to the Emperor, who wanted his military support against France – images of power which impressed them.[90] Diplomatic purposes also lay behind other, later entertainments. In 1527, for example, banqueting and disguising houses were built next to the Greenwich tiltyard for the pleasure of an impressive French embassy, which came to make an anti-Habsburg alliance with Henry. They were worked on and lavishly decorated by Holbein, Kratzer and other artists of international reputation, and they were the venue of the great celebrations which accompanied the signing of the treaties.

Many of the later Court festivities charted the stages in the king's sexpartite marital history. There were the royal weddings: river and street pageants, with '[w]ine also running at certain conduits plentifully', stately processions and banquets which accompanied Anne Boleyn's coronation in 1533; in 1536 Henry's river journey from Greenwich to Whitehall, with Jane Seymour, was the occasion of a great Thames pageant, including a 400-gun salute from the Tower, where Anne Boleyn had recently been buried.[91] There were also the christenings: Elizabeth's was scaled down when the king learned that Anne had not given him the anticipated son. But when Jane did, there was much rejoicing and Edward was baptized at a grand ceremony in Hampton Court on 15 October 1537. The solemn obsequies following Jane's death, nine days later on 24 October, befitted the mother of Henry's only legitimate son. Nevertheless, Jane and her successors were not crowned and the actual weddings were private, relatively low-key affairs. This reflects a general decline in the range and scale of celebrations and also of festivities and entertainments in the later Henrician Court. One occasion is worthy of mention, however, partly because it was a public, political statement about the papacy, but also because it illustrates Henry's sense of humour. On 17 June 1538 Henry, 'with his lords and certain ladies', watched from his private stairs outside Westminster Palace as one barge, manned by the king's men, engaged in battle with another crewed by the pope and cardinals. After firing reed darts at each other, they locked in combat and, it may not be surprising to learn, the papal crew was cast overboard. Meanwhile, 'two other barges rowed up and down with banners and pennants of the arms of England and St George, in which were sackbuts and waits, who played on the water, and so it finished'.[92]

The active involvement of London in the royal spectaculars of Henry VIII's reign illustrates his astuteness as well as the City's essential loyalty.

He was conscious of the Court's vulnerability to a metropolis out of control. This was shown by the speed of his firm response to the May Day riots of 1517. It was a demonstration both of royal authority and of popular royal mercy.[93] His government recognized too the political and economic importance and also the diplomatic value of London. Its size, wealth, proximity and river highway made it the obvious arena for displays of princely power and magnificence. In 1522, for example, king and emperor, riding to London from Greenwich, were met at Deptford by the mayor and aldermen, with Sir Thomas More as their orator. The two princes were then treated to a series of allegorical pageants in the City's streets.[94] London was also intimately involved in the celebration of royal weddings and consorts' coronations, especially as the Thames was frequently used to bring the king and current queen from Greenwich. So in June 1533,

all the crafts of London . . . in several barges decked after the most gorgeous and sumptuous manner, with divers pageants thereunto belonging, repaired and waited altogether upon the mayor of London; and so well furnished came all unto Grenewich, where they tarried and waited for the queen's coming to her barge: which so done, they brought her unto the Tower, trumpets, [shawms],[95] and other divers instruments all the ways playing and making great melody. . . .[96]

The greatest celebrations, however, occurred when Jane Seymour was delivered of the long-awaited male heir, Edward:

[T]he same night . . . their was new fiers made in everie streete and lane, people sitting at them banquetting with fruites and wyne . . . and hogsheaddes of wyne sett in divers places of the Cittie for poore people to drinke as long as they listed; the maior and aldermen riding about the cittie thancking the people, and praying them to give . . . praise to God for our prince.[97]

Age and declining health gradually changed this aspect of Court life as, indeed, it changed all others. In the 1530s Henry's active role in jousts and tourneys declined. The religious changes contributed to the decline of Court festivals. In his later years even Henry's active involvement in the making of music declined, although his volatility meant resurgences of activity, as in January 1543, when he was 'in good humour and high spirits . . . [and inclined] to invite and entertain [ladies] at Court', and in August, when he was the roaming hunter again. Thereafter exhaustion and a range of illnesses made him increasingly unfit for an active role in war, whilst at home his courtly activities were increasingly confined to gentler pastimes, such as 'playing at cards with the Lord Admiral and other intimates'.[98] Slowly but inexorably the curtain fell on the Henrician Court's long glittering run.

Notes

1 G. Walker, 'Henry VIII and the Invention of the Royal Court', *Hist. Today*, 47, 2 (Feb. 1997), 13–20; D. M. Loades, *The Tudor Court*, London, 1986, and Bargon 1992, p. 8.

2 D. Starkey, 'Intimacy and Innovation: The Rise of the Privy Chamber, 1485–1547', in idem, ed., *The English Court from the Wars of the Roses to the Civil War*, London, 1987, pp. 71, 118; idem, 'Representation through Intimacy', in Guy, ed., *Tudor Monarchy*, pp. 51–2, 55–67; idem, 'Court and Government', in Coleman and Starkey, eds, *Revolution Reassessed*, pp. 31–6; G. W. Bernard, *Power and Politics in Tudor England*, Aldershot, 2000, pp. 131–2; Walker, *Persuasive Fictions*, pp. 14–23.

3 D. Starkey, 'Court, Council and Nobility in Tudor England', in R. G. Asch and A. M. Birke, eds, *Princes, Patronage, and the Nobility: The Court at the Beginning of the Modern Age c.1450–1650*, Oxford, 1991, pp. 175–6.

4 Davies, *Peace, Print and Protestantism*, pp. 156, 238–9; *Cal. SP Ven.*, 2, no. 918 (p. 400); D. Cressy, 'Spectacle and Power: Apollo and Solomon at the Court of Henry VIII, *Hist. Today*, 32 (Oct. 1982), 17–19.

5 Whether or not the council met in Whitehall or Westminster Palace after 1529 has little practical significance. Henry did not commonly attend meetings anyway. Furthermore, Westminster Palace was within easy walking distance of him. Bernard, 'Court and Government', in *Power and Politics*, pp. 129–33.

6 *Trevelyan Papers*, I, p. 157; Thurley, *Royal Palaces*, pp. 126–7, 196–9; M. St Clare Byrne, ed., *The Lisle Letters*, 6 vols, London, 1981, 5, no. 1415.

7 *Cal. SP Ven.*, 2, no. 918 (p. 398).

8 Williams, 'Three Contrasts in Personality', p. 159; D. Willen, *John Russell, First Earl of Bedford*, London, 1981, pp. 101–11; D. Loades, *John Dudley Duke of Northumberland, 1504–1553*, Oxford, 1996, App. II; B. L. Beer, *Northumberland. The Political Career of John Dudley, Earl of Warwick and Duke of Northumberland*, Kent State Univ., 1973, pp. 8–10; R. Virgoe, 'The Recovery of the Howards in East Anglia, 1485–1529', in E. W. Ives, R. J. Knecht and J. J. Scarisbrick, eds, *Wealth and Power in Tudor England*, London, 1978, pp. 18, 20. They also benefited by appointment to local, regional and central offices.

9 Henry even attempted to use it as an instrument for the cultural assimilation of Gaelic lords. Ciarán Brady, 'Comparable Histories? Tudor Reform in Wales and Ireland', in S. G. Ellis and S. Barber, eds, *Conquest and Union: Fashioning a British State, 1485–1725*, London, 1995, p. 69.

10 The privy purse expenses include payments for repairing, painting and decorating the king's great barge, for 'dressing new barges', and for the wages of seventeen crewmen. *Privy Purse Expences*, pp. xiii–xiv, 44–5, 96, 135, 155, 169, 181, 195, 208, 211 247, 279, 281, 298–9.

11 The river was also used for important occasions. In January 1540 'did the kyng and all ye noblis of ye Reme . . . and every craft in your best a raye, went doun in ther barges to Grenwitche . . . and ther the kyng did mete and reseve on Black heth my lady An, the Deukes doughter of Kleve, and made her queene of Ingland'. C. Hopper, ed., *A London Chronicle*, Camden Miscellany, 4, Series no. 1, 73 (1859), p. 15.

12 Thurley, *Royal Palaces*, p. 67; Byrne, ed., *Lisle Letters*, 5, nos 1177, 1203 (1538), 1475 (1539).

13 N. Samman, 'The Progresses of Henry VIII, 1509–1529', in MacCulloch, ed., *Politics, Policy and Piety*, pp. 64, 65, 67.

14 Hall, fol. 8.

15 Samman, p. 64; E. Lodge, ed., *Illustrations of British History, Biography and Manners*, 3 vols, London, 1838, 1, p. 6.

16 Anglo, *Spectacle*, pp. 190–206; D. Loades, *Power in Tudor England*, London, 1997, p. 110; Biddle, ed., pp. 425–32.

17 From 5 July to 1 October according to the giest. *LP*, 8, no. 989.

18 R. Bell, 'Aston Court and the Progress of 1535', in Starkey, ed., *A European Court*, pp. 118, 121.

19 Hay, ed., *Anglica Historia*, p. 11; *LP*, 16, no. 1130 (p. 533).

20 *Privy Purse Expences*, pp. xxii, 251.

21 H. Ellis, ed., *Original Letters, illustrative of English History*, 11 vols in 3 series, London, 1824–6, 3 (3), pp. 208–9.

22 *LP*, 2(2), nos 3558, 3638, 3697, 3723, 3788, 3885; Byrne, ed., *Lisle Letters*, 2, p. 503 (1533); ibid., 5, nos 1449, 1452; *LP*, 4, no. 2407; Samman, pp. 69, 71–2.

23 Ellis, ed., *Orig. Letters*, 3 (1), p. 346; Byrne, ed., *Lisle Letters*, 2, no. 227.

24 M. St Clare Byrne, ed., *The Letters of Henry VIII*, London, 1936, pp. 70–1.

25 See above, Chap. 3, pp. 31–4.

26 D. Starkey, 'Castiglione at the Court of Henry VIII: Was There a Renaissance Court After All?', in G. J. Schochet, ed., *Reformation, Humanism and 'Revolution'*, I, Washington D.C., 1990, pp. 166, 175, 178–9, 181.

27 M. Vale, *War and Chivalry*, London, 1981, p. 171. Unfortunately, Henry seems to have regarded jousting skill as sufficient justification for appointing courtiers to military or naval commands. S Gunn, 'Tournaments and Early Tudor Chivalry', *Hist. Today*, 41 (June 1991), 21.

28 Anglo, *Spectacle*, p. 111; *The Great Tournament Roll of Westminster*, 2 vols, Oxford, 1968, I, pp. 44–8.

29 *Great Tournament Roll*, pp. 51–5; Anglo, *Spectacle*, pp. 111–12; Hall, fols 9–10.

30 Ibid., p. 45n1; Anglo, *Spectacle*, pp. 117–18; Hall, fols 15v–16.

31 Anglo, *Spectacle*, pp. 113–14; *Four Years at the Court of Henry VIII*, 2, p. 97.

32 S. J. Gunn, *Charles Brandon, Duke of Suffolk, c.1484–1545*, Oxford, 1988, pp. 8–10; idem, 'The Early Tudor Tournament', in Starkey, ed., *A European Court*, p. 47.

33 Thurley, *Royal Palaces*, pp. 192–3.

34 T. Hoby, ed., *Baldassare Castiglione, The Book of the Courtier*, London, 1974, pp. 35, 42, 98–9; Thurley, *Royal Palaces*, pp. 179–80, 182–91; idem, 'The Sports of Kings', in Starkey, ed., *A European Court*, p. 163.

35 *Cal. SP Ven.*, 2, no. 1287 (p. 559); see above, Chap. 3, pp. 41–2.

36 *Cal. SP Ven.*, 4, no. 105 (p. 61).

37 Thurley, *Royal Palaces*, pp. 165–6.

38 *Privy Purse Expences*, pp. 65, 240.

39 *LP*, 3 (1), no. 950.

40 *A Collection of Ordinances and Regulations for the Government of the Royal Household*, Society of Antiquaries, 1790, pp. 158–9.

41 *LP*, 16, no. 59; ibid.,17, no. 1212; ibid., 18 (2), no. 41.

42 Ibid., 16, no. 1130; see above, p. 58.

43 Thurley, 'Sports of Kings', p. 166.

44 Kipling, *Triumph of Honour*, pp. 13, 30.

45 Wolsey too was an active, important patron of the arts.

46 S. Foister, 'Holbein as Court Painter', in Starkey, ed., *A European Court*, pp. 58–63.

47 J. Blezzard and F. Palmer, 'King Henry VIII, Performer, Conoisseur and Composer of Music', *Antiquaries Journal*, 80 (2000), 249–55.

48 E.g. P. Holman, 'Music at the Court of Henry VIII,' in Starkey, ed., *A European Court*, pp. 104–5; D. Fallows, 'Henry VIII as a Composer', in C. Banks, A. Searle and M. Turner, eds, *Sundry sorts of music books*, London, 1993, pp. 27–36; Blezzard and Palmer, pp. 255–7, 262–9.

49 Walker, *Persuasive Fictions*, p. 112; N. Williams, *Henry VIII and his Court*, London, 1971, pp. 34–6.

50 Ellis, ed., *Orig. Letters*, 3 (2), p. 49; R. Bowers, 'The Cultivation and Promotion of Music in the Household and Orbit of Thomas Wolsey', in S. J. Gunn and P. G. Lindley, eds, *Cardinal Wolsey: Church, State and Art*, Cambridge, 1991, pp. 190–3; *Four Years at the Court of Henry VIII*, 1, pp. 78–9.

51 P. C. Herman, ed., *Reading Monarch's Writing*, Tempe, Arizona, 2002, pp. 13–26, 30–4, 228.

52 *Dieu et mon droit*, the royal motto. Ibid., p. 33.

53 Ibid., p. 227.

54 G. Walker, *Plays of Persuasion: Drama and Politics at the Court of Henry VIII*, Cambridge, 1991, pp. 7, 15–22.

55 *Cal. SP Span.*, 5 (2), no. 55 (p. 127).

56 See above, p. 55.

57 Williams, *Henry VIII and his Court*, pp. 40–7; Dickens, ed., *Courts of Europe*, p. 155; A. Weir, *Henry VIII: The King and his Court*, London, 2001, pp. 269–73.

58 Sylvester and Cavendish, eds, Roper, *Life of More*, p. 202.

59 W. G. Zeeveld, *Foundations of Tudor Policy*, Cambridge, Mass., 1948, pp. 3–11, 157–61, 164–5, 227–33; M. Dowling, 'The Gospel and the Court: Reformation under Henry VIII', in P. Lake and M. Dowling, eds, *Protestantism and the National Church in Sixteenth Century England*, London, 1987, pp. 36–40, 64–6.

60 Sylvester and Cavendish, eds, Roper, *Life of More*, p. 202; W. Hackmann, 'Nicolaus Kratzar: The King's Astronomer and Renaissance Instrument-Maker', in Starkey, ed., *A European Court*, pp. 70–1.

61 A plat was a pictorial representation. P. Barber, 'Henry VIII and Mapmaking', in ibid., pp. 146–50.

62 J. Carley, 'Greenwich and Henry VIII's Royal Library', in ibid., pp. 155–6; J. Backhouse, 'Arms and the Manuscripts: The King's Illuminated Books', *Hist. Today*, 41 (June 1991), 46.

63 Kipling, *Triumph of Honour*, pp. 31–40.

64 Ibid., pp. 39–40, 40–71.

65 S. W. Haas, 'Henry VIII's *Glasse of Truthe*', *History*, 64 (1979), 353–62.

66 Ibid., p. 358.

67 F. D. Logan, 'The First Royal Visitation of the English Universities, 1535', *EHR*, 106 (1991) 861, 865–9, 872–3, 877–84, 888.

68 Scarisbrick, *Henry VIII*, p. 519.

69 In civil law, divinity, Greek, Hebrew and medicine.

70 Williams, *Henry VIII and his Court*, pp. 245–6.

71 G. Walker, *The Politics of Performance in Early Renaissance Drama*, Cambridge, 1998, Chap. 3.

72 W. Sessions, '"Enough survives": The Earl of Surrey and European Court Culture', *Hist. Today*, 41 (June 1991), 48–52.

73 M. Dowling, 'A Woman's Place? Learning and the Wives of Henry VIII', *Hist. Today*, 41 (June, 1991), 38–42.

74 Hall, fols 133–4; Anglo, *Spectacle*, pp. 115–16.

75 Hall, fol. 202.

76 See above, p. 61.

77 Hall, fols 16, 55v; Anglo, *Spectacle*, pp. 118–20.

78 *LP*, 14 (1), no. 967.

79 Hall, fols 11v–12.

80 *Four Years at the Court of Henry VIII*, I, pp. 79–80, 90–1.

81 See above, Chap. 1, pp. 12–13.

82 Williams, 'Three Contrasts in Personality', p. 156; Thurley, *Royal Palaces*, pp. 46–8; W. Jerdan, ed., *Rutland Papers*, Camden Society, Series no. 1, 21 (1842), pp. 28–49; Starkey, 'The Field of Cloth of Gold, 1520', in idem, ed., *A European Court*, pp. 50–3.

83 *LP*, 3, no. 806; R. J. Knecht, 'The Field of Cloth of Gold', in C. Giry-Deloison, ed., *Francois Ier et Henri VIII. Deux Princes de la Renaissance (1515–1547)*, Lille and London, 1996, p. 42.

84 Ibid., pp. 43–6.

85 Ibid., pp. 46–51.

86 Ibid., p. 51; Williams, 'Three Contrasts in Personality', p. 156.

87 Scarisbrick, *Henry VIII*, p. 81; Knecht, 'Field of Cloth of Gold, pp. 37–40.

88 See below, Chap. 9, p. 171.

89 *Rutland Papers*, p. 51.

90 Ibid., pp. 59–100.

91 Williams, ed., *Eng. Hist. Docs*, V, pp. 720–1; Weir, *Henry VIII: King and Court*, p. 386.

92 W. D. Hamilton, ed., Charles Wriothesley, *A Chronicle of England, 1485–1559*, Camden Society, Series no. 2, 11, 2 vols (1875–7), I, pp, 66–71, 109–11.

93 See above, Chap. 3, p. 32.

94 Anglo, *Spectacle*, pp. 190–202; Hall, fols 96–98v; *Cal. SP Span.*, 2, no. 423.

95 Oboe-type instruments.

96 J. E. Cox, *Miscellaneous Writings and Letters of Thomas Cranmer*, Parker Society, Cambridge, 1846, pp. 244–7.

97 Hamilton, ed., Wriothesley, *Chronicle of England*, 1, p. 67.

98 *Cal. SP Span.*, 6 (2), pp. 223, 460; ibid., 8, p. 320.

Chapter 5

Henry VIII, His Councillors and Ministers

Henry VIII's relations with his councillors and ministers were determined partly by the king's constitutional authority, but also by this particular king's personality, his conception of kingship and his role in government. There were dramatic changes in the pronounced official conception of kingship during his reign, most notably stated in the acts in restraint of appeals and of supremacy. These statutes declared that the king exercised secular *imperium* over the English kingdom and spiritual *imperium* over its Church. The spiritual authority was supposedly given by God, not parliament, and Henry modelled his role on Solomon and David – hence his frequent use of their images. Nevertheless, his constitutional role in secular government was not significantly changed in theory or practice. Before, during and after the 1530s, government, exercised through the royal prerogative, was the right of God's anointed, the king. The 'ordinary' prerogative was limited by the common law, but he also enjoyed an extraordinary prerogative power for use in emergencies. Henry VIII's reign did not substantially change the *dominium politicum et regale* as defined by Sir John Fortescue in the fifteenth century. It is particularly important here to stress the *two* ongoing limits on royal authority: not only common law but also counsel. In the last pre-Tudor parliament (1483) the lord chancellor declared that 'the womb of this great public body of England' was 'where the king is himself, his court and his counsel'.[1] John Guy writes that, 'Whether expressed in Court, Council, or Parliament, it was counsel that made the exercise of royal power legitimate.' By reference to Sir Thomas Elyot (1531), Thomas Starkey (c.1535), Christopher St German (1531), even Stephen Gardiner (1535) and later Francis Bacon, he proceeds to show how counsel continued to be regarded as essential to legitimate government.[2]

Henry certainly recognized the value, indeed the practical necessity, of advice. His expulsion of the minions, for example, was a consequence of counsel.[3] He sought advice about the Amicable Grant in 1525. In June

1530 he called a meeting of prelates, nobles and lawyers and consulted them about an appeal to the pope for his divorce from his first wife, Catherine, or alternatively the summoning of a General Council. The response was unfavourable. At another meeting, in October, Henry sought the opinion of clergy and lawyers whether parliament could give the archbishop of Canterbury statutory authority to act. '[H]aving studied and discussed the affair', they answered that it could not be done. It is not surprising either that the king sought advice on such an unusual and important matter or that he was angry at the responses.[4] A more important consideration is whether he sought and took advice as a routine practice in the government of the realm. In order to see this in the right perspective, it is necessary to examine consultation and advice in the context of his overall performance as a personal monarch.

England was governed by personal monarchy: Thomas Starkey wrote that the 'hart' of 'thys polytyke body' was 'the kyng prynce & rular of the state'; in the 1560s Sir Thomas Smith described the Prince as 'the life [and] head' of the realm of England.[5] Did Henry fulfil the two essentials of personal monarchy: the personal projection of greatness and the effective control of government? *First*, there is no doubt that he fully and effectively represented the symbolic side of this royal office. In language, ceremony, ritual and reverential etiquette he also elevated the office and its occupant to a new majestic height. Smith described Henry's legacy when he wrote 'no man speaketh to the prince nor serveth at the table but in adoration and kneeling, all persons of the realm be bareheaded before him'. Regulations for making Henry's bed required the yeomen bedders to make the sign of the cross and kiss the bed 'where there handes were'.[6] Subjects and foreigners alike attested to the fact that the king had the physique, majestic bearing, presence and dignity to make such reverence, indeed 'adoration', seem natural and appropriate. Yet this is the man who also acted brutally to those around and near him and with total indifference to the public perception of him. He reputedly inflicted physical violence on Cromwell. On one occasion in 1535, as the Spanish ambassador reported,

He the other day nearly murdered his own fool, a simple and innocent man, because he happened to speak well in his presence of the Queen [Catherine] and Princess [Mary] and called the concubine [Anne] 'ribaude' and her daughter 'bastard'.[7]

When Mary refused to acknowledge the legitimacy of her father's second marriage or her own bastardy and exclusion from the succession, she was subjected to humiliation, deprivation, virtual imprisonment and enforced separation from her mother. She was not even allowed to see Catherine during her final illness. The king's cruel conduct was common knowledge. So Charles V received news about him

visiting . . . the daughter of his concubine, and refusing to see his own legitimate daughter, the Princess, whom he has spoiled of her princely estate, and caused to live under the same roof as the other.[8]

Perhaps the only certain thing about King Henry VIII is that he was an apparent mass of contradictions.

Secondly, he was capable of being the decisive factor in government at crucial moments, such as the 'Evil May Day' riots in London in 1517.[9] On the other hand, his response to the lengthy and most serious uprising of the reign, the Pilgrimage of Grace in 1536, was characterized by 'vacillation and inconsistency'.[10] In any overall assessment of Henry's kingship, however, his crisis response was less important than his ongoing involvement in government.

Policy formulation

He was, in this matter, characteristically both dominant and subservient, opinionated and yet susceptible to the opinions of others. Once again his inconsistency spawned a variety of contemporary and later assessments of him. French ambassador Marillac, writing in 1540, described him as tainted with three 'plagues', the second of which was 'distrust and fear'. Henry 'would fain keep in favour with everybody, but does not trust a single man. . . . The third plague, lightness and inconstancy . . . has perverted the rights of religion, marriage, faith and promise, as softened wax can be altered to any form.'[11] Here was a suspicious king, frequently making policy changes as he chose. Does this mean, however, that he could not be influenced, even manipulated? In 1536 Charles V was advised that Henry

liked always to be led as mildly and courteously as possible. . . . And whereas Your Majesty was so high in dignity and so powerful, it would be a greater virtue for you to treat him with all possible courtesy. . . . [As a result] Your Majesty would easily lead him wherever you liked, and absolutely dispose of him in every way.[12]

John Foxe astutely observed how current royal policy reflected those around the throne. When Anne Boleyn, Cromwell and Cranmer enjoyed his attention, 'what organ of Christ's glory did more good in the Church than he?' But 'when sinister and wicked counsel, under subtle and crafty pretences, had gotten once the foot in, thrusting truth and verity out of the prince's ears, how much . . . all revolted backward again'. Yet is this a description of a manipulated king? Foxe also stated that, 'while good counsel was about him, and could be heard, the king did much good'.[13] In other words he sought counsel before acting, which, as already observed, is what a king should do.

What, then, is the most accurate picture? Historians also offer varying images. To David Starkey, Henry 'was manipulable'. In apparent contrast, David Potter depicts him as a king who was in 'ultimate control of policy' and determined its 'broad outlines'. And Greg Walker sees a pragmatic Prince, 'clear in his overall strategic aims'.[14]

Royal control of policy was, however, limited from the very beginning by Henry's indecision, his laziness about State business (even, indeed especially, about signing documents)[15] and his enthusiastic preference for martial and artistic activities. For lengthy periods he was parted from his council, especially during the summer. Then he spent much time on 'progress' or hunting. Between 1509 and 1511 the core of the council, meeting on its own, managed business, because the young king was inexperienced in matters of State and, in any case, preferred to indulge his passion for the masque and the revel, the joust and the tourney.

The rise of Thomas Wolsey from 1511, however, eclipsed the council and the driving force of government was transformed from the conciliar to the ministerial.[16] In 1517 the papal nuncio in England, Francesco Chieregato, described Wolsey as doing everything:

The King occupies himself with nothing but scientific amusements. All negotiations pass through the Cardinal, who manages everything with consummate authority, integrity, and prudence. The King pays the Cardinal such respect that he speaks only through his mouth.[17]

This amounts to a misreading of the king. Wolsey presided in council and by letters or personal visits kept the king fully informed on State business.[18] However, whilst Wolsey shouldered the burdens of government, however, Henry would not relinquish ultimate control, especially in decision-making. It was, undoubtedly, a co-operative relationship in which king and minister together worked out policy before consulting the council. Furthermore, it was the minister who was constantly in the thick of State business and so, armed with the necessary facts and figures, could advise the king on the feasibility of particular policies. This gave him much influence, even though in the end it seems to have been the king who decided policy, especially in foreign affairs, and it was Wolsey who executed it.[19] Of course Henry's galaxy of weaknesses could be exploited, especially when he was encouraged to gallop away and make his fame by military exploits in France. Furthermore, the king's direct access to the council was steadily diminished. By 1522 Wolsey had trimmed the number of councillors attendant upon the king to just two, Sir Thomas More and Sir Thomas Neville.[20] Yet his dependence on royal response to his actions continued.[21] When in 1525 the attempt to raise a forced loan, the Amicable Grant, failed miserably, Henry blamed the venture solely on him. The peace with France later that year brought Wolsey's noble critics back to Court and to the king. And in the following year Henry complained about the lack of sufficient attendant councillors. Wolsey's response was the Eltham Ordinances, which purported to be a measure of household reform, including the provision of an effective council attendant upon the king: '[A] good number of honourable, virtuous, sad, wise, expert and discreet persons of his Council shall give their attendance upon his most royal person.' There followed a list of twenty councillors. Many would be absent from Court on their duties, but at least two of them would always be in attendance.[22] It was a device to separate the hostile nobles from Henry and to ensure that, whilst he had two resident councillors on hand, he had little more.

Wolsey did not last much longer before a matter close to the king's heart, political priorities and libido brought him down. His failure to procure for his royal master an annulment of his first marriage, to Catherine of Aragon, led to his dismissal from the lord chancellorship in 1529, his banishment to York and then, in 1530, his summons to face charges of treason for conspiracy. His death from natural causes during his journey southwards spared him the public humiliation of conviction in court, followed by execution. Whether Henry was pressured by a Court faction to destroy his chief minister, after many years of faithful toil in his service, is now questionable, indeed doubtful. One of the constant problems is that among the commonest contemporary sources about Court pressures upon the king and the way in which he could supposedly be influenced, even swayed by them, were reports by foreigners. According to Polydore Vergil the king 'smartly censured Wolsey' over his financial mismanagement in 1523 'and said that he would manage his affairs soon without any minister'. The cardinal behaved humbly and, we are told, within a few days had 'reconciled Henry to himself'.[23] Ambassadors, too, often depicted Henry as manageable, even malleable. But most foreign observers were ill-informed and influenced by their own dynastic loyalties. In the case of diplomats, facts could also be tailored to influence their own royal masters in particular directions.

And Vergil was biased because of his intense hostility towards Wolsey. The point is that we should not mistake Vergil's account of Henry's reconciliation with his minister as a sign of weakness. He remained in ultimate control of policy. When matters so personally dear to him as his passion for Anne Boleyn and the desire for a secure succession became urgent, he then became the driving force in both policy initiation and implementation.

Not for the last time the king demonstrated that a lengthy record of loyal active service provided no immunity against royal impatience, anger and rejection. After the Amicable Grant fiasco in 1525, when Wolsey was a vulnerable target of criticism, Archbishop Warham tried to reassure him: '[I]t hath been and ever shall be that whatsoever be in most of favour and most of counsel with a great prince shall be maligned and ill spoken of, do he never so well.'[24] As Peter Gwyn observed, 'If the remark fitted Wolsey's situation in 1525, how much better did it fit two years later,'[25] when the annulment of Henry's marriage first became an issue. Now, however, not only was Wolsey the target of political critics; he also became, to Henry VIII, a dispensable failure who deserved condign punishment for treachery. If Cavendish is to be relied upon, the cardinal's words to Sir William Kingston, uttered in his last hours, reveal that he understood the king so well:

He is sure a prince of a royal courage [= temper], and hath a princely heart; and rather than he will either miss or want any part of his will or appetite, he will put the loss of one half of his realm in danger.

He recalled that he could never 'persuade him from his will and appetite'. So he warned Kingston that, if he became a member of the king's council, he should be 'well advised and assured what matter ye put in his head; for ye shall never pull it out again'.[26]

After Wolsey's fall the ministerial focus of government was, to some extent, replaced by a conciliar one. The king, assisted by a confused medley of councillors, took direct charge of affairs.[27] In the process, however, he revealed his shortcomings. The inner council of Boleyns, the dukes of Norfolk and Suffolk, Gardiner and More was divided and incapable of advice based on consensus. Henry had no doubts as to what he wanted, but, after twenty years as king, he was still inexperienced in council management, indecisive and lacking direction, and so he made no progress towards a resolution of his problems. The muddle and mayhem ended only with the rise of Thomas Cromwell in 1532. He secured his place in the king's confidence when, in 1533–4, he achieved the annulment of his marriage and the recognition of Henry VIII as 'the supreme hede of the Churche of England'.[28] Although Cromwell worked with and through the council, the 1530s marked a return from conciliar to ministerial government. Cromwell engineered great benefits for his master: these included the wealth of the monasteries (1536 and 1539), First Fruits and Tenths (1534), the Statute of Uses (1536) and, by the Franchises Act (1536) and the start of Welsh union (1536), the centralizing of government. Yet, to what extent could he actually manage the king? Although Henry enjoyed substantial benefits from Cromwell's energy and skills, other influential councillors and courtiers, some of whom, especially Norfolk, were his critics and enemies, played their part. They too had contact with the king and, in varying degrees, enjoyed his favour. Cromwell's religious policies and his persuasion of the king into marriage with the 'Flanders Mare', Anne of Cleves, enabled Norfolk to secure his downfall and death.

For the remainder of the reign Henry ruled without a principal councillor-cum-arch-bureaucrat: no more Wolseys or Cromwells. But he did not rule alone, for he lacked both energy and interest. The year 1540 witnessed rather a shift back from ministerial to conciliar management or, as David Loades describes it, 'a more corporate style of government'.[29] The reorganization of the council, in 1534–6 and 1540, as a relatively small executive as well as advisory privy council, meeting virtually every day, ensured the continuity of government business.[30] Henry directed his energies elsewhere, to matters of religion, to continuation of the political centralization of the 1530s, to foreign policy and, especially from 1542, to renewed war with the Scots and French. Furthermore, his last years were riven by conflict, the product of personal rivalries and ambitions and, of course, of religious division. Such conflict was ongoing, bitter and at times even deadly, within and between the privy council and privy chamber.[31] Consequently the king was subjected to constant pressure from opposing sides, especially in the ongoing religious struggle. In 1546 George Blagge, known as Tom Thumb because of his 'square shape', was condemned to be burned alive for heresy. His contacts in the privy chamber secured his release, doubtless because the king, who nicknamed him the 'pig', enjoyed his company. When the king saw him again and called out 'Ah, my Pig', the reprieved man answered, 'Yea, if your Majesty had not been better to me than your bishops were, your *Pig* had been roasted ere this time!'[32] A more important and exposed target of the conservatives was Archbishop Cranmer. When, in 1543, Bishop Gardiner presented charges of heresy against Cranmer, by his own clergy at Canterbury

Cathedral, the king assigned to his archbishop the task of investigating the accusations.[33] As Henry undoubtedly remained a Catholic, how, then, does one explain his behaviour?

It might be confirmatory evidence of the commonly held view that the king was pliable, easily influenced and swayed, one way then another. On 4 January 1545 Chapuys advised the emperor,

I ought to know the character of the King sufficiently well to be sure that he was always anxious to reciprocate; nay even to exceed, any friendly approaches made to him and that any one who knew how to manage him might do almost as they liked with him, if he could be satisfied that his friendship would be returned.[34]

Chapuys, however, was talking about Henry's diplomatic role, which may have been very different from the way in which he conducted himself in domestic affairs. His idiosyncratic personality does pose a problem for historians. We have to grapple with conflicting images which have given rise to fundamentally different interpretations: in Starkey's words, Henry, on the one hand 'as puppet master', pulling all the strings, and, on the other, 'as the creature of factions, which pull him first one way and then the other'.[35] He suggests that it may simply be a matter of perspective: Henry believed that he managed all, whilst his courtiers and ministers thought and acted as if they managed him.[36] Walker's view of the king is a more positive one: he 'occupies the centre of the political arena, not because he was forced there by the contrary pressures of competing factions, but because he chose that ground for himself'.[37] In 1516 Ambassador Giustinian seemed to confirm such confident royal assertion of control, when he recounted Henry's comment:

I only wish to command my own subjects; but, on the other hand, I do not choose any one to have it in his power to command me, nor will I ever suffer it.[38]

This was, however, uttered in a conversation with a foreign diplomat, when a Prince would naturally wish to project images of strength and self-confidence. Nevertheless it does conform with Henry's conduct during the Blagge and Cranmer episodes in the 1540s. His whimsical, relaxed manner was indicative of a king in full control. This is not to assert that he was uniquely impervious to persuasive influences. During his last years, for example, he was surrounded by bitter in-fighting into which, as we shall see, he was sometimes drawn and which did have some effect on both religious and foreign policies. Ultimately, however, he pursued his goals to the end.

Henry's administrative oversight of his daily government

Whether a particular king was politically active or not, whether he was a Prince of talents or mediocrity, a monarch of Renaissance Europe was conceived to be a mover and a shaker, an image-maker and -breaker. He was not normally a devotee of administrative minutiae, drafting memoranda, checking accounts and writing screeds of correspondence. Tudors had Wolseys, Cromwells and Cecils for that sort of thing. Therefore it is, perhaps, more realistic in the early modern European context to single out the bureaucratic Henry VII, rather than the athletic, martial and artistic Henry VIII, as an exception. The former's devotion to administrative oversight was more uncharacteristic of the time than Henry VIII's avoidance of administrative tedium. However, the second Tudor did have an unusual reputation for laziness and lack of attention to daily, routine responsibilities. It figured frequently in diplomatic correspondence. In 1510 frustrated English bishops confided to the Spanish ambassador that '[t]he King . . . is young, and does not care to occupy himself with anything but the pleasures of his age. All other affairs he neglects.'[39] Wolsey willingly shouldered the burdens of daily administration, managed the council and presided over judicial proceedings in Star Chamber, leaving youth to pursue those pleasures.[40] Henry himself rarely attended formal council meetings after the beginning of his reign. When he was present the occasions were formal gatherings of the great council rather than council business sessions: on 2 May 1516, for example, when Wolsey delivered a formal oration to Henry, the earl of Northumberland was committed to prison for contempt and then king, queen, minister and council dined at Lambeth; or when the problems of sanctuary were debated before Henry in star chamber on 10–11 November 1519.[41] He might also preside when the council met to consider crucial business, such as Wolsey's successor as lord chancellor, on 23 October 1529.[42] As time passed, youth faded, but the pursuit of pleasure did not. In 1535 Chapuys informed Charles V that the English government feared a French attack on Calais and Guines.

Yet it seems to me as if this King cared not much for them and the others at this present moment, for he is more occupied with dancing parties and ladies than ever he was, and I see no sign at all of warlike preparations.[43]

Ambassadorial reports tended to be better-informed and more accurate on matters of foreign policy and European power politics because that was their diplomatic business. They were also often alert to the reason for the king's frustrating delays or avoidance of action in such matters.

On 18 March 1538 a portrait of Christina, duchess of Milan, was de-livered to the wife-hungry Henry. According to Chapuys it greatly pleased the king, 'so much so, that since he saw it he has been in much better humour than ever he was, making musicians play on their instruments all day along'. Two days later Henry visited one of his riverside palaces. There he issued orders 'for the erection of certain sumptuous buildings' before returning by river, 'surrounded by musicians', and visiting the duchess of Suffolk. Since then, he 'cannot be one single moment without masks'. The ambassador had two possible explanations for his conduct: celebrating his intention to remarry, or 'by way of dissimulation' whilst the French ambassador was still at Court.[44] There was a third possible and persuasive reason: the simple pursuit of pleasure.

Four years later frustration was still a recurrent theme of diplomats' correspondence. Attempts by Chapuys to negotiate a treaty were being held up because, according to Henry's commissioners, he had been 'lat-terly going from place to place for sport, without residing at any fixed spot'. As a consequence they had been unable to report to him or to get his 'final resolution' on the treaty. [45] A similar situation prevailed the following year, when the peripatetic king was again on the move, 'hunt-ing, or occasionally visiting some of his various Royal manors'. Whatever the reason – on this occasion Chapuys was convinced that Henry did not want to move against the French – such behaviour severely limited his participation in daily government.[46] The ambassador surmised correctly that, on this occasion, the king was playing diplomatic games. Usually, however, progresses, hunting and other pleasures between the many royal palaces – fifty-five by the time he died – were the reasons for his frequent movement away from London. This inevitably created practical problems for those entrusted with the execution of policy.[47]

Henry VIII's wide-ranging interests, his priorities, likes and dislikes together posed a particular problem, because of the rising importance of the sign manual at the expense of the signet. Under Henry VII the former had become the chief form of authentication. The king's signa-ture, the sign manual, required both the royal presence and willingness to put pen to paper, but Henry was both elusive and, when present, very reluctant. He was indeed notorious for his extreme dislike of putting pen to paper. On 8 July 1521 Richard Pace told Wolsey that, because of a headache, the king would not be able to write to Margaret of Savoy 'with his own hand, and you can order the matter as you please'. On 21 July Henry promised a letter for the French king 'of his own hand, but has now deferred the writing of it till tomorrow'. Officers of the privy chamber, always in attendance and with some knowledge of his idiosyncracies, were used to extracting the sign manual. This eased but never resolved the problem of royal reluctance. John Hussee's report of a conversation with the king in April 1536, however, offers a plausible alternative to laziness as an explanation of that reluctance. When Henry granted Viscount Lisle, lord deputy of Calais, licence to visit England, Hussee requested it in writing. 'But his Grace said it should not need, for his word was thereof sufficient'. Furthermore, when Henry did write letters, his manner was displeasing to at least one of his councillors. In the following reign Bishop Gardiner recalled that his 'fassion of writing' was what he called '"whetting," which was not all the moste pleasant unto me at al times'.[48]

Nevertheless, nothing is simple, straightforward and uncomplicated concerning Henry VIII, about whose place in government there are so many contradictory images. On the one hand, in his later years he introduced the dry stamp, which, when impressed on paper, produced an image of his signature, which was then inked in. It is easy to see this as the ultimate expression of royal laziness. However, the sign manual was now needed daily and was required for a wide range of business, including royal grants, pardons, appointments, passports, letters and financial warrants. So the dry stamp eased the daily routine burden, but, at the same time, Henry lost control and contact with so much government business.[49] Yet the image of a king who was in administrative matters indolent, or at best reluctant, is sometimes contradicted by the facts. In 1521, for example, Richard Pace informed Wolsey that Henry 'readeth all your letters with great diligence and mine answers made to the same not by my device but by his instructions'. When, on one occasion, he disliked Pace's reply to one of Wolsey's letters, he instructed the secretary to fetch pen and ink to the privy chamber. Thereupon he read the letters three times 'and marked such places as it pleased him to make answer unto'. Then, more characteristically, he commanded Pace to write his answer.[50] Undoubtedly age rendered Henry increasingly reluctant to put pen to paper. Yet his ego could cause him to wield the pen as a schoolmaster might do. When Sir William Petre first became secretary in 1544, he was reputedly 'dismaied for that the K[ing] crossed and blotted out manye thinges in a wrightinge w[hi]ch he had made'. Henry was supposed to have 'willed him not to take it in evill parte, "for it is I . . . that made both Crumwell, Wriotheslie and Pagett good Secretaries, and so must I doe to thee"'. If the tale is true, it must stand as one of the more impressive flights of royal fancy.[51] Furthermore, the Imperial ambassador Chapuys observed on a number of occasions that Henry liked to believe in his skills in government business, even if he did not back them with hard work. Yet he was prepared to work hard on the *Assertio* and his other books. In 1528 Brian Tuke told Wolsey that, 'Generally, in going and coming, he turns into my chamber to talk with me about his book.' A few weeks later Henry wrote to Anne Boleyn that the brevity of his letter to her was the result of a headache after writing for four hours.[52] However, the fact that such a short spell of writing could have that effect may indicate that being desk-bound was not a common experience for him.

Henry's place in the structure of politics

According to E. W. Ives, 'a strict definition of 'a [Tudor] faction' is 'a group of people which seeks objectives that are seen primarily in personal terms' – either securing benefits or denying them to their rivals and successfully advocating particular policies. He also argued that 'faction was endemic in sixteenth-century England, and that its objectives were patronage and political power'.[53] Although he acknowledges that the evidence is often scanty, he suspects and traces the operation of faction in the fall of Empson and Dudley and through Wolsey's rise, ascendancy, destruction of Edward Stafford duke of Buckingham and finally his own downfall.[54] The demise of Anne Boleyn in 1536, which Ives describes as 'the example of Tudor faction *par excellence*', ushered in 'an acute period of faction' for the next twenty years. Indeed, he insists that 'we must put Henry's personal monarchy in the context of faction'.[55]

Others pursue the same line of thought, arguing against Peter Gwyn's image of a king in control rather than that of an often-distracted monarch surrounded by jostling factions: that, for example, the removal of the 'minions' in 1519 marked Wolsey's success over a Court faction. The political hole left by Wolsey's fall in 1529 was filled by the aristocratic Boleyn and Aragonese factions, and the dominant characteristic of politics for the rest of the reign was faction.[56] G. R. Elton explained Thomas Cromwell's fall in 1540 as a faction coup carried through by the conservatives Norfolk and Gardiner.[57] David Starkey, in particular, has strummed the faction thesis. Although Wolsey defeated the challenge of the minions in 1519 'without becoming a faction leader himself', he had to become one in self-defence as Anne Boleyn's rise isolated and threatened him. 'So in the late 1520s (and not before) faction became the principal element in politics.' Furthermore 'in Tudor faction politics . . . the negative motive – doing somebody down – is at least as important in political alignment as the positive – getting something done'. This Starkey illustrates in the fall of Anne in 1536, Cromwell's destruction of those prominent Aragonese, the marquess of Exeter, Sir Edward Neville and Sir Nicholas Carew, in 1538–9, and Cromwell's own fall followed by the bitter in-fighting of Henry VIII's last years.[58] He also claims that privy chamber factions prevented a successful conservative counter-attack in the 1540s and made possible the establishment of Protestantism in Edward VI's reign.[59] Starkey's study of the privy chamber has revealed for him that this, the focus of power in the Court, vied with the council to influence and sometimes even manipulate the king. Henry VIII's style of government, characterized by his inconstant moods, priorities and limited engagement in government, gave faction, in both Court and council, 'an open invitation to flourish'. Furthermore, the polarization of the Court by Anne Boleyn's religious preferences illustrates that 'policy could be just as important as personality and place in faction'.[60]

In recent years a number of historians have expressed doubts, criticism and even rejection of faction as an important and continuing force during the sixteenth century. Simon Adams and Paul Hammer question both the endemic nature of factionalism and the identification of faction with patronage-hunting or policy promotion.[61] They narrowly define faction as 'a personal following employed in direct opposition to another personal following'. The essence of a faction struggle was 'a personal rivalry that over-rode all other considerations'.[62] The explanation of Henrician politics in factional terms has come under particularly harsh criticism. Consider, for example, Buckingham's fall. Henry and Wolsey suspected his intentions and the king was driven by his own fears to rid the kingdom of him. His death was the removal of an overmighty subject not of a faction leader.[63] In the same way G. W. Bernard's reassessment of the evidence leads him to the conclusion that 'it was Henry, not any faction, nor Anne Boleyn in any direct sense, that was responsible for the fall of Wolsey in 1529'.[64] Similarly he believes that Anne Boleyn's death was a consequence not of factional influence but of the king's acceptance of her guilt. Bernard concludes that 'on this and other occasions, Henry VIII was more in control and less the victim of factional manipulation than some recent accounts would claim'.[65]

The importance of faction in any study of the king is that its active presence and significance were harmful to images of kingship and to the realities of good governance. Faction was accepted as a feature of bad government and therefore of weak kingship. Historians who explore Henrician government in factional terms tend to reduce Henry to a factional tool or 'a mere cipher, swayed this way and that by whichever faction is perceived to have the ascendancy at a given moment'. Greg Walker rightly asserts that this neglects Henry's crucial role in the determination of policy: the 'constant element' in Henrician politics was not faction but 'the powerful, idiosyncratic, personality of the king'. He could accept criticism made to his face, even when it was outrageously bold. When Sir George Throckmorton told the king that, if he married Anne Boleyn, his conscience would be troubled, because 'it is thought ye have meddled both with the mother and the sister', he replied frankly and with unusual modesty, 'Never with the mother.' Frequently, however, critics such as William Peto and Elizabeth Barton were later punished. As for Throckmorton, in 1537 he signed a confession, '[w]ritten ... by the most unhappy man that ever I think did live in this world' and besought Henry to 'accept me into your favour and mercy'.[66]

The enduring characteristic of Henrician politics was not faction but often bitter, even mortal, conflict between ambitious politicians. Rivalries between powerful individuals – Wolsey and Norfolk, Cromwell and the duke, Gardiner and Cranmer – are often transformed by historians into faction conflicts, simply because such *prominente* had considerable followings. It is assumed that a great man's followers pursued his political objectives actively. Most of them, however, were just clients of a great patron: patronage hunters, not political warriors keen to fight his battles. And the ever-present hunt for patronage was a characteristic or purpose not of faction but of clientage. Faction had occasional appearances rather than a regular existence in Tudor politics. This is not to deny that, as Walker argues, the Henrician Court usually included 'individuals or groups' with a range of political opinions and religious affiliations. They provided Henry with a range of counsel which, ideally, provided a wise Prince with a broad spectrum of policy options. But they did not constitute factions.

How Henry took counsel and related to his council

It was the duty of the king's natural counsellors – nobles, churchmen, prominent gentry and, of course, ministers and members of his council – to give advice. Castiglione identified the objective of the ideal courtier as good counsel: tell the Prince what he needs to hear, not simply what will please him. Sir Thomas Elyot wrote in similar vein: 'Oportunitie and tyme for a counsayllour to speke do not depend on the affection and appetite of hym that is counsayled' – in brief, honesty had to take precedence over tact.[67] At the same time, as John Skelton wrote, the virtuous monarch took advice across the political spectrum. Henry VIII lived up to this ideal, because he took counsel widely,[68] formally, confidentially and even intimately! Parliament was one, occasional, source of counsel, which was explicitly stated in writs of summons to lords spiritual and temporal.[69] The king's council provided the regular, daily advice. During Henry VIII's reign nobles ceased to be as prominent on it, although they remained the king's 'natural councillors'. However, he often took advice from those outside the council and the nobility, especially with Court intimates, as Thomas Elyot complained. Sir William Fitzwilliam, for example, was Prince Henry's companion and educated with him. There-after he enjoyed royal favour in his career as courtier, soldier, lord admiral, household treasurer and trusted counsellor of King Henry VIII. During the 1530s Thomas Cromwell began to transform the large advisory coun-cil into a smaller executive privy council, whose members were chosen for their bureaucratic skills rather than their noble status. This process was not completed until 1540 after Cromwell's downfall: its nineteen members then included just eight nobles, some of whom, such as Nor-folk, Suffolk, the earl of Hertford and Lord Russell (Great Admiral), were liable to be absent for lengthy periods on military service. This trend provoked resentment and evoked a hankering for the past, as expressed in the concerns and complaints of the Pilgrims of Grace in 1536.[70] It is ironic therefore that, in the very same year, England's premier noble, the duke of Norfolk, informed the imperial ambassador,

[T]he King needs no chancellor and no council to deliberate and return an answer: he does all that himself without previous consultation.[71]

Perhaps the duke was simply projecting a desirable image of the English king's talent to a foreign diplomat. It was not, however, an accurate image because, as we have seen, he did seek advice. And he accepted it, even if it was not what he wanted to hear. Sir Francis Bryan, who later recollected 'I came to the court very young', was one of Henry's minions. Yet after 1519 he remained in the king's favour and household with regular access to him and with his licence 'boldly [to] speak ... the plain-ness of his mind ... [and] his Grace doth well accept the same'. When, in 1529, he was in Rome attempting to secure the king's divorce, he wrote bluntly to his royal master about Cardinal Campeggio, who was appointed papal legate to deal with the divorce:

As for what you write to us, that Campeggio is your servant, and will do what he can for you, these are fair words only because he wishes to have the bishopric of Durham.[72]

Bryan's frankness, which contrasted with the legate's calculated insincerity, did him no harm and he remained in favour.

The king's ministers, those men most prominent in his government, were, at the same time, those royal servants burdened with the ongoing responsibilities of offering advice or being consulted frequently on matters of complexity, importance and even 'urgent necessity'. How did Henry relate to them? Some of them, such as Thomas Audley, William Paget, William Petre, Richard Rich and Thomas Wriothesley, were amongst the new bureaucrats educated at Oxbridge and in the law schools. They began their careers in royal service in Wolsey's household or, during the 1530s, after the cardinal's fall, they were advanced by favoured politicians such as Bishop Gardiner and Thomas Cromwell. So Audley – described by Chapuys as a man 'suited to [Henry's] purpose' – became lord chancellor (1533), Paget clerk of the signet (c.1531), Petre a master in chancery (1536), Rich solicitor-general (1533) and chancellor of augmentations (1536) and Wriothesley secretary of State (1540). They were the beneficiaries of an irresponsibly generous king who, in the 1530s and 1540s, was in a state of royal flush. All of them received gifts of monastic land and were also able to purchase on favourable terms. Most of them flourished in the last years of the reign, when Henry had no successor to Cromwell.

Rich served the king well, prosecuting at many State trials, giving the testimony which condemned Thomas More in 1535 and which helped to destroy Cromwell in 1540. But Henry's gratitude was always a delicate creature and usually short-lived. As treasurer for the French war, Rich incurred the king's displeasure for his grossly over-stated expenditure for the 1544 campaign and 'resigned'. Petre, who became a principal secretary in 1544, was an administrator and clerk who dutifully executed royal decisions without offering counsel. Henry must have been well content with him, because he claimed that he taught him all that he knew. And he must have particularly appreciated Thomas Wriothesley for his legal skills, energy and loyalty, for he rewarded him with estates and ex-monasteries in eight counties and London, a wide range of local offices, the lord chancellorship and a barony in 1544. Yet Henry's favour was never certain. In 1546 he empowered the conservative chancellor and Bishop Gardiner to draw up charges of heresy against his last wife, Catherine Parr. When Wriothesley turned up to arrest her as she walked in the garden with her husband, Henry – now her protector – called him knave, beast and fool and sent him packing. Nevertheless he remained lord chancellor for the rest of the reign. As for William Paget, who rose from clerkships to privy councillor and a principal secretary in

1543, his diplomatic skills earned enduring royal favour. In the king's last years he became increasingly reliant on Paget, his confidant and contact with the political world. During Henry's final illness, the secretary's most prolonged absence from him was at the trial of the earl of Surrey.

Such were some of the 'new men' who played a prominent part in Henry's government in his later years. As a generalization, and allowing for the occasional exception, they were characterized by a reluctance to counsel the king as to what he should do in sensitive or controversial matters. They were dutiful but very self-serving, and therefore unwilling to go out on the limb of honest, frank, realistic but unwelcome advice. As More said of one of them, Richard Rich, he was 'very light of [his] tongue, a great dicer, and of no commendable fame'. Another, Paget, could persuade Henry 'to adopt suggestions of policy', but 'unlike Wolsey and Cromwell he did not attempt to pursue his own agenda. Such men suited a king who, in his later years, valued his servants less for their counsel than for the way their labours facilitated his ambitions.[73]

One can understand the reluctance of these men to risk the wrath of such an unpredictable king. It was, however, far more difficult for those men in whom Henry particularly placed his trust, in whom he confided and of whom he had the highest expectations. In Henry's view Stephen Gardiner, Thomas More, Thomas Wolsey and Thomas Cromwell all betrayed his trust. At that point their long, devoted service and its fruits were totally discounted. For two of them – More and Cromwell – it was fatal, whilst death by natural causes spared Wolsey a bloody humiliation. The fourth, Gardiner, survived on a tight-rope from which the pope had been pushed but Catholic orthodoxy remained teetering. His academic career at Cambridge, studying canon and civil law (1511–24), ended when he was taken into Wolsey's service. In 1529 he was employed to further the cause of Henry's divorce in Rome and, as Wolsey fell, so Gardiner rose to become the king's principal secretary. In 1535 he wrote *Of True Obedience*, a defence of the royal supremacy and a repudiation of papal authority.[74] Loyalty brought its rewards: in 1531 he became bishop of Winchester. Cromwell's rise, however, led to his loss of the secretaryship in 1534 and thereafter Gardiner and Norfolk formed the core of the conservative resistance to doctrinal change. They succeeded in bringing down Cromwell in 1540, but at the very end of the reign Henry repudiated Gardiner by deliberately excluding him from the executors of his will. When, in 1547, Sir Anthony Brown pointed out to the bed-ridden king that Gardiner 'hath done your highness most painful, long, and notable service', Henry replied,

I remembered him well enough, and of good purpose have left him out: for surely, if he were in my testament, and one of you, he would cumber you all, and you should never rule him, he is of so troublesome a nature.[75]

Mortal he might be, but even on his deathbed Henry had no doubts about his special ability to manage others:

I myself could use [Gardiner], and rule him to all manner of purposes, as seemed good unto me; but so shall you never do.[76]

The insecurity and uncertainty experienced by prominent politicians were exacerbated in this case by religious conflict. Gardiner was a casualty in Henry's assault on the conservatives in 1546–7.[77] He was fortunate insofar as his only penalty was exclusion. Surrey, in contrast, lost everything. So too, in the 1530s, did Thomas More. In his case the king's conduct in pursuing him to his death as a supposed traitor, even after he had resigned his office and gone into silent retirement, portrays a brutal, vindictive king. But was More 'the innocent victim'?

Despite More's projected 'otherworldliness', he actively sought a career in royal service: in 1515 he was on diplomatic service in Flanders and in 1517 he was appointed to the king's council.[78] Wolsey promoted his career, Henry desired his counsel and he became one of the few councillors in regular attendance on the king.[79] He served as diplomat, secretary with custody of the signet, parliamentary orator pursuing royal ends and, of course, regular counsellor. His choice as lord chancellor in October 1529, after Wolsey's fall, is therefore no surprise. What was surprising was More's acceptance of the office. Wolsey fell because he failed to secure Henry's divorce. As early as September 1527 More had informed the king that the proposed divorce was not acceptable. As lord chancellor, how could he conduct himself as a loyal servant? According to Nicholas Harpsfield, he had no choice about his promotion:

[The king offered the position] to Sir Thomas Moore, who refusing it, the king was angri with hym, and caused hym to accepte it.[80]

However, as chancellor, More was bound to be involved in moves to secure the divorce. Perhaps Henry thought that he could persuade him. He might tell his new chancellor

that if he could not therein with his conscience serve him, he was content to accept his service otherwise. . . . [He] would nevertheless continue his gracious favour towards him and never with that matter molest his conscience after.

Fine words! More, however, did not change his mind: he openly stated his views to the king and in his council, he covertly supported parliamentary resistance to the divorce in the commons, he communicated with the pro-Aragonese Chapuys, and in the lords in May 1532 he and the bishops publicly opposed attacks on the Church. It is not surprising that, as Chapuys wrote, Henry was 'very angry, especially with the Chancellor and the bishop of Winchester'. To make matters worse, three days later More resigned the chancellorship. As Guy points out, 'One simply did not "resign" in the Renaissance.' Perhaps it is not surprising that Henry's fine words were forgotten:[81]

[The king] labored to haue had hym perswaded on his [side and] bycause he could not be perswaded, he hated hym for it.

More would not shift his position to please the king. He fought, in an untenable position as lord chancellor, and he resigned only when he had lost.

In the process, however, he learned to read Henry very well. He advised the rising Thomas Cromwell that in his service of

a most noble, wise and liberal prince . . . you shall, in your counsel-giving unto his grace, ever tell him what he ought to do but never what he is able to do. So shall you show yourself . . . a right worthy counsellor. For if a lion knew his own strength, hard were it for any man to rule him.[82]

Henry's two greatest ministers and counsellors were similarly thrown over by Henry, despite long periods of onerous, conscientious service. There is, however, one important difference. Unlike More, neither Wolsey nor Cromwell can be charged with resistance to Henry on some issue which the king deemed vital to his self-interest. These men, both of relatively humble birth, certainly received great rewards for their services: for Wolsey, in Skelton's words an upstart of 'greasy genealogy', there were a cardinal's hat, honours, pomp and circumstance, power, wealth, York Place, Hampton Court and other palaces; for Cromwell, monastic lands, vicegerent of the supreme head of the English Church, offices, membership of the Order of the Garter and the earldom of Essex.[83] Nevertheless they earned them. Wolsey not only administered the realm and serviced Henry's wars. He also pandered to the royal appetite for masquings, banqueting and other entertainments. As Cavendish wrote,

[W]hat joy and delight the Cardinal had to see his prince and sovereign lord in his house so nobly entertained. . . . [N]othing was to him more delectable than to cheer his sovereign lord. . . .[84]

Henry once wrote lovingly to Wolsey:

I recommend me unto you with all my heart, and thank you for the great pain and labour that you do daily take in my business and matters, desiring you . . . to take some pastime and comfort, to the intent you may the longer endure to serve us.

Wolsey's failure to deliver the divorce killed that sentiment.

As for Cromwell, he was instrumental in so many changes which were to the personal advantage of Henry and to the authority and (in the short term) wealth of the monarchy. Yet he went to the Tower in June 1540, less than two months after his elevation to the peerage. Why? Cromwell had been responsible for negotiating Henry's disastrous marriage to Ann of Cleves. More serious for him, he was also suspected of heresy and accused of harbouring heretics in Calais. These undoubtedly influenced Henry, but some of the charges in the parliamentary attainder which condemned him seem far-fetched. They reek of calumny devised by bitter political rivals, in this case Norfolk and Bishop Gardiner, the religious conservatives.[85] In the same way an important part in Wolsey's fall was played by the hostility of the dukes of Norfolk and Suffolk, and especially of Anne Boleyn. If, as it seems, drip-fed political poison contributed to the end of Henry's two greatest ministers, it is a commentary on his susceptibility.

Over lengthy periods the king displayed a particular skill in maintaining a delicate balance between ambitious rivals and conflicting religious positions within the privy council. It enabled him to obtain a broad range of opinions and advice. His innate suspicion, quick anger with obduracy and his susceptibility to whispered accusation, however, caused that balance to break down a number of times, especially during the last weeks of his life. Then he turned on Bishop Gardiner and the Howards, perhaps influenced by the anti-conservative Seymour interest but possibly for apparently unrelated reasons.[86] Henry never fully trusted Gardiner's loyalty after April 1532, when he publicly rejected the royal demand that all ecclesiastical legislation should receive the king's assent. With typical modesty the king believed thereafter that only he could manage the bishop to his advantage. Gardiner's position remained reasonably secure until November 1546, when he proved obstinate to the king's offer of an exchange of certain lands. The bishop was banished from the privy council for several weeks. During that time, in early December, Norfolk and his son were dispatched to the Tower. On 26 December the bishop's name was removed from the list of regents for the royal minority – not for religious reasons, but because he was a 'wilful man, not meet to be about his son'. Meanwhile the declining king was personally active in the destruction of the Howards. With a shaky hand he wrote in additions to the draft of the articles against them. On 13 January Surrey was convicted of the treasonable charge that he had quartered on his heraldic shield the arms of Edward the Confessor, thereby asserting a claim to succeed the mortally ill Henry. Eight days later he was executed. So the greatest English poet of his day met the same end as so much other rich and diverse talent did during the reign of the second Tudor. On 27 January Norfolk was attainted by parliamentary statute for complicity in his son's treason. Four commissioners, appointed by letters patent (which were signed by the dry stamp) and including Edward Seymour earl of Hertford and Lord Chancellor Wriothesley, gave the dying king's assent.[87] The next day King Henry VIII died. The duke's life was spared but he remained securely shut away in the Tower. And Edward VI's uncle, Hertford, was ready to assume control.

Notes

1 J. Guy, 'Tudor Monarchy and its Critiques', in idem, ed., *Tudor Monarchy*, p. 78.

2 Ibid., pp. 79–89, 105 n. 7.

3 See above, Chap. 3, p. 35.

4 *Cal. SP Span.*, 4 (1), nos 354 (pp. 598–9), 366 (p. 616), 460 (p. 758).

5 Mayer, ed., Starkey, *Dialogue*, p. 33; M. Dewar, ed., Sir Thomas Smith, *De Republica Anglorum*, Cambridge, 1982, p. 88.

6 Ibid.; J. C. Brooke, ed., 'The Ceremonial of Making the King's Bed', *Archaeologia*, 4 (1786), 313.

7 *Cal. SP Span.*, 5 (1), no. 184

8 Ibid., no. 18.

9 See above, Chap. 3, p. 32; *Anglica Historia*, pp. 245–7.

10 A. Fletcher and D. MacCulloch, *Tudor Rebellions*, 4th edn, London, 1997, p. 34.

11 The first 'plague' was 'that he is so covetous'. *LP*, 15, no. 954.

12 *Cal. SP Span.*, 5 (2), p. 263.

13 J. Pratt, ed., J. Foxe, *Acts and Monuments*, 8 vols, London,1853–70, V, pp. 605–6.

14 Starkey, *Personalities and Politics*, pp. 139–40; D. Potter, 'Foreign Policy', in MacCulloch, ed., *Politics, Policy and Piety*, pp 131–2; Walker, *Persuasive Fictions*, pp. 22–3.

15 See below, pp. 88–90.

16 Sylvester and Harding, eds, Cavendish, *Wolsey*, pp. 12–13; see above, Chap. 3, p. 44.

17 *Cal. SP Ven.*, 2, no. 894.

18 J. Guy, *The Cardinal's Court*, Hassocks, Sussex, 1977, pp. 29, 30–2, 74.

19 Gunn and Lindley, 'Introduction', in idem, eds., *Cardinal Wolsey: Church, State and Art*, p. 22.

20 J. Guy, 'The King's Council and Political Participation', in Fox and Guy, *Reassessing the Henrician Age*, p. 134.

21 P. Gwyn, *The King's Cardinal*, London, 1990, pp. 23–4.

22 Williams, ed., *Eng. Hist. Docs*, V, pp. 517–18.

23 *Anglica Historia*, p. 307.

24 *LP*, 4 (3), app. 39; Gunn and Lindley, eds, *Cardinal Wolsey: Church, State and Art*, pp. 2–3.

25 Gwyn, *King's Cardinal*, p. 579.

26 Sylvester and Harding, eds, Cavendish, *Wolsey*, pp. 183–4; Gwyn, *King's Cardinal*, pp. 637–8.

27 *Cal. SP Span.*, 4 (1), no. 257 (pp. 451–2); J. Guy, 'The Privy Council: Revolution or Evolution?' in Coleman and Starkey, eds, *Revolution Reassessed*, p. 69.

28 26 Henry VIII c. 1, *Stats Realm*, III, p. 492.

29 Starkey, *Personalities and Politics*, p. 125; J. Guy, *Tudor England*, Oxford, 1988, p. 189; Loades, *Power in Tudor England*, pp. 55–6.

30 G. R. Elton, *Tudor Revolution in Government*, Cambridge, 1953, pp. 342–5, 351–2; Williams, ed., *Eng. Hist Docs*, V, pp. 524–5.

31 The extent to which this was driven by faction is considered below, pp. 90–2.

32 W. A. Sessions, *Henry Howard. The Poet Earl of Surrey. A Life*, Oxford, 1999, pp. 183, 379.

33 See below, Chap. 8, p. 164.

34 *Cal. SP Span.*, 8, no. 3 (p. 18).

35 Starkey, *Personalities and Politics*, pp. 138–9.

36 Ibid., p. 139.

37 Walker, *Persuasive Fictions*, p. 23.

38 *Four Years at the Court of Henry VIII*, p. 237.

39 *Cal. SP Span.*, 2, p. 41.

40 J. A. Guy, 'Wolsey, the Council and the Council Courts', *EHR*, 91 (1976), 481–92.

41 Lodge, ed., *Illustrations*, I, p. 13; Guy, *Cardinal's Court*, pp. 2, 24, 27, 33.

42 Ibid., p. 132.

43 *Cal. SP Span.*, 5 (1), p. 511.

44 Ibid., 5 (2), no. 220.

45 Ibid., 6 (2), no. 84.

46 Ibid., pp. 216–17; for Marillac's experience, see above, Chap. 4, p. 64.

47 E. W. Ives, 'Henry VIII: The Political Perspective', in MacCulloch, ed., *Politics, Policy and Piety*, pp. 21–3.

48 Byrne, ed., *Lisle Letters*, 3, no. 684; D. Starkey, 'Court and Government', in Guy, ed., *Tudor Monarchy*, pp. 201–4; *LP*, 3 (2), nos 1399, 1429; Muller, ed., *Gardiner's Letters*, p. 286.

49 Ives, 'Henry VIII: The Political Perspective', and Guy, 'Wolsey, Cromwell and Reform of Henrician Government', in MacCulloch, ed., *Politics, Policy and Piety*, pp. 14–15, 18–19, 56.

50 *State Papers Henry VIII*, 11 vols, London, 1830–52, I, pp. 79–80.

51 B. L. Yelverton MS, cit. C. Read, *Mr Secretary Walsingham and the Policy of Queen Elizabeth*, Oxford, 1925, 1, p. 423.

52 *LP*, 4 (2), nos 4409, 4597.

53 E. W. Ives, *Faction in Tudor England*, Historical Association, London, 1979, pp. 1–8.

54 Ibid., pp. 12–16. Barbara Harris identified factional rivalry in the nobility, especially between Buckingham and the Howards, and noted that Norfolk 'accepted appointment as lord high steward at his trial'. It was, however, one of his duties as earl marshal. Harris, *Buckingham*, pp. 58–60.

55 Ives, *Faction*, pp. 16–20, 25–9; idem, 'Faction at the Court of Henry VIII: The Fall of Anne Boleyn', *History*, 57 (1972), 175–83; idem, 'Henry VIII: The Political Perspective', in MacCulloch, ed., *Politics, Policy and Piety*, p. 29.

56 P. Servini, 'Government and Politics 1529–47', in J. Lotherington, ed., *The Tudor Years*, London, 1994, pp. 135–47.

57 G. R. Elton, 'Thomas Cromwell's Decline and Fall', in idem, *Studies in Tudor and Stuart Politics and Government*, 4 vols, Cambridge, 1974, I, pp. 189–230.

58 D. Starkey, 'From Feud to Faction', *Hist. Today*, 32 (Nov. 1982), 18–22.

59 Idem, *Personalities and Politics*, pp. 8–9.

60 Ibid., pp. 27–9, 30, 95–101.

61 S. Adams, 'The Patronage of the Crown in Elizabethan Politics: The 1590s in Perspective', and P. E. J. Hammer, 'Patronage at Court, Faction and the Earl of Essex', in J. Guy, ed., *The Reign of Elizabeth I*, Cambridge, 1995, pp. 20–45; 65–86. John Guy shows how Henry created political affinities, through which royal patronage was distributed in the counties and royal control was asserted. So patronage was linked to such affinities, not to factions. Guy, *Tudor England*, pp. 165–9.

62 S. Adams, 'Faction, Clientage and Party: English Politics, 1550–1603', *Hist. Today*, 32 (Dec. 1982), 34.

63 Davies, *Peace, Print and Protestantism*, pp. 165–6; M. Levine, 'The Fall of Edward, Duke of Buckingham', in A. J. Slavin, ed., *Tudor Men and Institutions*, Baton Rouge, 1972, pp. 33–48.

64 Bernard, *Power and Politics*, p. 74.

65 Ibid., pp. 85–99.

66 Walker, *Persuasive Fictions*, pp. 13–14, 18–19, 21, 22–3; J. A. Guy, *The Public Career of Sir Thomas More*, Brighton, 1980, p. 209; *LP*, 12 (2), no. 952. See also Potter, 'Foreign Policy', in MacCulloch, ed., *Politics, Policy and Piety*, pp. 131–2. He finds little evidence that faction pressures determined Henrician foreign policy.

67 S. E. Lehmberg, *Sir Thomas Elyot: Tudor Humanist*, Austin, 1960, p. 119.

68 He did not, however, welcome counsel from the lower orders. In 1536 he responded angrily to the Lincolnshire rebels' demands: 'I never have read, heard, nor known that princes' councillors and prelates should be appointed by rude and ignorant common people. . . . How presumptuous then are ye, the rude commons of one shire, and that one of the most brute and beastly of the whole realm, and of least experience, to find fault with your prince, for the electing of his councillors and prelates.' M. H. and R. Dodds, *Pilgrimage of Grace*, p. 136.

69 E.g. House of Lords Record Office, *Journals of House of Lords*, Vol. I, p. 61.

70 Lehmberg, *Sir Thomas Elyot*, pp. 115–18; Fox and Guy, *Reassessing the Henrician Age*, pp. 138–9, 142–4.

71 *Cal. SP Span.*, 5, no. 61 (p. 161).

72 Starkey, *Personalities and Politics*, pp. 69–70; Walker, *Persuasive Fictions*, p. 110; *LP*, 4 (3), no. 5519.

73 S. T. Bindoff, *The House of Commons, 1509–1558*, 3 vols, London, 1982, III, pp. 42–4, 92–3, 192–4, 663–5; S. E. Lehmberg, 'Sir Thomas Audley: A Soul as Black as Marble?', in Slavin, ed., *Tudor Men and Institutions*, pp. 7, 14–21; *LP*, 6, no. 160; A. L. Rowse, 'Thomas Wriothesley, First Earl of Southampton', *HLQ*, 28, 2 (Feb. 1965), 107, 110–13, 116–17; Sylvester and Harding, eds, Roper, *Life of More*, p. 246; F. G. Emmison, *Tudor Secretary*, Chichester, 1961, pp. 47–64; S. R. Gammon, 'Master of Practises. A Life of William, Lord Paget of Beaudesert, 1506–63', Ph.D., Princeton, 1953, pp. 153–4.

74 G. Redworth, *In Defence of the Catholic Church: The Life of Stephen Gardiner*, Oxford, 1990, pp. 66–7.

75 Pratt, ed., Foxe, *Acts and Monuments*, V, p. 691.

76 Ibid., p. 692.

77 See below, pp. 98–9.

78 Guy, *Public Career of More*, pp. 6–12.

79 Ibid., pp. 11–18; Eltham Ordinances, Williams, ed., *Eng. Hist. Docs*, V, p. 518.

80 E. V. Hitchcock, ed., Nicholas Harpsfield, *The Life and Death of Sir Thomas Moore, knight*, London, 1932, p. 222; A. Fox, *Thomas More, History and Providence*, Oxford, 1982, p. 173.

81 Fox, *More*, pp. 173–4; J. Guy, *Thomas More*, London, 2000, pp. 152, 154, 156–7, 160–1, 163, 172; *LP*, 5, no. 1013; Sylvester and Harding, eds, Roper, *Life of More*, p. 224.

82 Ibid., pp. 224–5, 228; Hitchock, ed., Harpsfield, *Thomas Moore*, p. 222; Guy, *Thomas More*, pp. 156, 180.

83 Davies, *Peace, Print and Protestantism*, p. 159.

84 Sylvester and Harding, eds, Cavendish, *Wolsey*, p. 30.

85 *HLRO, Orig. Acts*, 32 Henry VIII, no. 14; S. Brigden, 'Thomas Cromwell and the "Brethren" ' in C. Cross, D. Loades and J. J. Scarisbrick, eds, *Law and Government under the Tudors*, Cambridge, 1988, pp. 32–3, 47–8; idem, 'Popular Disturbance and the Fall of Thomas Cromwell and the Reformers, 1539–1540', *HJ*, 24, 2 (1981), pp. 266–7; Byrne, ed., *Letters of Henry VIII*, p. 28.

86 Redworth, *Gardiner*, pp. 241–3; Starkey, *Personalities and Politics*, pp. 156–9.

87 Sessions, *Henry Howard*, pp. 358–62, 366–72, 388–409; J. A. Muller, *Stephen Gardiner and the Tudor Reaction*, London, 1926, p. 142; Redworth, *Gardiner*, pp. 36–8, 51, 239, 242–7; H. L. R. O., Orig. Acts, 37 Henry VIII, no. 32; *LP*, 21 (2), nos 753, 759, 770 (86), 771 (36); Gammon, *Master of Practises*, pp. 183–6; M. A. R. Graves, *The House of Lords in the Parliaments of Edward VI and Mary I*, Cambridge, 1981, pp. 14, 15.

Chapter 6

Henry VIII in His Parliaments

The nature and place of parliaments

The medieval parliament was known as the 'High Court of Parliament' because it dispensed royal justice. It was, however, much more than this. Long before 1509 the primary purpose of parliaments was to fulfil political functions which benefited both royal government and the community: to assist the king with advice (when he sought it), the grant of taxes (initiated by the commons when he requested them), and the enactment, amendment or annulment of laws. Parliaments also provided the crown with opportunities to inform the governing elite about intended actions and policies.[1] At the same time the elite was able to express its opinions, air grievances and promote legislation for particular interests in the community. These activities were a natural consequence of the growing belief in parliament as 'the body of the whole realm', in other words as a representative institution. When a king summoned a parliament (for he alone determined the frequency, occasion and length of meetings), he breathed into life an institution 'whose decisions bound everyone because everyone was present in it either in person or by proxy'.[2]

In the old, medieval High Court of Parliament the commons presented petitions to the lords for grievances to be redressed. Over the course of time, however, the lords ceased to sit in judgement on those petitions. Parliament became a truly bicameral institution in which the two houses were co-equal in legislative authority. During the reign of the first Tudor, this was confirmed by the judges: in 1489 they declared that the assent of *both* houses was necessary for the enactment of a new law. In another judicial decision the judges ruled, in 1516, that the first estate of bishops and abbots did not have to be present in the house of lords when a bill was passed. This was a recognition that, unlike many Continental representative assemblies, an English parliament was not a meeting of the three social estates.[3] At the same time one more important, indeed fundamental, structural change was taking place. In pre-Tudor England the king called and met the two-chamber parliament. However, in 1523 Christopher St German wrote of statutes made by king, lords and commons of the whole realm in divers parliaments. The act to end payment of 'exactions' to the papacy (1534) made specific reference to 'your Royall Majestie and your Lordes Spiritual and temporall and Commons, representyng the holle state of your Realme in this your most high Court of Parliament'. And eight years later Henry VIII told the speaker and some members of the commons or 'Nether House':

[W]e be informed by our judges that we at no time stand so highly in our estate royal as in the time of Parliament, wherein we as head and you as members are conjoined and knit together into one body politic.

So parliament was now regarded as a bicameral trinity, of which the crown was an integral part. Henry VIII was saying that king *and* parliament had become king-*in*-parliament. It may help to explain why it was that he ended the old royal practice of adding provisos to acts after a parliament had served the king's purpose and been ended. On the other hand, this is not necessarily true of the entire reign. Ninety surviving provisos to acts passed between 1510 and 1523 bear only the sign manual and no endorsement by lords and commons.[4]

During the reign of the second Tudor, parliaments were to prove vital to the furtherance of his interests and aspirations: in particular, for the resolution of his succession problems and for the funding of his wars. They had an additional value, in G. R. Elton's words, as 'the premier point of contact between rulers and ruled, between the Crown and the political nation'. The institution of parliament 'fulfilled its function as a stabilising mechanism because it was usable and used to satisfy legitimate and potentially powerful aspirations'.[5] It follows that parliaments were also valuable to the members of the elite, to cities, towns, rural localities and economic interests.

Henry VIII's awareness of this is observable in his active response to bill promotion by individuals, lobbies and communities. Many private bills were endorsed by him with the sign manual and this royal imprimatur strengthened their chances of a successful parliamentary passage. In the early parliaments of his reign between 1510 and 1515, however, the young king's enthusiasm caused him to emulate his father, who, at some stage, signed every act, public and private, as well as all provisos in 1497 and 1504. So he endorsed all but two of the 115 acts as well as some of the provisos. It is not possible to tell how many of these bore the sign manual when they entered parliament – a sign that he chose to support them out of 'royal grace' or because they were important to him. But it is clear from the journals of the house of lords that some were endorsed during or even after the session. Thereafter, as the passing of time reinforced his distaste for routine administrative toil, the proportion of acts bearing the sign manual dropped dramatically: to just over one-third in the 1530s and to a mere 41 out of 227 acts in the 1540s. From 1529 on these were genuine sign manual bills, endorsed when they entered parliament. Some were personally beneficial to the king, but the majority were grace bills for favoured individual subjects, their relatives and a variety of local interests.[6]

One might have expected London to have been one of the more prominent and frequent beneficiaries here. Its success rate, however, was very low in Henry's reign, despite the fact that it was an active and organized parliamentary lobby under the control of the court of aldermen. This lack of success was not primarily the consequence of royal disapproval or veto. It is true that, in 1521, Wolsey let the City know of Henry's anger at the sympathy shown by Londoners towards the recently executed duke of Buckingham. The king threatened to punish the City 'with such sharp and grevous punyshement which they be not nor shalbe able to beere'. On the other hand, when parliament cancelled Henry's loan debts in 1529, he intervened to ensure the passage of two London bills. He also promised that, unless an emergency occurred, he would never demand a penny from them for the rest of his life; indeed, he would happily agree to anything they promoted for the good of his realm and of the City. During his reign, however, London's frustrated efforts and high rate of bill failures were normally consequences of either opposition from rival lobbies or mere lack of time.[7] The occasional act, as in 1512 (for juries), 1514 ('for the packership of cloth') and 1531 (concerning vacant land in Cheapside and improvement of the City's water supply) were but oases in a legislative desert.[8] Nevertheless, London's undiminished expectations continued to fuel its efforts.

Although parliaments were valuable and important, before the 1530s their competence and authority were clearly limited in two ways. First, statute could not deal in matters spiritual. These were the preserve of the Church and its two assemblies: the southern (Canterbury) convocation, which sat concurrently with parliament, and the northern (York) assembly, which met afterwards. On August 1547 Stephen Gardiner wrote that 'Our late soveraigne lord made no alteration in his tyme withowt a convocation of bishops and open debating of the mattier.' That was not appropriate when he wrote but it would have been much closer to reality before the 1530s.[9] Secondly, as might be expected, the propertied membership of parliaments had never attempted to encroach in any general way upon the sanctity of titles to property. Such limitations would disappear in an attempt to satisfy the aspirations and urgent needs of Henry.

Henry and the house of commons

Membership

The king's very active involvement with the other component parts of parliament was evident throughout his reign. There was, for example, a dramatic increase in the number of new or restored parliamentary constituencies returning members to the commons. Such additions or restorations were the undisputed prerogative right of the crown. Of course one cannot assume that the impulse for such changes originated with the king.[10] It has been variously argued that enfranchisement was commonly a royal response to pressure from powerful courtier patrons or from local communities desirous of a parliamentary voice. Sometimes the real initiator may have been the king's trusted minister, in particular Wolsey (until 1529)[11] and, in the 1530s, Cromwell. Whatever the origin, any proposal for enfranchisement required the royal imprimatur. Furthermore, it was given for the addition of about forty-five members.[12] Some of the new constituencies were created within the crown's duchies of Cornwall and Lancaster and so would return reliable royal servants. Henry's conquest of Tournai in 1513 was followed by his fulfilled promise to give its French inhabitants representation in the forthcoming parliament of January 1514. Calais was similarly treated in 1536. In 1543 the county palatine and city of Chester were enfranchised and, when the principality of Wales was incorporated into 'this his Realme of Englande', its counties and shire towns became single-member constituencies.[13] The extension of parliamentary representation to Cheshire and Wales can be seen as:

1 a practical consequence of their annexation into what was acknowledged, in the Statute of Supremacy (1534), as 'the Ymperyall Crowne of this Realme';[14] and
2 an expression of Henry VIII's fashionable acceptance that king-in-parliament represented (or should represent in its membership) the entire realm.

Management, co-operation and discord

Although, in normal circumstances, parliamentary management was a function of the king's ministers, Henry was actively involved with the two houses. At the very beginning of his reign the arrest of Empson and Dudley announced to the world his apparent intention to put right the wrongs of his father's financially rigorous rule. When his first parliament met, in 1510, he gave his assent to a number of measures, including one which protected landowners against untrue inquisitions, and another which strictly limited the time in which prosecutions under statutes penal were allowed.[15] However, behind this masquerade of the altruist stalked the reality of the warrior king. Henry needed money for war. As he had ended some of his father's unpopular financial practices he was surely entitled to some recompense. This he duly received: the traditional life-grant of tunnage and poundage in 1510; fifteenths and tenths in 1511/12 and 1512; the introduction in 1514 of a subsidy or income tax with an estimated yield of £160,000; another in 1515, designed to make up the shortfall of £110,000 in the first subsidy (but producing only £45,637); and yet one more tax, a fifteenth and tenth, in the same year.[16] No-one could have been pleased with the tax performance. The king did not receive his promised due, whilst parliamentary critical faculties were sharpened by repeated royal demands for war revenue.

Then, in 1515, a political parliament-focused crisis erupted over the 'Hunne affair'. The death of Richard Hunne, a London merchant and Lollard, whilst in the bishop of London's custody, triggered a furious anti-clerical outburst.[17] Many suspected murder and would not accept the Church's verdict of suicide. When parliament met that year, the commons clamoured for punishment of the guilty clerks in the secular courts. The king responded by organizing a formal disputation between canon lawyers for the two sides and over which he presided. Although the result was inconclusive, it was a significant early indicator of Henry's interest in theology and affairs of the Church. Nor did his involvement end there. When Henry Standish, the Franciscan anti-clerical spokesman in the disputation, was accused of heresy in October 1515, the king organized another disputation. Its task was to consider the validity of the charge against Standish, and it was conducted before members of both lords and commons and the common law judges. Henry then sought the judicial opinion of the judges, who pronounced Standish's accusers guilty of *praemunire*. The drama ended when, before both lords and commons, Henry's own minister, Cardinal Wolsey, humbled himself on his knees and begged the royal pardon.

Whereas, in the Hunne affair, there tended to be parliamentary accord within the trinity of king, lords and commons (the lords spiritual only excepted), this was not the case when parliament met again in 1523. It was chief minister Wolsey who had to suffer the slings and arrows of outraged members. But the real target was royal government and the issue was excessive financial demands to sustain Henry's seemingly pointless military intervention on the Continent. Commons' members were willing to speak out about his policies, frankly, bluntly and without seeming fear of royal reprisals. Some objected that 'If all the money were brought to the king's hands then men must barter cloth for victuals, and bread for cheese, and so one thing for another.' One member, Thomas Cromwell, drafted a speech (which he may have delivered). In it he condemned the acquisition of Thérouanne, which had cost, in money and lives, 'more then [twenty] suche vngracious Dogholes cowld be worthe'.[18] It was a disturbed, noisy, even at times heated parliament where, Thomas Cromwell wrote,

we communyd of warre, pease, Stryffe, contentyon, debatte, murmure, grudge, Riches, pouerte, penurye, trowth, falshode, Justyce, [equity, deceit, oppression, magnanimity, activity], force, attempraunce, Treason, murder, Felonye, [conciliation], and also how a [commonwealth] myght be ediffyed and al[so] contenewid within our Realme.[19]

Although he was writing with tongue in cheek, Cromwell captured the atmospherics of that parliament. It was at the beginning of that same parliament that the commons' speaker, Sir Thomas More, made the first known formal request for the king

to give to all your Commons here assembled your most gracious licence and pardon, freely, without doubt of your dreadful displeasure, every man to discharge his conscience, and boldly in every thing incident among us to declare his advice. And whatsoever happen any man to say that it may like your noble majesty, of your inestimable goodness, to take all in good part.[20]

There were clear limits. Free speech applied only to matters put before members and not other subjects about which they might wish to voice their opinions. Furthermore it excluded 'licentious' talk. No-one could have realized then what was to come: the crises of succession and religion, the frequency of parliaments and the dramatic changes which statute would work upon the political, religious and socio-economic landscapes of the kingdom. Furthermore, Henry was to discover how bold the knights and burgesses of the 'Nether House' could be. In 1529 he sought the cancellation of his obligation to repay a forced loan. John Petit, an 'eloquente and welspoken' citizen of London and member of the Grocers' Company, 'stode agaynste the byll', saying that he could not accept it 'for I know not my neighbores estate. They perhaps borowed it to lend the kyng.' But as a loyal, devoted subject, 'I know myn owne estate, and therefor I freely and frankly gyve the kyng that I lente hym.' Henry was clearly amused. Thereafter he 'wolde [ask] in the parlamente tyme, in hys waighty affayres, yf Petite were of his syde'.[21] The issues of the 1530s were of a different dimension and scale, but members of the commons were still willing to question and challenge their king. This was particularly true of the 'Aragonese' faction (Catherine of Aragon's supporters) and other devout Roman Catholics. When Henry sent for Sir George Throckmorton, who had spoken against the act in restraint of appeals, he was told that, whilst Throckmorton '[i]ntended no harm to the King . . . he was one that durst speak for the common wealth'.[22]

During the 1530s Henry continued to experience commons' criticism, often bluntly outspoken, about his succession-related marital policies, his steps to schism and his assumption of supremacy over the Church. One of the most persistent vocal choruses of opposition, however, was not related to these fundamental issues about legitimacy and spiritual authority. It concerned Henry's attempt to limit the harmful effect of the *use* (or trust) on his feudal revenues. These were feudal obligations due to the king from his tenants-in-chief. The most important were, in effect, death duties: for example, minor heirs became royal wards and adult heirs had to pay a relief or entry fine. The development of the use or trust, however, enabled landowners to avoid such obligations. This was because the corporate body of trustees (or *feoffees to uses*), to whom legal estate in their property had been surrendered, never died. Surprisingly, Henry was not greedy. As the imperial ambassador, Chapuys, informed Charles V in February 1532, the government bill sought to recover only 'the third part' of his legal rights. 'But', he added, the king 'has not yet succeeded, and the demand has been the occasion of strange words against the King and Council'.[23] Continuous resistance had worn royal patience thin when, on 18 March, Henry met a deputation of commons' members. Far from being the aloof and remote king, he revelled in the public occasion, was an accomplished actor on the political stage and an effective communicator. On this occasion he was the wounded monarch:

Me thynketh that you shoulde not contende with me that I am youre Sovereygne Lorde and kyng, consideryng that I seke peace and quyetnesse of you; for I have sent to you a byll . . . in the which thyngs I am greatly wronged.

He was a king with right on his side:

I have offered you reason, as I thynke, yea, and so thynketh all the Lordes.

He was also becoming a weary Prince:

[I]f you wyll not take some reasonable ende now, when it is offered, I wyll serch out the extremitie of the lawe and then wyll I not offre you so moche agayne.

On this occasion the potent mix of artistry, regality and formidable presence was of no avail. In the belief that his rebuke and ultimatum would subdue the commons, the bill was resubmitted. 'But', as Edward Hall relates, 'many frowarde and wylfull persones, not regardynge what myght ensue . . . woulde neither consent to the byll . . . nor yet agree to no reasonable qualificacion of the same'.

Hall observed that there were also in the house those who 'would gladly have had the bill assented to' because they 'understood and saw the mischief to come'. He styled them 'wise men', perhaps because they understood their king.[24] It is common and popular to associate Henry VIII with bold action, impetuosity and imperious impatience with those who would frustrate or constrain him. What are less frequently appreciated are his tenacity, his powers of endurance and his capacity to mount and sustain a prolonged campaign in order to achieve his cherished objectives. For years he laid courtly siege to Anne Boleyn's virginity and he laboured even longer to secure a settled succession. So too with uses. In 1532 he ended the parliamentary session with the matter unresolved. He then switched his line of attack to the law courts, where, in 1535, he obtained a judgment in his favour in a test case. Armed with this he was able to secure, in 1536, a statute which gave him not just a fraction but all of his feudal dues. Had he not warned the commons that he 'would search out the extremity of the law' and 'not offer you so much again'! The whole process had begun with an initial agreement between Henry and the nobility in 1529. Despite fierce resistance in the lower house, he persevered until he was rewarded in 1536 with the Statute of Uses. This, however, contributed to the most serious rebellion of the reign, the Pilgrimage of Grace, and was a cause of continuing governing class discontent.[25] Finally, in 1540 political realism took precedence over greed, when Henry acquiesced in the restriction of his feudal rights in the Statute of Wills.

The Statute of Uses does not exhaust the catalogue of government initiatives which aroused parliamentary discontent, criticism, even opposition during the frequent sessions of the 1530s. The request for a peacetime tax in 1532 produced a smaller offer than expected. Robert Fisher, burgess for Rochester, said that 'there was never such a sticking at the passing of any Act in the Lower House as was at the passing of the [Treason Act in 1534]'.[26] In 1539 the bill for proclamations engendered 'many liberal words' and underwent substantial amendment before it passed into law. For most of the time Henry displayed a resilience and self-confidence in his parliamentary dealings. In particular he generally respected freedom of speech as a liberty of the commons. In 1512 he signed into law a bill which protected an individual, Richard Strode, from reprisals for promoting a measure against Devonshire tinners in a previous parliament. The act also declared that suits against any 'for any bill, spekyng, reasonyng or declaryng of any mater or maters concernyng the parliament to be ... treated of, be utterly voyd and of none effect'.[27] The first recorded speaker's request for free speech occurs in Henry's reign (1523); so does the first recorded royal grant thereof (to Speaker Moyle in 1542). Henry and his ministers, however, would never allow untrammelled freedom of speech. The royal response to Sir Thomas Moyle qualified his request.[28] It is also necessary to qualify G. R. Elton's statement that Henry 'allowed attacks on his policy and even on his private concerns to pass without action more drastic than an explanatory address'.[29] For example, the king might make lighthearted references to John Petit, but the wretched Londoner was imprisoned by Sir Thomas More in the Tower, where he 'was layd in a doungeone apon a padd of strawe'. By the time that he was released he 'hadd caght hys dethe ... [and] dyed immediately aftere'. Although Petit was imprisoned for heresy, More had no evidence against him.[30] It was not the only occasion on which the authorities acted against someone after an impetuous, tactless parliamentary performance. In 1539 Thomas Broke, member for Calais, spoke against the Catholic Six Articles bill.[31] Sir William Kingston, comptroller of the royal household, threatened him for his heretical speech: 'Tell this tale the xii day of July next [when the act would come into force] and I will bring a faggot to help to burn you withal.' According to John Foxe, Kingston

offended in a manner the whole House, and caused them to say, 'It was very unseemly, that a gentleman of the House should so ungodly be used, where it was equally lawful for every man reverently to speak plainly his mind.'[32]

In mid-July 1539, just after the act had come into force, Broke was accused of assisting a heretic and imprisoned for most of the next three years.

Others who spoke out of turn were simply encouraged to stay away. George Throckmorton agreed to accept Thomas Cromwell's advice 'to live at home, serve God, and meddle little' [33] As an additional life insurance policy he wrote to Henry in 1537, seeking his pardon, acknowledging 'his error' and praying 'for the prosperous estate of the King and his little son Prince Edward'.[34] It should be added that Sir Marmaduke Constable, another member of Throckmorton's group who shared unsympathetic views of royal policies, also wrote to Cromwell in January 1534 excusing himself from parliament. The king may not have been personally involved in the process whereby difficult members were encouraged to remove themselves. However, he could and did respond angrily to those who spoke out of turn. During a commons' debate in 1539 John Gostwick, a religious conservative, accused Archbishop Cranmer 'openly in a parliament for his preaching'. Henry 'mervelously stormed at the matter, calling openly Gostwick *verlett*, and saied that he hadd plied a vilonyous parte so to abuse in open parliamente the primate of the realme, speciallie being in favour with his prince'. Gostwick was ordered to apologize to Cranmer or – and this is significant in a parliamentary context – the king would 'both make hym a poore Gostewycke, and otherwise punishe hym, to th'example of others'.[35]

Henry was capable of presenting a justification of his policies, actions, government and ministers in a reasonable and reasoned manner. During the 1532 session of the Reformation Parliament Thomas Temys, a parliamentary burgess of Aragonese sympathies, warned of the dangerous consequences of their monarch's intention to end his marriage, such as the 'bastardyng the Lady Marie, the Kynges only childe'. He moved that the house should petition Henry to take Catherine back. Later, when Henry summoned the commons' speaker and some members to an audience about religious matters, he took the opportunity to respond to Temys and to defend himself:

[H]e marveiled not a litle, why one of the Parliament house spake openly of the absence of the Quene from hym, whiche matter was not to be determined there, for he saied it touched his soule.

His marriage to his brother's widow was

voyde and detestable before God, whiche grudge of conscience caused me to abstein from her compaignie.

He insisted that the reason was not

folishe or wanton appetite: for I am forty-one yere old, at which age the lust of man is not so quicke, as in lustie youth [a 'fact' which did not prevent him from seeking fulfilment of a 'wanton appetite' with five more wives in the royal nuptial bed].[36]

Temys does not seem to have suffered any unpleasant reprisals for his conduct. That may be regarded, however, as no more than characteristic of the king's inconsistent, erratic behaviour. When Sir William Roche, newly elected for the 1545 parliament, protested against the benevolence which was currently being collected, the privy council dispatched him to the Fleet for 'divers contempts, crimes and misdeeds' against the king.[37] When Richard Rede, an alderman, refused to contribute to the benevolence, Henry thought that, as he 'would not disburse a little of his substance' for the defence of the realm, 'he should do some service with his body'. So he was conscripted to fight the Scots and sent north. There he was to be subject to 'the sharp military discipline of the Northern Wars', whereby he 'may . . . feel the smart of his folly'.[38] Rede died on service in Scotland. Although he was not a member of the commons, his case illustrates once again Henry's propensity for harsh retaliation against those who crossed him. As Roche's case demonstrated, election to parliament was no guarantee of immunity. Furthermore, the treatment meted out to Rede and Roche, both London aldermen, must have sent a warning to England's wealthiest city that the king expected its financial support.

Henry and the house of lords

Membership

The monarch had far greater impact on the composition of the lords than of the commons. During his reign Henry VIII enlarged the number of permanent[39] seats of the lower house from 296 to about 341, an increase in size of less than one-sixth. Furthermore, whilst his ministers and councillors were able to ensure the return of reliable, active, trusty men, who would oversee and advance royal interests, the government had little overall influence on the choice of members in any particular parliament. In contrast, the crown controlled the composition of the upper house. It consisted of two orders of parliamentary peerage, the lords spiritual and temporal. The presence of both, however, was not necessary. When, in 1516, the judges advised Henry that he could hold a parliament without the bishops, abbots and priors, it was because they, like the nobles, were summoned individually, by royal writ, as tenants-in-chief of the crown to counsel the king. He could not, however, manipulate the membership by withholding or issuing summonses as it suited him. Over the course of time, peerage became identified with 'lordship of parliament' and, as a consequence, automatic summons had come to be regarded as a prescriptive right. As parliament approached in 1536, Lord Chancellor Audley wrote to Viscount Lisle, deputy of Calais, that '[Y]e shal not nede to com . . . but I sent you the wrytt, bycause it ys the order that every nobilleman shuld have his wrytt of somonz of a parlament'.[40] Lisle's case illustrates the fact that a summons did not necessarily mean attendance. Lord Sandys had to stay on duty as captain of Guisnes in 1539–40; Suffolk was on service in the north in 1543.[41] According to Chapuys in 1534, the king ordered the archbishop of York, the bishops of Durham and Rochester and Lord Darcy to stay away. Richard Hilliard, the secretary of Cuthbert Tunstal (Durham), who was a firm supporter of Queen Catherine, recorded that on this or some other occasion the out-of-favour bishop was not far from London, on his long journey south, when he received a letter from Secretary Cromwell. Because of the wintry conditions, difficulties of such a long journey, the bishop's age and Henry's 'special affection' for him, it pleased the king 'to grant him leave to stay at home'. One wonders whether Tunstal was moved by this touching gesture from a caring king.[42]

Not only was Henry able and willing to manipulate attendance, he also exercised the power to determine membership. Two archbishops and nineteen bishops were regularly summoned to parliaments. So too were twenty-seven heads of monastic houses, until Henry added three more: Tewkesbury by 1512, Tavistock (1514) and Burton-on-Trent (1532). Although he had no control over ecclesiastical organization until 1534, it was normal for the monarch to nominate his preferred choice to any vacancy. As supreme head, however, Henry had the right to appoint bishops and to control the diocesan structure, duly adding six new bishoprics. The dissolution of the monasteries removed the regulars and so, during his reign, the lords spiritual were transformed from a majority (48) to a minority (27) of the house of lords.

In contrast the lords temporal grew in number. This change too was due to royal action, because it was the monarch's exclusive right to elevate subjects to noble rank. To a great extent those who sat on the benches of the temporal lords were there simply because they had inherited titles; faces changed as sons succeeded fathers; titles disappeared as lines became extinct. But in one important respect the crown's role was vital. Although the king did not advance men to noble status as a means of parliamentary management, when he rewarded friends, servants, powerful regional men and military commanders with titles he was adding reliable and loyal subjects to the upper house. When Henry became king in 1509 there were only forty-two nobles. He soon restored to favour and to noble title members of families whose heads had been cast out by his father and even attainted: for example, William Courtenay earl of Devon and John Tuchet Lord Audley. He was also, perhaps surprisingly, careful after the fashion of his father in the land settlements which he negotiated with them.[43]

Thereafter every grant of a peerage 'served one basic purpose: to project the image of a munificent prince, glorified in the distribution of honours'. Helen Miller believes that this is why Henry created many of his new peers during the very public occasion of a parliament: the earl of Wiltshire (1510); Thomas Howard, created earl of Surrey for life when his father, the victorious general at Flodden, was elevated to the dukedom of Norfolk; Charles Brandon (who distinguished himself at Tournai) made duke of Suffolk, and Baron Herbert raised to the earldom of Worcester (1514); and in 1523 five barons, including the king's old servant Henry Marney and also Arthur Plantagenet Viscount Lisle, whose creation ceremony was followed by the usual feast, at which he was to have 'the preeminence as a bride'.[44] In 1525, when no parliament sat, the king created his illegitimate son Henry Fitzroy duke of Richmond and Somerset, Henry Brandon earl of Lincoln and Sir Thomas Boleyn Viscount Rochford. A number of others, including three of his friends – Lords Ros, Clifford and FitzWalter – were promoted. Thereafter most of Henry's noble creations occurred during the parliament time: seven (and three promotions) in 1529; one in 1532; Anne Boleyn's brother George in 1533; Jane Seymour's brother Edward (as Viscount Beauchamp), Thomas Cromwell and two others in 1536; Lord Chancellor Audley in 1538; three barons in 1539; Thomas Cromwell, created earl of Essex in April 1540, and his son Gregory made a baron in December 1540; John Dudley as Viscount Lisle in 1542; William Parr, Queen Catherine's brother, in 1543; Thomas Wriothesley, his treasurer of the wars, and two northern commanders, William Eure and Thomas Wharton, in 1544; and Thomas Poynings, serving at Boulogne, in 1545. Of all those created in or after 1529, only Audley and Gregory Cromwell were not ennobled when a parliament had been called or was in session.[45] The deliberate timing of the other creations, in order to coincide with parliaments, was important. It 'provided the opportunity to create a peer "with the assent of parliament" presumably as a way of associating the commons as well as the lords with the celebrations'.[46]

Some of those whom Henry VIII honoured were friends and social companions or kinsmen. A number were his generals, amongst whom was Edward Stanley. The king commanded that he should be proclaimed lord for such valiant acts as he did against the Scots at [Flodden] . . . and because he won the hill or *mount* against the Scots . . . and also in consideration that his ancestors bare in their crest the *eagle*, named him the Lord Mounteagle.[47]

Others were trusty royal servants, who, however, were not simply being rewarded. When Henry granted Thomas Poynings a barony he stated that one reason for doing so was 'to encourage him to serve us the better'. The evidence certainly supports Helen Miller's conclusion that 'In the eyes of Henry VIII a grant of nobility was as much a call to further effort as a reward for past services.'[48] On the other hand, especially under this king, it could be followed by disaster, downfall and death: for example Henry Courtenay, marquess of Exeter, after thirteen years; George Boleyn after three; and Thomas Cromwell only ten weeks after promotion to the earldom of Essex. The unpredictable second Tudor varied both the size and composition of the nobility. He did so in a variety of ways: not only by creations, but also by the termination of noble titles, as a consequence of condemnations for treason by trial or parliamentary attainder, by the restoration in blood of convicted nobles' heirs, and in 1539 by the issue of writs. Such actions were rarely prompted by the need or wish to strengthen parliamentary support. Nevertheless they did have a significant progressive effect on membership and the king's relationship with the house. By the end of the reign the majority of lords temporal were 'new nobility' – men ennobled during the reign.

Management, co-operation and conflict

Stanford Lehmberg argues, with some justice, that 'the story of the Reformation Parliament should be read in terms of partnership and co-operation rather than antagonism and opposition'.[49] The changing lords' membership should have encouraged that. Not only were many nobles Henry's creations. After 1534 the lords spiritual owed allegiance and obedience to him as king and supreme head. Ironically, yet understandably, they provided the focus of opposition to his policies in the critical decade of the 1530s: in support of Catherine and against the move to schism and royal supremacy.[50] In 1529 the bishops 'both frowned and grunted' at a commons' bill to regulate probate fees. When another bill, against pluralism and non-residence, was debated in the upper house, 'the Lords spiritual would in no wise consent'. Henry 'caused eight lords and eight of the commons to meet in the Star Chamber at an afternoon, and there was sore debating of the cause'.[51] Nobles and commons combined to force the lords spiritual to accept the bill. In the following years Henry employed a variety of tactics. He invoked the law, such as *praemunire* in 1530–1. He resorted to rapid response, persuasion, coercion and exploitation of the commons' anti-clericalism in order to get his way. Of course, many of his actions were prompted by others. He received much practical advice, especially from Thomas Cromwell during the years of the Reformation Parliament. But some of his interventions, particularly his personal parliamentary appearances, were probably the product of royal initiative. He was, in a very literal sense, king-in-parliament. When, in March 1532, the lords spiritual would not approve a bill harmful to papal interests, Chapuys reported that

the King has been at the Parliament three times lately, and has played his part so that the [bill] . . . has been passed. . . . The lords [temporal], who were about thirty, all consented, except the earl of Arundel, so that the majority was for the King.[52]

In the same year clerical resistance to his ambitions caused him to send for the speaker and twelve members of the commons and eight lords:

Welbeloved subiectes! We thought that the clergie of our realme had been our subjectes wholy, but now wee have perceived that they bee but halfe our subjectes, yea, and scarce our subiectes.[53]

And, so saying, he caused copies of the clergy's oaths to pope and king to be given to them for discussion in the lower house. Repeatedly, as we shall see, the royal performer displayed skill, learning and artistry, as well as formidable presence and authority when he strutted onto the public stage. As for the lords spiritual, the royal supremacy and the end of the monasteries irrevocably weakened their position in the lords. By 1547 the pro-papal regulars had all gone and, over the years, Henry was able to place reliable nominees into vacant bishoprics.

Henry VIII: image projector, performer and PR man

The art of parliamentary management was an important element in Henry's effective and successful use of parliament. It was, however, in C. S. L. Davies' words, 'sometimes rather roughly applied'. He cites, as examples, Thomas Cromwell's order to Canterbury to quash its parliamentary election and return the king's choices (1536), and the 'blatant intimidation' used to extract the Submission of the Clergy from the southern convocation (1532).[54] The heavy-handed approach, however, was exceptional. The king was usually much more concerned to inform, promote and persuade. The lord chancellor was a key figure in the informing process. At the ceremonial opening of parliament the ancestor of the monarch's address from the throne was the lord chancellor's speech. In 1529, for example, Thomas More performed that function. He informed the assembled members of the two houses that the king, who was the 'shepherd of his people', had brought security, peace and commercial prosperity to them by negotiating the treaty of Cambrai earlier that year. The diplomatic effort, however, had been very expensive and so he needed parliament to cancel his debts. Also, as many laws had become obsolete and 'new errors and heresies' had appeared, parliament would be asked to enact necessary reforms. So, through the lord chancellor, the king explained and justified what he required.[55] In the same way when, in 1531, Henry sought parliamentary support for divorce from Catherine, Chancellor More informed lords and commons in turn of the European universities' favourable opinions.[56]

The king usually had a parliamentary manager or managers, who bore the chief workload and burden of responsibility for translating royal wishes and policies into statute. Much of Henry's success during the 1530s, for example, can be attributed to Thomas Cromwell.[57] Care was also taken to secure the election of both privy councillors and some of the king's friends. In addition the growing importance of professional bureaucrats appears to have been acknowledged by Henry in the terms of the act 'for placing of the Lordes in the Parliament Chamber' (1539). It stated the order in which the peerage should sit and it gave places to the officers of State even when they were commoners. Although its prime concerns were rank, order and degree, it was also further proof of Henry's concern for parliamentary efficiency. The upper house already had judges and law officers to advise it on the common law and bill drafting. The act now made provision for experts on administration and diplomacy. The secretaries were to sit there 'to aunswere of such letters or thinges passed in counsell whereof they have the custodie and knowledge'.[58]

The king himself proved to be a very capable manager. He often took bold initiatives in order to prompt parliament into action. This was very evident in the long struggle to secure the Statute of Uses.[59] On occasions he attended debates, an action which usually signified his support for a particular measure. In 1531, for example, he appeared during the passage of a savage bill which declared that all those guilty of murder by poison would be 'commytted to execucion of deth by boylynge'.[60] In 1532 he forced a commons' division on the Annates Bill. And in 1536, according to a London clergyman, Thomas Dorset,

The King came in among the burgesses in the Parliament, and delivered them a Bill, which he desired them to weigh in conscience, and not to pass it because he gave it in, but to see if it be for the common weal of his subjects. On Wednesday next he will be there again to know their minds.[61]

Three years later Henry was actively involved in proceedings on the Six Articles Bill, amending the draft, presiding over the lords' debates and, in the process, 'confounding' all with his learning.

Henry's awareness of the value and importance of parliament, expressed in such activity, extended to a concern about efficiency. An act of 1515 empowered the 'Speker and Commyns', instead of the crown, to license the absence of members. This was to counter an ongoing problem that, long before sessions ended, many 'of their owne [authorities] depart and goeth home into their Countrees, Whereby ... grett and weighty maters ar many tymes gretly delayed.'[62] The king also displayed a positive attitude towards the privileges of the lower house, not only free speech but also freedom from arrest. When a member, George Ferrers, was arrested for debt in London in 1542, the commons sent their sergeant-at-arms to release him by authority of his mace. In the past only the lord chancellor's authority had been sufficient warrant, but Henry VIII gave his full and formidable support to the change. He promptly called to him his lord chancellor and judges, the speaker 'and other of the gravest persons of the Nether House' and declared that he would not have the privileges of the house 'infringed in anie point'. It was at this point that he made the well-known and oft-quoted statement that 'We at no time stand so highly in our estate royal as in the time of Parliament'. It followed, therefore, that 'whatsoever offence or injury ... is offered to the meanest member of the house [during the parliament time] is to be judged as done against our person and the whole court of parliament'.[63] This might be seen as a public expression of Henry's sense of parliamentary unity. It can be argued, however, that this simply illustrated his managerial and public relations skills, which masked his true autocratic instincts. According to John Guy, Henry 'disliked representative assemblies out of "imperialism" and emulation of the French'.[64] If that was the case, he was nonetheless a realist, to the extent that he recognized that parliaments had to be used to achieve some of his objectives.

Throughout his reign Henry VIII and his ministers displayed a talent for getting what he wanted from parliament. Between 1510 and 1523 it repeatedly voted taxes, including a new one, the subsidy, to fund his wars. And in 1529 he secured the cancellation of his debts. In order to create a suitable parliamentary climate the king, in turn, allowed the commons to legislate on grievances: against his father's financial mal-practices (1510) and against clerical abuses (1529). The Reformation Parliament (1529–36) carried through a revolution which, in effect, created the royal supremacy. It enriched the crown with the wealth of the monasteries and in 1545 planned the dissolution of the chantries 'at the Kinges Majesties Pleasure'.[65] The Act of Supremacy, which enacted that the king and his successors were to have the office of supreme head of the Church of England 'annexed and unyted to the Ymperyall Crowne of this Realme', also gave substance to Henry's ambitions for imperial status.[66] This and his later parliaments also concurred with his desired changes in the succession, consequent upon his marriages and annulments. He was granted taxes even during peace-time in the 1530s. When he resumed war with the Scots and French in the forties, parliament, without protest, voted £670,000 in seven years, even though he was concurrently levying forced loans (in 1542) and illegal benevolences (in 1544 and 1546).[67]

Treason legislation of various kinds figured frequently in the business of parliament. This was partly a consequence of the revolutionary changes in the 1530s, but it also reflected the often harsh, even brutal, nature of Henry's rule. With each royal marriage parliament gave the new queen and the rearranged succession the security of the treason law.[68] In 1534, when Henry became supreme head, the existing treason legislation was updated to accommodate this. In addition, statutory attainders and confirmations thereof featured frequently: the duke of Buckingham (1523); certain Welshmen in 1532; two acts in 1533; Bishop Fisher and Sir Thomas More in 1534; three in 1536 (including Thomas Fitzgerald, his five uncles and Lord Thomas Howard); the marquess of Exeter 'and many others'[69] in 1539; five acts, including Thomas Cromwell's attainder, in 1540; Catherine Howard and two clerks in 1542; and Norfolk and Surrey in 1547. The king's government also secured other laws. Some, such as reforms in the law, sumptuary regulations, provision for the 're-edification of townes', and poor laws, were designed to meet contemporary concerns about order, stability and economic improvement. The proclamations bill (1539) was intended to make government more efficient by improving enforcement of proclamations. Although it was controversial and stirred up opposition, it ended up in the statute book. So too did two of Henry's cherished measures, concerning uses and the six articles of faith.[70]

It seems as if he could get whatever he set his heart on. An unusual, indeed remarkable, feature of the parliamentary history of his reign was the way in which lords and commons were even willing to grant him delegated legislative power. The Act in Restraint of Annates, for example, was passed in 1532, but Henry was left to decide when or if to enforce it. He was empowered to vary the terms of the Second and Third Succession Acts (1536 and 1544).[71] In 1536 he was also authorized, for the term of three years, to repeal, 'revoke and abrogate' the whole act extending English laws and courts to Wales or 'any thing therin conteyned'. Wales was shired and the king was duly left to appoint the new shire towns, a right renewed later in 1536 and in 1539.[72]

On the other hand, as we have already seen, Henry VIII certainly experienced criticism and opposition quite often: over taxation (in 1523, when Wolsey's request for a 4s tax rate was scaled down to 2s over two years), and over the cancellation of his debts (in 1529 and especially during the 1530s). But the self-assured king displayed skill in handling parliaments, which were characterized by collaboration rather than conflict. As he grew more experienced, he recognized the limits beyond which he could not go. Secretary Petre recorded in 1545 that he could even take failure in his stride:

The bill of books, albeit it was at the beginning set earnestly forward, is finally dashed in the Common House, as are divers others, whereat I hear not that his Majesty is much discontented.[73]

Henry's virtuoso performance on Christmas Eve 1545, at what proved to be his very last parliamentary appearance, was a personal response to the 'eloquent oration' of the commons' speaker at the end of the session.

I most hartely thanke you all, that you haue put me in remembraunce of my dutye, which is to endeavor my self to obtein and get suche excellent qualities and necessary virtues, as a Prince . . . ought to haue, of which giftes I recognise my self bothe bare and barrein. . . . I cannot a litle reioyse when I consider the perfite trust and sure confidence, whiche you haue put in me, as men hauing undoubted hope, and unfeined belefe in my good dooynges and iust procedinges for you. . . . I cannot choose, but love and favor you, affirmyng that no prince in the world more favoreth his subiectes then I do you.[74]

Petre, who was present, wrote afterwards to his fellow secretary Sir William Paget that the king spoke

so kingly, or rather fatherly, as peradventure to you that hath been used to his daily talks should have been no great wonder (and yet saw I some that hear him often enough largely water their plants[75]), but to us, that have not heard him often, was such a joy and marvellous comfort as I reckon this day one of the happiest of my life.[76]

At the end of the closing formalities, after all the completed parliamentary bills had received the royal assent (or veto, the final royal instrument of control), 'his grace rose and departed'.[77] Henry had taken his final curtain call.

Notes

1 E.g. in the lord chancellor's opening address.

2 G. R. Elton, *The Tudor Constitution*, 2nd edn, Cambridge, 1982, p. 236.

3 See below, p. 114.

4 Elton, *Tudor Constitution*, p. 277 cit. R. Holinshed, *Chronicles of England, Scotland and Ireland*, 6 vols, London, 1808, III, pp. 824–6; *Stats Realm*, III, p. 464. Proviso figures calculated from *HLRO, Orig. Acts*.

5 G. R. Elton, 'Tudor Government: The Points of Contact. I. Parliament', *TRHS*, 5th Ser. 24 (1974), 200.

6 M. A. R. Graves and C. R. Kyle, '"The Kinges most excellent majestie oute of his gracious disposicion": The Evolution of Grace Bills in English Parliaments, 1547–1642', *PER*, 18 (Nov. 1998), 38–41.

7 H. Miller, 'London and Parliament in the Reign of Henry VIII', *BIHR*, 35 (1962), 136–49.

8 Ibid., 137, 139,146.

9 Muller, ed., *Gardiner's Letters*, p. 367.

10 J. Loach, *Parliament under the Tudors*, Oxford, 1991, pp. 35–6.

11 A. D. K. Hawkyard, 'The Enfranchisement of Constituencies, 1509–1558', *Parliamentary History*, 10, I (1991), 4–6.

12 In some cases the enfranchisement date is uncertain, e.g. Berwick-upon-Tweed (Northumberland) and Orford (Suffolk). Ibid., 2–3.

13 Calais, 27 Henry VIII, *c*.63; Chester, 34/35 Henry VIII, *c*.13; Wales, 27 Henry VIII *c*.26, 34/35 Henry VIII, *c*.26, 35 Henry VIII, *c*.11.

14 *Stats Realm*, III, p. 492.

15 I Henry VIII, *c*.12 and *c*.4; also the act against escheators 'for making false returns' (*c*.8).

16 1 Henry VIII, *c*.20; 3 Henry VIII, *c*.22; 4 Henry VIII, *c*.19; 5 Henry VIII, *c*.17; 6 Henry VIII, *c*.26; 7 Henry VIII, *c*.9, *Stats Realm*, III, pp. 21–2, 43–4, 105–19, 156–75, 195–9.

17 See above, Chapter 2, p. 19.

18 R. B. Merriman, *The Life and Letters of Thomas Cromwell*, 2 vols, Oxford, 1902, I, p. 39. Hall, fol. 109v; M. A. R. Graves, *The Tudor Parliaments*, London, 1985, pp. 43, 54, 61–2.

19 Merriman, *Life and Letters of Cromwell*, I, p. 313.

20 Sylvester and Harding, eds, Roper, *Life of More*, p. 205.

21 J. G. Nichols, ed., *Narratives [of the Days of the Reformation]*, Camden Society, Series no. 1, 77 (1859), pp. 25–6.

22 *LP*, 12 (2), no. 952.

23 *LP*, 5, no. 805.

24 Hall, fols 102–3.

25 Davies, *Peace, Print and Protestantism*, pp. 233–4.

26 26 Henry VIII, *c*.13; Lehmberg, *Reformation Parliament*, pp. 204–5.

27 4 Henry VIII *c*.8, *Stats Realm*, III, p. 53.

28 S. E. Lehmberg, *The Later Parliaments of Henry VIII, 1536–1547*, Cambridge, 1977, pp. 276–7.

29 Elton, *Tudor Constitution*, p. 266.

30 Nichols, ed., *Narratives*, pp. 26–7.

31 See below, Chap. 8, pp. 162–3.

32 Pratt, ed., Foxe, *Acts and Monuments*, V, p. 505.

33 *LP*, 6, no. 1365; Bindoff, *Commons*, III, p. 453.

34 *LP*, 12 (2), no. 952.

35 Nichols, ed., *Narratives*, pp. 251, 253–4; Lehmberg, *Later Parliaments*, p. 74.

36 Hall, fol. 205; Lehmberg, *Reformation Parliament*, pp. 147–8.

37 Roche was duly replaced in a by-election. Bindoff, *Commons*, III, p. 203; Lehmberg, *Later Parliaments*, pp. 205, 278.

38 *LP*, 20 (1), no. 98.

39 Tournai and Calais were only briefly represented.

40 H. Miller, 'Attendance in the House of Lords during the Reign of Henry VIII', *HJ*, 10, 4 (1967), 330.

41 Idem, *Henry VIII and the English Nobility*, Oxford, 1986, pp. 118–19.

42 29 Jan. 1534, *Cal. SP Span.*, 5 (1), p. 26; Miller, 'Attendance in Lords', 331–2.

43 Miller, *Henry VIII and Nobility*, pp. 7–9.

44 Ibid., pp. 12–18; J. Enoch Powell and Keith Wallis, *The House of Lords in the Middle Ages*, London, 1968, pp. 551–2, 557–8.

45 Ibid., pp. 18–35.

46 Ibid., pp. 12–13.

47 Ibid., pp. 552–3.

48 Miller, *Henry VIII and Nobility*, p. 34.

49 Lehmberg, *Reformation Parliament*, p. 255.

50 See below, Chap. 8, for a fuller study of Henry's role in the religious changes and his handling of opposition.

51 Hall, fols 188v–189v.

52 *LP*, 5, no. 879.

53 Hall, fol. 200.

54 Davies, *Peace, Print and Protestantism*, pp. 231–2; Elton, *Tudor Constitution*, pp. 296–8.

55 Guy, *Public Career of More*, pp. 113–14.

56 Ibid., pp. 156–8; Pratt, ed., Foxe, *Acts and Monuments*, V, pp. 55–6.

57 Graves, *Tudor Parliaments*, pp. 78–81.

58 31 Henry VIII, *c*.10, *Stats Realm*, III, pp. 729–30.

59 See above, pp. 110–11.

60 22 Henry VIII, *c*.9, *Stats Realm*, III, p. 326.

61 *LP*, 10, no. 462.

62 6 Henry VIII, *c*.16, *Stats Realm*, III, p. 134.

63 Holinshed, III, pp. 824–6; see above, p. 105.

64 J. Guy, 'Thomas Cromwell and the Intellectual Origins of the Henrician Revolution', in Fox and Guy, *Reassessing the Henrician Age*, pp. 172–3.

65 27 Henry VIII *c*.28 and 31 Henry VIII *c*.13; 37 Henry VIII *c*.4.

66 26 Henry VIII, *c*.1, *Stats Realm*, III, p. 492.

67 Davies, *Peace, Print and Protestantism*, pp. 213–14.

68 25 Henry VIII *c*.22; 28 Henry VIII *c*.7; 32 Henry VIII *c*.25; 35 Henry VIII *c*.1.

69 31 Henry VIII, *c*.15.

70 See above, pp. 110–11 and below Chap. 8, pp. 162–3.

71 See below, Chap. 7, p. 140.

72 27 Henry VIII, *c*.26, 28 Henry VIII, *c*.3 and 31 Henry VIII, *c*.11; *Stats Realm*, III, pp. 569, 653, 730.

73 G. W. Bernard, *War, Taxation and Rebellion in Early Tudor England*, Brighton, 1986, pp. 120–1; *LP*, 20 (2), no. 1030.

74 Hall, fols 260v–261.

75 I.e. weep.

76 *LP*, 20 (2), no. 1030.

77 Hall, fol. 262.

Chapter 7

Wills, Wives and *Rex*

Political stability and dynastic security depended, to a significant extent, on the breeding of royal heirs by king and consort. Consideration must be given, therefore, to Henry VIII's place in the sorry procreative record of the Tudor dynasty. His parents had eight children, but by the time he succeeded as king in 1509 his sisters Margaret and Mary were the only other survivors. Henry's attempts to secure the dynastic future were also beset with problems. In his reign, however, these were not only biological and physical but also political: problems not only about potency and fertility but also questions about the legitimacy of some of his marriages and of some of his children. Perhaps the most important single reason why Henry is riveted in the English folk-memory is that he had so many wives. The wives have, in turn, spawned a considerable literature, in particular Catherine of Aragon[1] and Anne Boleyn.[2] To some extent this may be the consequence of their central position in the process whereby Henry's hunt for a divorce resulted in schism and royal supremacy.[3] Although, with the exception of Catherine Parr,[4] there are relatively few studies of his later consorts,[5] there are also various collective studies of his six wives.[6] Many of these studies appeared in the 1980s and 1990s, indicating a continuing interest in the subject and an awareness of its importance. Who were these women, all but one of whom were able either to captivate a formidable king or were made captives in his service? Why were his marriages to two living queens annulled and why were two wives executed? Was a king who went through the wedding service five times in only ten years and five months (January 1533–July 1543) really in control?

Marriage was an important part of kingship and so it is important to understand its role and purposes in Henry's governance. It is commonly assumed that royal marriages served political ends, in particular to provide legitimate – preferably male – heirs. This would ensure an accepted, unchallenged succession and provide the essential precondition for political stability and dynastic security. However, Henry's first marriage, to the twenty-year-old Catherine when he was only seventeen, was simply, he declared, in respect of his father's wish. One does not have to accept his word: his reason may have been to secure the good favour of the Habsburgs, especially as war with France was his goal, or to avoid repayment of Catherine's dowry. Whether or not breeding Tudors was a major or pressing consideration with the young king, it certainly became a growing concern as the years passed. When his third wife, Jane Seymour, died in October 1537, the forty-six-year-old Henry had only one legitimate son and two bastardized daughters – the succession hung on far too slender a thread. Therefore it must have been an important inducement to marry again. By then, plagued with varicose ulcers, his health was declining, especially since the disastrous fall from his horse and the end of his jousting career in 1536. In 1538 he was critically ill and for a fortnight many believed him to be near death. The once fine figure was transformed by lack of exercise and over-indulgence into an obese hulk. There were also reports of his impotence. Even as preparations were underway in 1539 for the arrival of his fourth wife, Anne of Cleves, Henry's leg pained him and he was afflicted with constipation. He was not in the fine physical shape which might have been expected or at least hoped for in a newly-wed. Perhaps his condition rendered procreation increasingly unlikely and what he was now seeking was companionship, which he appears to have enjoyed in his last years with Catherine Parr. In 1539, however, expectations of more children were still being voiced.[7] When Henry became besotted with the fifteen-year-old Catherine Howard and then wedded and bedded her, he ceased to consult the doctors about impotence. In April 1541, scarce nine months after their wedding, Ambassador Marillac reported rumours around Court that 'this Queen is thought to be with child, which would be a very great joy to this King. . . . [T]he young lords and gentlemen of this Court are practising daily for the jousts and tournaments to be then made.'[8]

It is clear from such episodes that children – heirs – remained a prime purpose of Henry's marriages, because a secure succession was a perpetual priority. Furthermore, although the Tudors emerged as the victors of the fifteenth-century dynastic conflict known as the Wars of the Roses, members of the rival house of York still lurked in the political wings, awaiting their chance. Henry VIII, always ultra-sensitive to challenges or threats, pursued a dual policy designed to guarantee a Tudor future: the elimination of challengers, real or potential; and the securing of sons and heirs.

The elimination of challengers, real or potential

It paid Henry to be cautious, especially in the case of Poles and Courtenays. Although he executed Edmund de la Pole, earl of Suffolk, as a security precaution in 1513,[9] there was no vindictive policy or revenge campaign against old Yorkist families. Edward Stafford, duke of Buckingham, for example, flourished as a great regional magnate during the early years of Henry VIII's reign. Margaret Pole was created countess of Salisbury in 1513. The king also restored the fortunes of Henry Courtenay, earl of Devon, whom he raised to be marquess of Exeter, privy councillor and constable of Windsor Castle. For a quarter of a century he was Court-companion of Henry, who rewarded him with estates and offices. But their short sighted, provocative actions, an innately suspicious and over-reactive king, and changing circumstances combined to destroy men who were potential claimants to the crown. Buckingham, a powerful, danger-ous subject of royal blood, was not, as Polydore Vergil and Skelton claimed, the victim of Wolsey's malice but that of his own folly. He accepted prophecies of the king's death and reputedly said 'that if the King should die, he meant to have the rule in England'. This would mean the removal, even death, of the king's five-year-old daughter, Mary. Buckingham's trial and execution in 1521 can be seen as no more than sensible precautions taken by the ruling family under threat.[10]

In the late 1530s more potential claimants were victims of the volatile political world created by the European Reformation, the break with Rome and the shuffling alliances between the English, French and Habsburg Princes. Furthermore the king had become paranoid about threats, real or imagined, to his person, crown or Church. In 1538 Henry Lord Mon-tague became one of the victims of the king's ongoing and deepening hostility towards his brother, the diplomatically active Reginald (from 1536 Cardinal) Pole.[11] Exeter's credentials were fatally undermined by his association with the Poles and his wife's earlier connection with the Nun of Kent. He died with Montague on 9 December. Both men contributed to their downfall by their own indiscretion: Montague did not keep his hostility to the religious changes private, whilst Exeter sang 'political songs of a subversive nature in his garden'. At the same time the coun-tess of Salisbury was interrogated. In 1539 she was attainted by statute and imprisoned in the Tower. The sixty-eight-year-old countess was executed in May 1541 in response to a Yorkist conspiracy. So the con-scientious royal gardener weeded out the politically noxious white roses.[12] None of their indiscretions, however, had come close to those of Henry Howard, earl of Surrey, who paid for them with his life. It is not clear whether Surrey's trial and execution and his father's statutory attainder were driven by the king or a rival faction.[13] Neither, however, could allow the Howards to be alive, well and free when the new reign began.

Sons and heirs

The elimination of claimants, potential or active, was not enough in itself to secure the succession. It was necessary to provide male heirs of the body. The actual choice of a consort, however, was normally determined by more short-term political considerations. Eric Ives itemizes them as: someone of suitable status befitting a monarch; someone who brought the king diplomatic advantage; and someone whose marriage to him did not disrupt the delicate equilibrium of internal politics.[14] In Henry's case, however, only two marriages met these principles of choice: those to his two foreign wives, Catherine of Aragon and Anne of Cleves. Furthermore, although he chose Anne, sister of the fellow schismatic William duke of Cleves, for diplomatic reasons, his decision to remarry was driven by the need for heirs.[15] In contrast his choice of Anne Boleyn, Jane Seymour and Catherine Howard was not the simple consequence of sober political considerations but the result of love, lust or both. Politics, however, were never absent from the marital process. The susceptible king's choice of next wife could be and often was influenced by ministers, prominent noble families and their aristocratic networks, who were motivated neither by the needs of state nor by those of the king's body, but rather by personal and familial concerns. Not only were the fortunes of the Boleyns advanced by the king's choice of Anne; despite the contrary opinions of Chapuys, it is clear that Anne's grandfather, the conservative duke of Norfolk and his Howard kin warmly and actively supported her elevation into the royal nuptual bed.[16] This would strengthen his relationship with Henry and open up access to royal favour.

Henry it was who always made the final decisions. At the same time, those decisions could be and so often were influenced, managed, even determined by others. So Anne's downfall, increasingly possible as Henry became disenchanted with her failure to produce a male heir, was assisted by a mixture of conservatives, the pro-Catherine 'Aragonese faction', Cromwell and ambitious Seymours. The increasingly familiar story continues. When, after Jane Seymour's death, Henry sought a fourth wife, Cromwell was instrumental in persuading the king into marriage with Anne of Cleves. This can be seen as a diplomatic alliance. Nevertheless Henry sought wives with physical appeal. Cromwell is reported to have said that 'the King, my master, is not one to marry without having first seen and known the princess who is to be his companion for life'.[17] Prospective foreign brides presented an obvious problem here. When, in 1537–8, Henry pursued Christina, the sixteen-year-old widowed duchess of Milan, it was not only for diplomatic advantage but also in response to reports about her beauty. So he sent Holbein to sketch her. He was impressed by what he saw. She, however, was repelled by what she heard, 'for her Council suspecteth that her great aunt [Catherine of Aragon] was poisoned, that the second was innocently put to death, and the third lost for lack of keeping in her childbed'.[18] Henry switched attention to France, seeking a closer, marriage-based alliance. He proposed that he cross to Calais, where the French king might assemble '7 or 8 damsels of Royal blood . . . to visit him, when he would choose one' as his next wife. Francis' refusal to muster high-born women 'to be passed in review as if they were hackneys for sale' is hardly surprising.[19] The French ambassador, Castillon, reinforced the point when he asked Henry if he would like to mount them one after the other and keep for himself the one whom he found to be the *plus doulx*.[20] Castillon reported that the king 'laughed and blushed at the same time, and recognized then that the way he had taken was a little discourteous'. Yet his desire to meet prospective wives was understandable. As he exclaimed to the ambassador, 'By God! I trust no one but myself. The thing touches me too near.'[21] If he could not meet face-to-face, he needed to be informed about the physical desirability of a prospective bride. So he commissioned Holbein to paint a portrait of Anne of Cleves. The result did not present Henry with the prospect of legitimately bedding a beautiful woman. Nevertheless he appreciated that the proposed marriage had a diplomatic purpose. He was, after all, a monarch who was willing to listen to advice, ponder it and even act on it. Although, after Jane's death, Cromwell recorded that he was not inclined to marry again, some of his Council urged him to do so 'for the sake of his realm'. In response he had 'framed his mind, both to be indifferent to the thing and to the election of any person from any part that with deliberation shall be thought meet'.[22]

Henry VIII, however, was also a man driven by powerful impulses of love, passion or simple fulfilment of sexual urges. These could be important political wildcards, with dramatic impact on royal marriages and policies, Court politics and international diplomacy. In his early years as king he exercised some discretion, assisted by the fact that a monarch and his consort normally had separate households, which included their own personal bedchambers. The king would normally journey to the queen's bed for the purposes of nuptial pleasure and procreation. Such physical arrangements, however, facilitated extra-marital pleasures, usually on Henry's part (though, later, also by one of his queens, Catherine Howard). When his first wife was pregnant in 1510, he took as his mistress Lady Elizabeth FitzWalter, married sister of the duke of Buckingham. Sir William Compton, the king's groom of the stool, assisted his master by arranging the affair. When Elizabeth's sister and a close confidante of Queen Catherine, Lady Anne Herbert, became suspicious, she passed word on to Buckingham. He surprised Compton in his sister's chamber at Court and a furious quarrel followed. The king spoke angrily to the duke, who left the Court. Meanwhile, the Spanish ambassador, Luiz Caro, reported,

The lady's husband, too, carried her off to a convent 60 miles hence, and then the Queen's favourite [Lady Anne] and her husband, as having caused all this, were turned out of the Palace by the King, who would have turned off some other women, also suspected of tale-bearing but that he thought the scandal too great. All the Court knew that the Queen was vexed with the King, and he with her.[23]

Only the day before Luiz Caro penned his letter, Catherine wrote to her father, King Ferdinand of Aragon, that, although she had earlier been delivered of a still-born daughter, she and Henry were cheerful. And she thanked God for such a husband![24] Perhaps she was just putting on a brave face, or she was simply learning that royal marriages were designed to satisfy diplomatic and succession needs, not sexual appetites. Henry was not an exceptional Prince when he regarded it as his right to plant his royal standard anywhere. Throughout the rest of the reign there were rumours of liaisons, possible or actual, tidbits of gossip and evidence of royal conquests. It was characteristic of the wayward, insensitive king that Chapuys wrote, on 1 July 1536,

[W]ithin eight days after publication of his marriage [to Jane Seymour], having twice met two beautiful young ladies, he said and showed himself somewhat sorry that he had not seen them before he was married.[25]

Very few of his relationships – whether brief encounters or longer, active liaisons – resulted in children. He sired one child – a daughter – by Joan Dobson (Dingley?) and there may have been others.[26] He had, however, only one acknowledged bastard, Henry Fitzroy. He was born in 1519, issue of the king's five-year-long liaison with Elizabeth (or Bessie) Blount. As a maid of honour she had first gained Henry's attention because 'in syngyng, daunsyng, and in all goodly pastymes [she] exceeded all other'. So, Hall wrote, '[S]he won the kynges harte' or, more probably, stirred his loins.[27] By the time or soon after she gave birth, she had been rewarded for her various services by an arranged marriage with Gilbert Tailboys.[28] Queen Catherine was deeply wounded when she learned the news of Fitzroy's birth, but that mattered little to her husband, who lavished attention on his first son. He was tutored at Cambridge by Richard Croke, who had taught the king Greek. Then, in 1525, Henry VIII began to groom him for kingship. He was brought to Court, in April he was elected to the Order of the Garter and in June he was created duke of Richmond and Somerset, earl of Nottingham and keeper of the city and castle of Carlisle. The Venetian ambassador Lorenzo Orio observed that 'he takes precedence of everybody' and the king 'loves him like his own soul'.[29] In 1526 he became titular head of the council in the north and in 1529 lord lieutenant of Ireland. Queen Catherine was angry at the elevation of this product of her husband's infidelity. Orio wrote that

[she] remains dissatisfied, at the instigation, it is said, of three of her Spanish ladies, her chief counsellors; so the King has dismissed them the Court – a strong measure, but the Queen was obliged to submit and to have patience.[30]

The young duke was brought to Court again in 1530 in order to shelter him from an outbreak of the plague – another affront to Catherine – but eventually, on 22 July 1536, he fell victim to tuberculosis.

By then the king had married for a third time, but he was still without a legitimate male heir. His first wife Catherine had, on three occasions, given birth to a boy but they had survived only briefly: the first from 1 January to late February 1511, the second dying within a month in 1513 and the third, in 1514, lasting but a few hours. However, when, during the 1520s, Henry determined on a new marriage, he was not driven only, or even chiefly, by the need for male heirs. In 1525/6 he ended a lengthy liaison with Mary Boleyn, wife of William Carey, one of his gentlemen of the privy chamber, probably because he had fallen for her sister. Anne Boleyn, however, would lie in his bed only if she could wear a crown. She allowed certain intimacies – so Henry could write to her in 1528 'wishing myself (specially an evening) in my sweetheart's arms, whose pretty dukkys I trust shortly to cusse'.[31] But it was seven years before she yielded her body to him. During that time the queen aged from forty to forty-seven years, Henry entered his forties and still he had no legitimate son. In his prolonged siege of Anne, passion had taken precedence over political priorities.

Once Anne became pregnant in 1532 and Henry's wife in January 1533 his priorities shifted. It was as if her primary role ceased to be lover and companion and became provider of heirs. Furthermore, in his sexual behaviour he displayed a callous indeed brutal indifference towards her.

Already in August 1533 he was committing adultery and, when Anne protested, he 'told her that she must shut her eyes and endure as well as more worthy persons, and that she ought to know that it was in his power to humble her again in a moment more than he had exalted her'.[32] He had at least one more mistress in 1534; early next year he was bedding Queen Anne's cousin and lady-in-waiting, Madge Shelton; and by January 1536, when Anne had a miscarriage, she was distressed by the extravagant attention which he was paying to a Mrs Semel, alias Jane Seymour. In February 1536 Chapuys, loyal to the memory of Henry's Spanish first wife who had died a month before, reported to his emperor with pleasure that the ever-sensitive king 'has not spoken ten times to the Concubine [Anne], and that when she miscarried he scarcely said anything to her, except that he saw clearly that God did not wish to give him male children'.[33]

Questions may be asked about fertility and, in particular, about Henry's potency. One of the charges against Anne Boleyn was her revelation to her sister-in-law that he was impotent.[34] In his conversation with his trusted physician, Dr William Butts, he certainly acknowledged problems with his fourth wife, Anne of Cleves: that 'he could not know her'. As Henry informed Thomas Cromwell, this was because he found her physically repellent, so that 'he was struck to the heart, and left her as good a maid as he found her'. He turned this into a justification of non-consummation: the condition of her body was such that she came to him not as a virgin and, therefore, she was not his lawful wife. He insisted that 'he thought himself able to do th[e]act with other'.[35] In brief, his problem was neither biological nor general, as his personal record and Dr Butts' observations would appear to confirm.[36] What is far more significant, in a study of his style, priorities and techniques as a ruler, is his characteristically inconsistent, selfish, often wayward and certainly short-sighted pursuit of personal gratification – often at the expense of longer-term and desirable political objectives, above all a secure succession. At the same time the central, often critical, role of marriage in his reign probably influenced his attitude to its place in the 'Henrician Reformation': so he elevated it to the position of an essential sacrament, on a par with the eucharist.[37]

Henry's marital record

As Christina duchess of Milan cynically revealed, when Henry had run only half his marital course he had already acquired an unenviable European reputation.[38] In his defence it might be argued that, no matter how much a monarch loved his wife, his marriage had to be productive of heirs and its unquestioned legitimacy was the essential precondition of unchallenged hereditary succession. When King Ferdinand of Aragon, Catherine's father, learned of Henry VII's death, he instructed the Spanish ambassador in England to tell the seventeen-year-old Henry VIII 'that his age and position as a King without heirs render it imperatively necessary for him to take a wife without delay, and to beget children'.[39] Henry duly activated the marriage treaty and betrothal of 1503 when he married Catherine on 11 June 1509. They were crowned in Westminster Abbey on 24 June.

In the years which followed, Catherine proved to be a devoted, dutiful and responsible queen, who, for example, was governor of England in 1513 during Henry's absence in France and the English victory at Flodden. When she wrote to him after the battle, she ended, '[P]rayng God to sende you home shortly, for without this noo joye here can bee accomplisshed.'[40] There were many glimpses of a happy, if not always harmonious, relationship: when, for example, she kissed her young husband and thanked him after New Year revelry. But the relationship was plagued by a poor procreative record, not only short-lived sons[41] but a stillborn daughter in 1510 and another dead after a few hours in 1518. Only Mary, born in 1516, survived to rule. The king comforted his wife when young Henry died in 1511. But as early as 1514 a Venetian reported a rumour that Henry meant to repudiate his wife, 'because he is unable to have children by her, and intends to marry a daughter of the French Duke of Bourbon'.[42] That passed. It was only when he sought to possess Anne Boleyn that he displayed a remarkable tenacity and persistence of purpose in ending the marriage.

For her part Catherine was equally resolute in her resistance to the annulment of their marriage on the grounds that her first marriage, to Henry's brother Arthur, had been consummated. In these circumstances, according to two passages in Leviticus, the second marriage was prohibited in divine law. The papal dispensation which had been granted in 1503 permitting them to marry was therefore invalid. When Catherine was visited by Wolsey and Campeggio, the two cardinals appointed 'judges indifferent' to hear the case, she excoriated Henry's minister:

But of thys trouble I onely may thanke you my lorde Cardinal of Yorke, for because I have wondered at your hygh pride and vainglory, and abhorre your voluptuous life and abhominable Lechery, and litle regard your presumpteous power and tyranny, therefore of malice you have kindled thys fyre. . . .[43]

But Catherine was isolated and eventually Henry had his way. The pursuit of his objectives, however, led him into drastic courses: schism and 'uncompromising Erastianism'; the bastardization of his daughter Mary; and the brutal treatment of the 'holy maid of Kent' Elizabeth Barton, the Friars Observant, London Carthusians and other critics such as John Fisher bishop of Rochester and, above all, Sir Thomas More.[44] Although the catalyst of change was Anne Boleyn and the dynamic was 'the great love that he bare her in the bottom of his stomach', Henry had ceased to be besotted by the time that the process was complete.[45] Anne's personal qualities were an important element in this process of change. This was already evident when the king was courting but had not yet bedded her, because Cavendish, in retrospect, described her then as beginning 'to look very hault and stout'.[46] According to Chapuys, writing in 1529, '[I]f the said Lady Anne chooses, the Cardinal will soon be dismissed.'[47] This opinion was confirmed by Cavendish's account of a dinner conversation between Henry and Anne. When the king attempted to defend his chief minister, she attacked him for 'what things hath he wrought within this realm to your great slander and dishonour'.[48] Eventually she had her way: Wolsey was dismissed in 1529 and four years later, in 1533, she became queen and consort. But there were many who hated her and she was potentially very vulnerable. Even when she was married many continued to describe her as adulteress, concubine, harlot or whore.[49] As Henry's partner, then wife and queen, she was foolishly proud, unwisely intolerant of personal restraint, tactless enough to argue with him, criticize his clothes in public and, with her brother, make fun of his writings 'as of productions entirely worthless'.[50]

Anne also put herself in a very exposed religious position by her active evangelical interests,[51] in particular her French connections, her liking for vernacular scripture[52] and her protection[53] and promotion of those of similar mind. During her years as Henry's prospective second wife, she was able to take advantage of his love for her and his increasing hostility to Rome. She worked to secure the removal of Wolsey, who was busily persecuting evangelicals, and, presumably to this end, brought the king's attention to the writings of two of the cardinal's virulent critics, Simon Fish and William Tyndale. Having read Tyndale's *Obedience of a Christen Man*, Henry is reputed to have exclaimed with delight, '[T]hys booke ys for me and all kynges to reade.'[54] Whilst Cranmer entered her father's service, Anne, employing the knowledge and advice of Henry's doctor, William Butts, became patron and protector of other Cambridge evangelicals, such as Hugh Latimer, her chaplains William Latymer, John Skip and Matthew Parker, and William Shaxton. Seven new bishops, appointed between 1532 and 1536, were Anne's clients. She also encouraged the dissemination of vernacular texts and set a personal example by her own use of Tyndale's 1534 *New Testament*.[55] Henry was not inflexibly opposed to the use of the vernacular, yet on this point he remained conservative and was unenthusiastic about an author-ized English Bible. Furthermore Anne was unpopular in many quarters, especially amongst papists and enemies of the evangelicals. This is not enough to label Anne a Lutheran, for she also retained Catholic beliefs and observed Catholic practices.[56] So long as her relationship with the king remained passionate, with standoffs and warm reconciliations – a sign of continuing love – she was safe,[57] but once Henry's ardour cooled she was at risk and her enemies could exploit her vulnerability with fatal effect. During the years of courtship Anne had been in control: Henry believed he was manoeuvring her towards the royal bed, but she was scheming her way towards a royal diadem. She made the fatal mistake of thinking that, once wedded, she would retain control. She would not accept that, as the king's consort, it was her role to be the accepting, dutiful subordinate, who turned a tolerant blind eye to his liaisons, whilst she fulfilled her prime function as the mother of his sons and heirs. Anne was doomed.

In 1536 the king's second marriage was invalidated (17 May), Anne Boleyn was executed (19 May) and he married Jane Seymour (30 May). Jane, a woman of gentle status and conservative religious position, seems to have won Henry, who devotedly spent much time with her.[58] Her security was also strengthened, because both the king's previous wives were dead and so no-one could question the legitimacy of this marriage. At the same time, however, the Succession Act, passed by the parliament of June–July 1536, declared Mary and Elizabeth, the issue of the first two marriages, to be illegitimate and excluded from inheritance of the crown. Henry, aged forty-four and in physical decline, had no direct legitimate heirs. In August he was reported as telling Cromwell that 'he felt himself already growing old, and doubted whether he should have any child by the Queen'.[59] In these circumstances he was hyper-sensitive to any betrothal or marriage which promoted the dynastic ambitions of others and seemed to threaten a vulnerable king. This explains the prompt and terrible response to the contract to marry made between Thomas Howard and Margaret Douglas in April 1536. Margaret was Henry's niece and therefore, until he and his third wife had children, she was very import-ant as a potential successor.[60] The same parliament which passed the Succession Act also enacted a statutory attainder of Thomas Howard. He was accused, beyng ledde and seduced by the Devyll . . . [of contracting] hym self by craftye faier and flateryng Wordes to and with the Lady Margarete Dowglas beyng naturall Doughter to the Quene of Scottes eldest suster to oure sayd Sovereign Lord; by the whiche it is vehemently to be suspected that the sayd Lord Thomas falsely craftely and trayterously hath ymagined and compassed, that in case oure seid Sovereign Lord shuld die wythout heyres of his bodye, whiche God defend, that then the sayd Lord Thomas by reason of maryage in so highe a blodde . . . shuld aspyre by her to the Dignyte of the seyd Imperyall Crowne of this Realme.[61]

Howard was attainted of high treason and condemned to death. He was not executed but simply languished in the Tower until his death the following year. His offence – betrothal – was not treasonable when it occurred and there is no evidence of sinister treasonable intent. Statutes of attainder did not require either: that is why they were so useful to Henry, as he had found with Elizabeth Barton in 1534.[62]

Henry's vulnerability was lessened with the birth of Prince Edward on 12 October 1537. It was not possible to test the endurance of Henry's affections for Jane Seymour, who died in childbed only seventeen months after their marriage. He cherished her legacy, a son, Edward, born twelve days before her death. London rejoiced with celebratory street fires, banquets, church bells ringing till 10 at night, and also 'shot at the Tower that night above tow thousand gonns'.[63] Yet the succession hung on a single slender thread. There was no guarantee that the infant prince would survive. Three sons born alive during his first marriage survived for periods ranging from fifty-three days to a few hours. Matters were not improved by an unconsummated marriage to Anne of Cleves (January–July 1540). At least it was terminated quickly, with the compliance of Anne, who was rewarded with a financial settlement of £4,704 a year and extensive properties, including Hever Castle, Bletchingley and especially Richmond Palace. He visited her; she was welcome at the royal Court and often in attendance.[64] It paid to be compliant with the king's wishes.

Henry's interest continued to fluctuate between wiving and swiving. In the person of Catherine Howard, however, he seems to have briefly fulfilled both urges. On 28 July 1540, only nineteen days after the annulment of Henry's previous marriage, he wedded her at Oatlands. From the very beginning this marriage between the gross and besotted forty-nine-year-old monarch and the attractive, graceful fifteen-year-old was a recipe for disaster. It was also very characteristic of Henry's rule. Catherine had been dangled before him by the conservatives, seeking to build on the downfall and death of Thomas Cromwell. Henry had taken the bait because, as so often, self-gratification took precedence over long-term considerations, such as secure monarchy and political stability. In the shorter term the wayward behaviour of the greedy, self-indulgent, vacuous and sexually broad-ranging Catherine ended her marriage and, in the Tower on 13 February 1542, her life. Some of her Howard relatives, including the duke of Norfolk, fell out of favour with the king. For Henry it seems to have been a public humiliation and a major blow to his masculine self-esteem. Some reports describe a sad, lonely royal cuckold, looking old and grey.

One wonders, therefore, why he took the plunge yet once more. Undoubtedly he had not lost courtly and companionable interest in women. Indeed some accounts suggest that they enabled him to toss aside his grief rapidly. On the very day that the bill of attainder condemning Catherine Howard to death entered parliament he made 'hearty cheer' with more than sixty ladies of the Court at supper. He paid particular attention to 'the same lady whom [Thomas Wyatt] did some time ago repudiate on a charge of adultery'. Ambassador Chapuys added sardonically that 'She is a pretty young creature and has sense enough to do as the others have done should she consider it worth her while.' The king was also rumoured to have 'taken a fancy' to two other women.[65] Perhaps, at this point, he was simply taking refuge from grief. Within twelve months, however, Chapuys was observing,

Nowadays things have changed; he has given orders that the Princess [Mary] is to go to Court for [the Christmas] festivities, accompanied by a great number of ladies; he is having workmen day and night at Hampton-Court preparing the lodgings for the said ladies.[66]

But gone were the many and sometimes lengthy liaisons of his earlier years. The ambassador also reported that there was no rumour of Henry's intention to marry again. Why, then, did he marry again only a few months later, on 12 July 1543? Age, obesity and a pain-wracked body must have impacted adversely on his sexual drives and also reduced, if not removed, the possibility of siring more children. The simple explanation may be that he was lonely or, as Loades suggests, he simply wanted 'to obtain that "heart's ease" which had consistently eluded him since the early days of his reign'.[67]

Henry's choice, the twice-widowed thirty-one-year-old Catherine Parr, was influenced by neither political nor diplomatic considerations. Catherine was well-read, a competent scholar and an active patron with evangelical interests.[68] She enjoyed discussing the scriptures with both her friends and her indulgent husband. She was not, however, equipped for the instruction of the king's children and Henry did not assign her the task. Indeed, as Maria Dowling shows, she was a late starter 'who began to be learned, not in young girlhood, but after her marriage to the King'. Nor was she as prominent in the advancement of the evangelical cause as was once believed. She did not have an important political role nor was she a controversial leader of an evangelical faction or movement. In 1546 Bishop Gardiner's attempt to obtain her arrest secured the initial support of the king, who even signed the articles drawn up against her. This seems to have been no more than the impulsive action of a man exasperated by his wife's presumptuous boldness in their theological discussions. When Catherine, warned of what was happening, submitted totally to Henry she was forgiven. She was, like Henry's previous wives, very exposed and vulnerable to the current in-fighting in the Court. In 1546 the imperial ambassador wrote of 'rumours here of a new Queen', possibly the widowed duchess of Suffolk, attributed to the supposed 'sterility of the present Queen'.[69] It was symptomatic of her constant insecurity, despite what amounted to a low-key role. Catherine's position in the religious politics of the 1540s, Dowling concludes, has been greatly exaggerated. Her importance to Henry's rule in his last years was to be rather a companion, sometimes a nurse and, perhaps, someone who supplied some desired 'heart's ease'.[70]

The succession: uncertainty and change

Until 1533 Henry had one legitimate heir of the body, Princess Mary. The rapid sequence of marriages thereafter raised the number of surviving children to three, but also altered the status of two of them. The result was a series of changes to the order of succession. There was only one constant: the uncertain future of the Tudor dynasty. Whatever part conviction, conscience or passion played as a motive for the termination of his first marriage, there is no doubt that concern about the succession played a key part. When Henry first focused his desire on Anne Boleyn in 1525/6 he had been a married king for sixteen years and had only one child, Mary. It would have been diplomatically and, at home, politically more advantageous if he had married into one of Europe's great dynasties. Instead he wedded an upstart who was widely regarded as the cause of Queen Catherine's misery. As so often happened during his reign, personal self-fulfilment took precedence over all else: the present mattered more than the future.

The end of his first marriage, the confirmation of his second and the birth of Elizabeth, all during 1533, were acknowledged in the first Succession Act in 1534. It enacted that the marriage between Henry and Catherine was 'utterlie voyde [and annulled]' and that his second marriage 'shalbe establisshed and taken for ... perfecte ever hereafter'. The statute then detailed an order of succession, in which the sons of Henry and Anne and any sons by future wives would take precedence over the infant Princess Elizabeth. It made no mention, however, of Princess Mary. Naturally she was not specifically included in the order of succession, but nor did the act declare her to be a bastard and therefore without a legitimate place in that order. This was less likely to be an accident of omission than a deliberate but tacit act of insurance.[71]

When, in due course, Anne fell from royal grace and her head fell from the block, a second Succession Act (1536) declared that Henry's first two marriages were null and void and that the issue of both were illegitimate and therefore excluded from the succession. It directed the succession through the sons of Jane Seymour and other wives, and then through daughters of the same. This statute is a tribute to Henry's political control, because it also empowered him to designate further successors by letters patent or his will.[72] A third Succession Act was passed in 1544, when Henry's sixth marriage showed no signs of improving on the past thirty-five years' lean harvest of one legitimate and male heir. Mary and Elizabeth were slotted into the succession after Edward, but if they failed to accept conditions laid down by Henry the crown would pass to others designated by him in his letters patent or last will.[73] The succession statutes were another example of how he seemed able to obtain virtually anything he desired from parliament. The order of succession appeared to be secure in his hands with his will as the final statement. The succession provisions of his will, dated December 1546, repeated the terms of the third Succession Act. But Henry made the places of Mary and Elizabeth conditional on marrying with the consent of those privy councillors whom he appointed to govern during his son's minority. Also, in accordance with the terms of the 1536 act, he designated further heirs in case his three children died without issue. He passed over the progeny of his elder sister Margaret, who had married into the Stuart dynasty, and named Frances and Eleanor, the daughters of his second sister Mary.[74]

By the time Henry's will was drawn, it was evident that he would not survive until his son attained his majority. Therefore it was of major importance as the instrument by which he laid down arrangements for

Edward's government. There is an ongoing debate about the authenticity of the will, the circumstances of its drafting, and the extent to which others had an input, simply because so much is hidden from posterity. During his final weeks in December 1546–January 1547 the increasingly immobile king lived in growing isolation, as Sir Anthony Denny and Sir William Herbert of the privy chamber controlled access to him. They did so in the interest of the 'reformers' whose rivalry with the conservatives intensified. It culminated in the reformers' triumph with the death of Surrey, attainder of Norfolk and exclusion in disgrace of Gardiner. Henry's isolation leaves questions unanswered. Did he fear the Howards' power after his death or was he prompted by the reformers to bring them down? Did he seek a Protestant Church or was he unaware of the religious position of the Seymours and their allies? Did he really believe that the terms of his will would ensure strictly corporate government by privy councillors and prevent an ambitious politician from making himself Protector? Denny and Herbert stop us at the door. The king must have been conscious of an unsure future following his death. He needed stability, which may have seemed more likely with Seymours than Howards. But access to his thoughts is denied us. He was ill and isolated. When he expressed concern about the 'greatly decayed' nobility, Sir William Paget, ally of Edward Seymour, earl of Hertford, helped him to devise a list of those to be ennobled or promoted to 'higher places of honour'. But Henry's proposed gifts of estates to them was disputed by Paget, who, after the king's death, related, 'All which I sayde was to little, and stode moch with him therin.' There was even pressure on Henry to use as gifts the Howard inheritance, which the imprisoned Norfolk offered to the king for his heir in December. The terms of the royal legacies were settled and, in Henry's presence, the gifts clause was inserted in his will. Denny controlled the dry stamp with which the will was sealed. When King Henry VIII died on 28 January 1547, the reformers had already taken charge.[75]

At least in the short term the king eventually achieved a guaranteed succession under a legitimate male heir. He ensured that his daughters would not rule with undesirable consorts and he kept out the kings of Scotland, England's traditional enemy, both politically acceptable and sensible precautions. But the trail to that objective of a sure succession upon his death had involved so much pain, death, upheaval and destruction. Furthermore, in the strict terms of a secure succession as the prerequisite of a politically stable future, Henry VIII was not a success. Too often a longer-term vision, based upon considered political judgement, was sacrificed to short-term personal gratification.

Notes

1 E.g. by A. Du Boys, *Catherine d'Aragon et les origines du schisme Anglican*, Société générale de librairie catholique, Paris, 1880. English translation by C. M. Yonge, 2 vols, London, 1881; Mattingley, *Catherine of Aragon*; M. A. Albert, *The Divorce*, New York, 1965; J. E. Paul, *Catherine of Aragon and her Friends*, London, 1999; M. M. Luke, *Catherine the Queen*, London, 1968; see also the various works of J. Gairdner (e.g. 'Mary and Anne Boleyn', *EHR*, 8 (1893), 53–60; 'The Fall of Cardinal Wolsey', *TRHS*, 2nd Series, 13 (1899), 75–102; 'New Light on the Divorce of Henry VIII', *EHR*, 11 (1896), 673–702, 12 (1897), 1–16, 237–53).

2 E.g. by M. L. Bruce, *Anne Boleyn*, London, 1972; H. W. Chapman, *Anne Boleyn*, London, 1974; C. Erickson, *Mistress Anne*, New York, 1984; E. W. Ives, *Anne Boleyn*, Oxford, 1986; R. M. Warnicke, *The Rise and Fall of Anne Boleyn: Family Politics at the Court of Henry VIII*, Cambridge, 1989.

3 See below, pp. 134–5.

4 M. A. Gordon, *The Life of Queen Katherine Parr*, Kendal, 1952; A Martiensson, *Queen Katherine Parr*, London, 1973; B. Kemeys and J. Raggatt, *The Queen Who Survived: The Life of Katherine Parr*, London, 1992; K. Snowden, *Katherine Parr Our Northern Queen*, Pickering, 1994; S. E. James, *Kateryn Parr: The Making of a Queen*, Ashgate, 1999.

5 On Anne of Cleves: M. Saaler, *Anne of Cleves: Fourth Wife of Henry VIII*, London 1995; R. M. Warnicke, *The Marrying of Anne of Cleves: Royal Protocol in Early Modern England*, Cambridge, 2000. On Catherine Howard: L. B. Smith, *A Tudor Tragedy: The Life and Times of Catherine Howard*, London, 1961. Apart from W. Seymour's *Ordeal by Ambition: An English Family in the Shadow of the Tudors* (London, 1972) there is, ironically, little specifically on Jane Seymour, the queen who gave Henry the one male heir who survived.

6 E.g. by M. Cowan, *The Six Wives of Henry VIII: The King Seen through the Eyes of Each of His Ill-Fated Wives*, London, 1968; A. Weir, *The Six Wives of Henry VIII*, London, 1991; A. Fraser, *The Wives of Henry VIII*, London, 1992; D. Loades, *The Politics of Marriage: Henry VIII and his Queens*, Stroud, 1994.

7 *LP*, 14 (2), no. 400 (p. 140).

8 *LP*, 16, no. 712.

9 See above, Chap. 1, p. 3.

10 *LP*, 3 (1), no. 1284 (p. 492); Gwyn, *King's Cardinal*, pp. 159–72.

11 See above Chap. 3, p. 47.

12 M. L. Bush, 'The Tudors and the Royal Race', *History*, 55 (1970), 38, 40–1.

13 See above, Chap. 5, p. 99.

14 E. W. Ives, 'Marrying for Love: The Experience of Edward IV and Henry VIII', *Hist. Today*, 50 (Dec. 2000), 48.

15 Warnicke, *Marrying of Anne of Cleves*, pp. 4–8.

16 Idem, 'Family and Kinship Relations at the Henrician Court: The Boleyns and Howards', in Hoak, ed., *Tudor Political Culture*, pp. 32–3, 35–8, 43–6, 53.

17 *Cal. SP Span.*, 5 (2), no. 225 (pp. 530–1).

18 *LP*, 14 (2), no. 400 (p. 141).

19 *Cal. SP Span.*, 6 (1), no. 4 (p. 6).

20 'Ne vouldriez vous point, Sire encores monter sur toutes l'une après l'autre et après retenir pour vostre personne celle qui yroit le plus doulx?' *LP*, 13 (2), no. 77.

21 Ibid.

22 Ibid., 12 (2), no. 1004.

23 Ibid., 1 (1), no. 474.

24 Ibid., 1 (1), no. 473.

25 Ibid., 11, no. 8.

26 E.g. Sir John Perrot (by Mary Berkley) and Thomas Stukely were widely reputed to be his sons, but there is no evidence to justify such claims. A. Weir, *Britain's Royal Families: The Complete Genealogy*, London, 1996, p. 155. This also applies to Mary Boleyn's son, Henry, born in 1525. Starkey, *Personalities and Politics*, p. 95.

27 Hall, fol. 114v.

28 In June 1522 husband and wife were granted Rokeby Manor in Warwickshire. *LP*, 3 (2), no. 2356 (18).

29 *Cal. SP Ven*, 3, nos 1037, 1052.

30 Ibid., 3, no. 1053.

31 Byrne, ed., *Letters of Henry VIII*, p. 82.

32 *LP*, 6, no. 1069 (p. 453).

33 Ibid., 10, no. 351 (p. 134).

34 *Cal. SP Span.*, 5 (2), p. 126; *LP*, 10, no. 908 (p. 378).

35 Ibid., 15, no. 823 (p. 391); J. Strype, *Ecclesiastical Memorials, relating chiefly to religion and the reformation of it under King Henry VIII, King Edward VI and Queen Mary I*, 3 vols in 6, Oxford, 1820–40, 1 (2), pp. 461–2.

36 Warnicke, *Marrying of Anne of Cleves*, pp. 166–7, 204–5, 266. He also used witchcraft or some other evil external force as a possible explanation for his impotence in this case. Ibid., pp. 205–6, 266–7.

37 D. MacCulloch, 'The Religion of Henry VIII', in Starkey, ed., *A European Court*, p. 162.

38 See above, p. 130.

39 *Cal. SP Span.*, 2, no. 3 (p. 8).

40 Ellis, ed., *Orig. Letters*, 1 (1), p. 89.

41 See above, p. 132.

42 *Cal SP Ven.*, 2, no. 479.

43 Hall, fol. 181.

44 D. Loades, *Politics, Censorship and the English Reformation*, London, 1991, p. 64; Scarisbrick, *Henry VIII*, pp. 321–3.

45 Sylvester and Harding, eds, Cavendish, *Wolsey*, p. 37.

46 'High and mighty', ibid., p. 37 and n. 9.

47 *Cal. SP Span.*, 4 (1), no. 135.

48 Sylvester and Harding, eds, Cavendish, *Wolsey*, p. 98.

49 Amongst them Chapuys, whose lengthy accounts of the Henrician Court and her place within it were always coloured by his loyalty to Catherine of Aragon.

50 Chapuys to Charles V, 19 May 1536, *Cal. SP Span.*, 5 (2), no. 55 (pp. 127–8).

51 E. W. Ives, 'Anne Boleyn and the "Entente Evangelique"', in Giry-Deloison, ed., *Deux Princes de la Renaissance*, pp. 84–7, 92–102.

52 French scriptures had been available to her during her years at the French Court, 1514–21. Warnicke, *Rise and Fall*, pp. 109–11; Ives, 'Anne Boleyn and the "Entente Evangelique"', 91–4.

53 Ellis, ed., *Orig. Letters*, 1 (2), pp. 45–6; Ives, 'Anne Boleyn and the "Entente Evangelique"', 91–2, 97–9.

54 Warnicke, *Rise and Fall*, pp. 111–13; 'The Reminiscences of John Louthe, Archdeacon of Nottingham', in Nichols, ed., *Narratives of the Reformation*, p. 56.

55 Dowling, 'Gospel and the Court', pp. 51–5; idem, 'Anne Boleyn and Reform', *JEH*, 35 (1984), 35–40; Ives, *Anne Boleyn*, pp. 303–13.

56 Warnicke, *Rise and Fall*, pp. 108–9.

57 Ives, *Anne Boleyn*, pp. 240–5.

58 Loades, *Politics of Marriage*, p. 159; Seymour, *Ordeal by Ambition*, pp. 47–8, 52–4.

59 *LP*, 11, no. 285 (p. 121).

60 Margaret was daughter of Henry's elder sister by the earl of Angus.

61 *Stats Realm*, III, p. 680.

62 D. M. Head, '"Beyng ledde and seduced by the Devyll": The Attainder of Lord Thomas Howard and the Tudor Law of Treason', *Sixteenth Century Journal*, 13, 4 (1984), 4–5, 10–16.

63 Hamilton, ed., Wriothesley, *Chronicle of England*, I, pp. 65–7.

64 Saaler, *Anne of Cleves*, pp. 78–93.

65 Weir, *Henry VIII: King and Court*, pp. 456–7; *Cal. SP Span.*, 6 (1), no. 230.

66 Ibid., 6 (2), no. 84 (p. 186).

67 Loades, *Politics of Marriage*, p. 135.

68 Kemeys and Raggatt, *Queen Who Survived*, pp. 53–8.

69 *Cal. SP Span.*, 8, no. 204.

70 Dowling, 'Gospel and the Court', pp. 60–2, 70.

71 25 Henry VIII, *c.*22, *Stats Realm*, III, pp. 471–4; Lehmberg, *Reformation Parliament*, p. 198; M. Levine, *Tudor Dynastic Problems, 1460–1571*, London, 1973, pp. 64–5; idem, 'Henry VIII's Use of his Spiritual and Temporal Jurisdictions in his Great Causes of Matrimony, Legitimacy and Succession', *HJ*, 10, 1 (1967), 5–8.

72 Ibid., 8; 28 Henry VIII, *c.*7, *Stats Realm*, 3, pp. 655–62.

73 35 Henry VIII, *c.*1, Ibid., 3, 955–8; Lehmberg, *Later Parliaments*, pp. 193–4.

74 Levine, *Tudor Dynastic Problems*, pp. 163–4; Starkey, *Personalities and Politics*, p. 159.

75 E. W. Ives, 'Henry VIII's Will: A Forensic Conundrum', *HJ*, 35, 4 (1992), 779–804; idem, 'Henry VIII's Will: The Protectorate Provisions of 1546–7', *HJ*, 37, 4 (1994), 901–11; Starkey, *Personalities and Politics*, pp. 158–67; Haigh, *English Reformations*, pp. 166–7; H. Miller, 'Henry VIII's Unwritten Will: Grants of Lands and Honours in 1547' in Ives et al., eds, *Wealth and Power*, pp. 87–96, 105; R. A. Houlbrooke, 'Henry VIII's Wills: A Comment', *HJ*, 37, 4 (1994), 891–9.

Chapter 8

The Conscience of a King

Henry VIII's idiosyncratic nature was most evident in the many variations and frequent shifts in his religious positions. Practical considerations, such as the diplomatic situation, could sometimes influence his conduct and even trigger particular actions. Nevertheless the evidence strongly suggests that shifts in his position were not mere acts of political realism or cynicism but were driven by conviction. Certainly one must raise an eyebrow about the celebrated 'divorce'. Henry first expressed doubts about the validity of his first marriage in 1527, after eighteen years in wedlock and only as his relationship with Anne Boleyn became close and intense. Yet the persistence and energy which he displayed in pursuit of his cause point to other and even stronger driving forces than love or lust.[1] When he addressed the papal legates, Wolsey and Campeggio, who sat as judges on the 'great matter' between 31 May and 23 July 1529, Henry focused on two related concerns. The first was whether or not the pope had the power to dispense marriage to a brother's wife. The actual dispensation was flawed but for Henry that was not the real issue. Such a marriage was, as stated in Leviticus, forbidden by divine law, and papal action could not set that aside. And secondly, as a consequence of this, his marriage would be without sons, thereby preventing a secure succession and putting at risk the future political stability of the kingdom. Whatever doubts there may be about the sincerity of Henry's belated discovery and acceptance of Leviticus, there is no doubt about the high priority and continuing importance which he attached to national security and stability. One essential prerequisite was an unquestioned succession which was accepted by all. This could be achieved only by the siring of sons: in 1527 Anne Boleyn was only twenty, whereas Catherine was more than twice her age: forty-two.[2]

Even before the divorce crisis and certainly before the 1530s Henry's loyalty to the papacy was not unqualified. He did not dispute papal authority, or indeed any other earthly authority, *per se*, but only when it infringed upon his. The 'Hunne affair'[3] in 1514–15, for example, provoked him to declare that he was England's king by 'the ordinance and sufferance of God' and that his royal predecessors had never had 'any superior but God alone'. He warned that 'we shall maintain the right of our crown and of our temporal jurisdiction as well in this point as in all others'. It was a clear, early statement of his sovereignty, long before the divorce crisis. At the same time he could be the dutiful Roman Catholic. His first war against France was ostensibly in the pope's defence. *Assertio Septem Sacramentorum*, his assault on Martin Luther, earned him the title *Fidei Defensor* from a publicly grateful pope. He sported the insignia of papal sword, rose and cap. Even in 1529, the year of the legatine court, he staged a *Te Deum* for the pope. But in July Campeggio referred the divorce back to Rome. By this time English scholars were rallying around Henry to publicize his 'cause', amongst them Thomas Cranmer, Edward Fox, Stephen Gardiner and John Stokesley. Supportive works rolled off the press: for example, *Gravissimae censurae* (and the English translation, *Determinations of the Universities*), which, in 1531, presented the favourable opinions of seven European universities and proceeded to deny the pope's power to dispense marriages, and *Glasse of the Truthe*, in the writing of which Henry had a modest hand. The text *Collecteana satis copiosa* went further. Not only did it justify the English resolution of Henry's divorce, as the *Glasse* had done; it also projected doctrines of royal supremacy and *imperium*. These arguments of English scholars either persuaded their king, or confirmed him in his opinion, that he wielded independent authority over Church and State.[4]

King or minister?

The king's role in the translation of these doctrines into constitutional reality and political practice has been the subject of varied interpretation, ongoing debate and disagreement. That is hardly surprising, given the major, even fundamental, changes which resulted in the English State and Church. A. F. Pollard, for example, depicted Henry as the sole architect of Reformation in the 1530s. It was a Reformation which was not doctrinal but constitutional, subordinating Church to State. Thomas Cromwell's role was restricted to 'subordinate matters'.

G. R. Elton reversed the roles of king and minister, arguing that Cromwell was, in Rosemary O'Day's paraphrase, 'the architect, the builder and the master craftsman of the English Reformation'. According to Elton,

Henry's greatness lay 'not in originality, and it is doubtful if he was the architect of anything, least of all the English Reformation'. Elton argued that Cromwell masterminded a plan which fulfilled Henry's desire for a divorce, regardless of the papacy, 'by destroying the papal power and jurisdiction in England and by creating in England an independent sovereign state'. He concluded that 'The Henrician Reformation reflects the ideas – one may say, the political philosophy – of Thomas Cromwell.'

J. J. Scarisbrick stands closer to Pollard, asserting 'that [Henry] was the true source of the really important events of his reign – the wars, the divorce, the breach with Rome'. By the time divorce became an issue, Henry had 'acquired much more confidence and control (which he never wholly surrendered thereafter)'. His minister Cromwell interpreted his will and crafted the process by which it was implemented, but Henry was the architect.[5] At about the same time, but in stark contrast, David Starkey acknowledged that Cromwell, who 'had given policy its new clarity and urgency . . . and had master-minded the parliamentary strategy of 1532', was the 'architect of the Reformation'.[6]

One thing is certain: that Henry's obsessive concern about his first marriage was the starting point of change. That does not mean that he devised the solution whereby he became supreme head of the Church in an *imperium* which acknowledged no other authority apart from God. However, the evidence suggests that, as revealed by Virginia Murphy, the idea and the drive to implement it antedated Cromwell's 'ministry'. Foxe, Gardiner, Lee, Stokesley and Henry's other writers were the men who, between 1527 and 1531, did the donkey-work of research and drafting the series of 'king's books', such as Robert Wakefield's treatise, the *Collectanea*, 'Henricus octavus', the *Gravissimae censurae* and *Glasse of the Truthe*. Henry directed the royal propaganda campaign and in some of these works he had a direct hand.[7] On one occasion this king, who so disliked heaving pen onto paper, told Anne Boleyn

that my book maketh substantially for my matter; in looking whereof I have spent above four hours this day, which caused me now to write the shorter letter to you at this time, because of some pain in my head.[8]

Such labour by a reluctant royal pen-pusher is an indication of how serious the issue was to him. In the process, the work of his writing team brought him into contact with important historical sources and with great authorities, such as St Augustine and St Ambrose.[9] As Virginia Murphy's work shows, the king's books 'allow us to follow the development of the king's thinking through the entire course of the controversy'[10] from 1527. In particular, they indicate the clear imperial and anti-papal direction of his ideas from at least 1530.[11] And from that point one can follow the practical application of his thinking, in what became known later as the Reformation Parliament.

The steps to supremacy, 1530–1534

Henry's first victim in the process of assuming papal authority was the English clergy. In the first session of the Reformation Parliament (1529) he approved measures against mortuary fees, pluralism and non-residence of clergy. Then, in July 1530, fifteen clergy, including four bishops who were amongst Catherine of Aragon's chief divorce advocates,[12] were charged with *praemunire* for acquiescing in Wolsey's exercise of his power as a papal legate.[13] When the southern convocation of the Church met, four days before parliament reassembled in January 1531, Henry demanded a subsidy of £100,000. In return he would grant to the clergy 'his generall and gracious pardon of all their trespasses of penall lawes and statutes of this Realme'.[14] In these actions Henry was probably motivated by tactical and financial needs.[15] He was willing to exploit widespread anti-clericalism in his dealings with a beleagured clergy, although there are also clear signs of a personal anti-clerical temper. There were also clear signs of clerical resistance. The Canterbury convocation presented Henry with a list of conditions upon which supply depended. Amongst them was a demand that he confirm all the ancient privileges of the English Church and a challenge to the validity of the anti-clerical acts of 1529. An impatient, aggressive king responded with a demand that convocation recognize him as 'sole protector and supreme head' with 'the cure of his subjects' souls'.[16] Henry's demands and assertions now shifted fundamentally, and the fact that he had been reading *Collectanea satis copiosa* explains why.[17]

Convocation responded by debating and, in February 1531, finally accepting a modified version of Henry's demand about his supremacy: he should be styled 'singular protector, only and supreme lord and, *as far as the law of Christ allows*, even supreme head'.[18] The qualifying clause rendered it largely meaningless. Furthermore Henry's promised statutory pardon to the clergy passed parliament before the end of the session. Meanwhile he made no progress towards a divorce at Rome. Nevertheless Henry was now thinking and talking in terms of royal supremacy and imperial authority. With a new minister at the helm, Thomas Cromwell, Henry was able to transform them from words into statutory facts in the parliamentary sessions of 1532–4. The commons' Supplication against the Ordinaries, which in 1532 attacked the freedom of clerical legislation from royal control, led the clergy to surrender its independence in the Submission of the Ordinaries. This received statutory confirmation in 1534. The act in Restraint of Appeals (1533) prevented Catherine of Aragon from appealing to the pope for a judgement on her marriage because it ended judicial connections with Rome. The act's preamble described England as 'an Impire . . . governed by oon Supreme heede and King having the Dignitie and Roiall Estate of the Imperiall Crowne of the same'.[19] In the following year further statutes transferred to the crown papal revenues (annates) and granted to the king 'as supreme head' the first year's revenue of any new incumbent in a church living and a ten per cent income tax on all clerical livings. That title of 'supreme head' was recognized as already existing, in a skilfully drafted statute, also of 1534: the king 'justely and rightfully is and oweth to be the supreme heed of the Churche of England', and he, his heirs and successors were to be 'takyn, accepted and reputed' as such. The title, powers and possessions were 'annexed and unyted to the Ymperyall Crowne of this Realme'.[20] Henry had achieved rather more than a divorce.

What was the nature of the resulting supremacy? If this is less than obvious, it is because it was 'idiosyncratic and highly personal to Henry'.[21] Although he did not go so far as to lay claim to the *potestas ordinis* – the right to minister the sacraments and other priestly powers of the ordained clergy – he did exercise the *potestas jurisdictionis* when, for example, he appointed bishops, controlled the enactment of ecclesiastical laws and, above all, confirmed or altered doctrine. In late 1537/early 1538 his enthusiastic and confident belief in his theological knowledge and understanding caused him to make extensive and frequent, though belated, amendments to *The Institution of a Christian Man* (1537). It was the product of a bishops' committee. Many of the changes in this so-called 'Bishops' Book' were incorporated in the *Necessary Doctrine and Erudition of a Christian Man*, which was published in 1543. The fact that it is known as the King's Book is an acknowledgement of Henry's careful examination of the text before it went to press.[22] Cranmer's rejection or disagreement with many of Henry's corrections may reflect the limitations of the king's theological knowledge. It could not, however, have been because Henry's doctrinal authority was only advisory. In 1540 the Act Concerning True Opinions empowered him to pronounce on doctrine without having recourse to statute.[23] To the king it must have been a statutory support for what Richard Rex calls 'his almost priestly view of his supremacy'. That extended, however, not only to doctrinal review, but also to visitations, dispensations from canon law and, by the initiative of the supreme head's chosen deputy or vicegerent, Thomas Cromwell, a planned (albeit unfulfilled) revision of the canon law.[24]

King and church: Henry's role and priorities

It has been argued that Henry had determined to 'control and manage' the English Church from the moment he became king. According to John Guy, this was simply part of a wider, ongoing early Tudor campaign against agencies and interests which impeded or constricted princely objectives and ambitions: he cites, for example, franchises and liberties, but also churchmen, the Church, appeals to Rome and 'Henry VIII's attacks on benefit of clergy and sanctuary'.[25] A statute of 1512, placing new restrictions on benefit of clergy, was obviously at variance with Pope Leo X's Lateran Council pronouncement of 1514 that even criminous clerks could not be tried in secular courts. The following year the abbot of Winchcombe's condemnation of the act, in a sermon at St Paul's Cross, provoked Henry to join in the dispute. He was at his most censorious and majestic when he summoned a conference and presided over it at Baynard's Castle. Proceedings began with the new cardinal, Wolsey, on his knees before Henry, pleading the clergy's cause but dutifully declaring that 'he would assent to nothing that would tend to annul or derogate from his royal authority for all the world'. It ended with Henry's grand pronouncement that, as king, he had no superior but God and would maintain 'the rights of our Crown and of our temporal jurisdiction'.[26]

Another of the Church's liberties, sanctuary, came under attack both in the common law courts and in the king's council between 1517 and 1522. So long as he was in royal favour and power, however, Wolsey, as minister, lord chancellor and papal legate, was able to straddle the divide, smooth ruffled feathers and ease tensions.[27] And so, before Henry's desired divorce became an issue, such matters did not result in a volatile relationship with the papacy. Relations between the monarch and pope were stable. The fact that the king exercised much control over an English Church which was, in many ways, autonomous of Rome did not strain those relations – the 'Hunne affair' must be viewed as a rare exception.[28] Henry displayed a confident willingness to approach his Holiness: for example Leo X in 1513, on behalf of the Friars Observant, and in 1513–15 for Wolsey's promotion to the cardinalcy.[29] That royal–papal relationship was of course briefly reinforced by Henry's anti-Lutheran *Assertio*. When the pope was formally presented two copies by John Clerk, he opened one and redde therof successyvely v. lefes with owt interruption. . . . His Holynes in redyng, at soche place as he lykyd (and that seemyd to be att every second line) mad ever some demonstracion, *vel nutu vel verbo*, whereby it apperyd that he had great pleasure in redyng. . . . His Holynes sayd, that he wold nott a thowght that soche a boke shold haue com from the Kyngis Grace, who hath been occapied necessarily in other feattis, seeyng that other men whiche hath occapied them selffis in stody all ther liffes, cannot bryng forth the lyke.[30]

All this vanished with the divorce issue and its resolution. In one respect, however, there was a consistent trait in Henry's relations with the Church before and after the resolution of that issue: greed. Wolsey served him well when he extracted unprecedented sums of money from the clergy, including a frequent ten per cent income tax during the 1520s and an additional payment of £118,000 by the ecclesiastical provinces in 1523. Another payment of equal amount for the clerical pardon of 1531 marked the first step in the Reformation process. It presaged the rapacious way in which Henry VIII would exploit his position as supreme head. In 1534, when payments to Rome ceased, they were replaced by first fruits and tenths: every new incumbent of a Church living had to pay his first year's income to the crown and an annual ten per cent income tax there-after. But worse was to come.

Dissolution of the monasteries

Within a few years of his recognition as supreme head, Henry had achieved not only the suppression of the 750 monasteries and convents in England and Wales and some religious houses in Ireland but also the destruction of shrines and relics. It can be argued that these pro-cesses were practical consequences of his changing position on the doc-trine of purgatory, rather than expressions of his insatiable appetite for revenue and capital assets. This was evident in his proposed alterations to the Bishops' Book in 1537/8. The injunctions of 1536 and 1538, which ordered the destruction of relics and forbade both pilgrimages and burn-ing of candles for the dead, amounted to an implicit attack on purgatory. As Cromwell was empowered to issue injunctions in his capacity as vicegerent, these may have been an expression of his own Protestant leanings. Nevertheless the King's Book, in which Henry was personally involved, was dismissive of the doctrine of purgatory.[31]

But few if any Henrician 'policies' were coherently assembled or sys-tematically and consistently implemented. The dissolution of the lesser houses in England and Wales was justified to parliament in 1536 by the 'manifest synne, vicious, carnall and abhomynable lyvyng [which] is dayly usyd and commytted' in those where the congregation numbered less than twelve. This was not presented as the first step in surpressing the entire monastic system. So the act acknowledged that in 'dyverce and greate solempne Monasteryes of this Realme . . . Religyon is right well kept and observed'. They were, however, 'destytute of suche full nombers . . . as they ought and maye kepe'. Therefore they were to supplement their numbers with such members of the suppressed houses 'as shalbe assigned and appoynted by the Kynges Highnes'. There was also a loophole in the suppression of the lesser houses, because the king was empowered to issue letters patent exempting any house from the terms of the statute. Hoyle argues that there was a consistent Henrician policy, which intended complete dissolution from the very beginning. But the government recognized that such a general assault would cause parliamentary discontent and dissent, not assent. 'Gradualism was the key.' So reform was the ostensible motive for the 1536 statute and the reason which Henry gave to the Lincolnshire rebels.[32] This does not, however, satisfactorily explain why Henry re-endowed some monasteries in 1536–7 or why as many as seventy or eighty houses, most of which had petitioned for exemption from the statute, were allowed to continue. And, whilst it was the task of Cromwell's commissioners to expose corruption, abuses and moral decay, in July 1536 they advised him about 'the nunnery of Pollesworth in the county of Warwick, wherein is an abbess named dame Alice Fitzherbert . . . a very sad, discreet, and religious woman . . . and in the same house under her rule are 12 virtuous and religious nuns'. It was their opinion that

ye might do a right good and meritorious deed to be a mediator to the King's highness for the said house to stand and remain unsuppressed, for, as we think, ye shall not speak in preferment of a better nunnery nor of better women.[33]

Such considerations justify the view that the dissolution statute of 1536 was not the first step in the execution of a preconceived plan against the monasteries. It was a professed measure of reform. It was the rebellions of 1536–7 which may have played a significant part in shifting the government's priority from reformation to termination. The articles of Lincoln, addressed to King Henry in October 1536, were central to the thinking of the rebel leader, Robert Aske. The first concerned

the suppression of so many religious houses [whereby] the service of our God is not well [performed] but also the commons of your realm unrelieved, the which as we think is a great hurt to the commonwealth and many sisters be [put] from their livings and left at large.

Similarly, in his detailed answers to his interrogators' questions, Aske emphasized that 'the suppression of abbeys was the greatest cause of the insurrection, which the hartes of the comens moste grudged at'. He went on to expound at length on the social and economic as well as spiritual importance of the religious houses to the north of England. Hoyle, however, disputes this. He argues that there is a lack of supporting evidence for Aske's assertion that monasteries occupied a special place in the north. And he concludes that opposition to the dissolution during the Pilgrimage was 'largely the result of Aske's own preoccupations'.[34] Nevertheless the active role of monks in the rebellions may have caused Henry to rethink his attitude to the monasteries. His anger was expressed to the duke of Norfolk, when he wrote to him in February 1537:

How discreetly you paint those persons that call themselves religious in the colours of their hypocrisy, and we doubt not but the further you shall wade in the investigation of their behaviours the more you shall detest the great number of them.[35]

Monks who had reoccupied monasteries during the Pilgrimage were afterwards turned out again by the duke of Norfolk, Henry's military commander against the rebels. Houses which had supported the rebels were closed. In 1537 treasonable abbots and a prior were convicted and executed and the king seized their monasteries and property. Yet even as late as July 1537, the abbot and convent surrendered Chertsey Abbey to Henry simply because 'the King intends to found anew the late monastery of Bissam, Berkshire, and establish them as abbot and convent of Bissam, and endow them with the possessions of the late monastery'.[36] Only in 1538 was there an apparent decision to end the system by means of 'voluntary' surrenders or, in cases of refusal, dissolution. That decision was confirmed when, in June 1538, Abbot Cordrey surrendered Henry's recent refoundation of Bisham. Between 1538 and 1540 the process was completed. Midway through the process, in 1539, past and future surrenders were given legal validity by the statute 31 Henry VIII c.13 and the court of augmentations was established to administer the crown's new gains. Although Henrician policies tended to develop in fits and starts and to manifest the royal characteristic of changeability, from 1538 at least this was not the case with the monasteries.[37]

It is nonetheless possible that duplicity, another Henrician characteristic, concealed an earlier determination to be rid of them all for financial reasons. A surge of anti-clericalism when Wolsey fell, at the end of the 1520s, provided a sympathetic climate of public opinion which the king could exploit. In the early thirties there were already proposals and schemes afoot to strip the Church of assets, including episcopal estates.[38] In 1536–7 Henry secured the dissolution of eight Irish monasteries. It was confirmed in an act which made no mention of reform.[39] It was another matter, however, to secure the English parliament's assent to dissolution. A measure to strengthen the crown's finances by the transfer of ecclesiastical wealth may have failed in 1534. A more acceptable reason was needed. In 1535–6, two roaming commissions compiled a comprehensive survey of ecclesiastical resources, the *Valor Ecclesiasticus*, and visited all religious houses. By the time parliament met again, in 1536, the government was fully informed on the monasteries' wealth and it had assembled, for propaganda purposes, an often distorted, exaggerated, unreliable picture of immoral and corrupt monastic communities. This justified the Dissolution Act of 1536. The clause allowing for the reprieve of smaller houses which were not corrupt seemed to confirm that reform was the motive. As already noted above, some were duly reprieved, indeed as many as a quarter or a half of the 453 houses affected by this act. Most of these reprieves, however, were not granted but simply sold, often for very large sums of money. Thereafter the government dealt individually with religious houses, securing their 'voluntary' surrenders by contract. In 1539 parliament was asked not to dissolve the larger monasteries but, to a large extent, simply to acknowledge and confirm what had happened. So the second bill of dissolution was enacted into law. If the ongoing motive was money, as argued cogently and most recently by Hoyle, it illustrates Henry's capacity for duplicity. He later advised the Scots that, if they planned to dissolve monasteries, they should conceal their real intentions and tell the public that reform was their purpose. In 1539 parliament not only legitimized Henry's acquisition of the larger religious houses; it also authorized him to create much-needed new bishoprics, which would obviously be funded from his newly acquired wealth. In this way dissolution and reform were publicly linked. The implication is that Henry would practise what he preached. Indeed he personally drafted a plan for fourteen new sees funded from the income of twenty dissolved abbeys.[40] The end-result, characteristically, was just six new dioceses,[41] each with the income of one abbey.

In the decision to dissolve, as in most matters, Henry's motives cannot be taken for granted. His shift away from purgatory and therefore prayers for the dead lessened the value of monasteries. He seems to have been unimpressed by their spiritual condition. During the 1530s he feared them as potential foci of resistance to the royal supremacy. And then there is the financial motive. As so often, opinions on Henry are divided. There is the confident assertion, with a conclusive ring: '[I]t is generally accepted that, for Henry at least, money was the main motive.' On the other hand, there is the more qualified assessment: 'Whether the King's motives were partly religious or wholly fiscal cannot be concluded from the surviving evidence.'[42] One thing is certain: Henry was a greedy, rapacious king, who coveted wealth and power, and the acquisition of the religious houses augmented both. But, at the same time, the effects were damaging, in some respects disastrous. The widespread destruction of magnificent buildings, the plundering and dispersal of artworks and libraries were 'acts of licensed vandalism'.[43] The dissolution missed great educational opportunities. Henry's creation of a few colleges and some regius professorships is understandable, because they commemorated his name and signalled to future generations that here was a great royal patron of learning and education. They certainly did not compensate for the damage done and the losses incurred by the dissolution.[44]

Then, in 1545, parliament empowered Henry to dissolve colleges and chantries whenever he chose. Although it accorded with Henry's current convictions, because the prime function of chantries – prayers for the dead – rested on his discarded belief in purgatory, the purpose of this dissolution act was to provide a financial life-line for a king burdened with the enormous costs of his current wars. At the same time, however, it constituted a major threat to the universities. Dr Richard Cox warned Secretary Paget that, around the king, '[there] is such a number of importune wolves that be able to devour colleges, chantries, cathedral churches, universities ... and a thousand times as much'.[45] Fortunately Catherine Parr, Sir Thomas Smith who was the new Cambridge professor of civil law, and others interceded with the king. He responded favourably, the universities were spared and, not long after, he died without fully implementing the terms of the statute.[46] Nevertheless, by 1547 almost a quarter (34 of about 140) of the secular colleges in England and Wales had been dissolved.[47]

We may deplore such short-sighted royal greed. Later Tudor generations, however, looked back on Henry with different perspective and priorities from the modern historian. Queen Elizabeth's godson, Sir John Harington, recorded: 'The Monks Hymn to Saunte Satan, chauntede daily in their cells, till goodlie Kynge Henry spoyled their singing.'[48] The Protestant John Hooper, martyred in 1555, condemned idolatrous images. Citing the idols of Walsingham, Canterbury and Hales Abbey in

Gloucestershire, he wrote that 'They flourished most a little before their desolation in the reign of the king's majesty that dead is, Henry the VIII, of a blessed memory.'[49]

Religious change and Henry's relations with Erasmian humanism

Hooper's reflection is a reminder that Henry was also unconvinced, even sceptical, about pilgrimages to shrines, many of which were housed in monasteries. As befitted a monarch, he gave money or paid for candles on the traditional religious festivals. He also made routine offerings at shrines whilst on summer progress or other travels. In his earlier years as king he even journeyed for that specific purpose. After the birth of his son Prince Henry in January 1511, he went to the priory of Our Lady at Walsingham in Norfolk in order to give thanks. The young king walked the last mile barefooted and lit candles at the shrine, but such public displays of Christian devotion were not repeated.[50] Indeed during the 1530s shrines and relics, like the monasteries which often housed them, became targets of royal hostility. In 1536 Vicegerent Cromwell's injunctions prohibited pilgrimages. Further injunctions in 1538 ordered the clergy that in sermons, at least four times each year, they were to instruct their hearers

not to repose their trust . . . in wandering to pilgrimages, offering of money, candles or tapers to images or relics, or kissing or licking the same. . . . That such feigned images as ye know of in any of your cures to be so abused with pilgrimages or offerings . . . ye shall, for avoiding of that most detestable sin of idolatry, forthwith take down. [They were to admonish their parishioners that] if they abuse [images] for any other intent than for remembrances, they commit idolatry . . . to the great danger of their souls; and therefore the king's highness, graciously tendering the weal of his subjects' souls, hath in part already, and more will hereafter, travail for the abolishing of such images.[51]

The supreme head was as good as his vicegerent's word. A vigorous campaign of iconoclasm destroyed many images and exposed some frauds in the process. At Boxley in Kent there was

found, in the Roode of Grace, which has been had in great veneration, certain engines and old wire, with old rotten sticks in the back of the same, which caused the eyes to move and stir in the head thereof, like unto a lively thing, and also the nether lip in likewise to move as though it should speak.

The Rood was brought to Court, where it 'performed' before the king. It was reported that Henry 'hardly knew whether more to rejoice in the exposure or to grieve at the long deception'. Other images were brought to London and publicly burnt, amongst them Our Lady of Walsingham at Chelsea in July 1538.[52] The annotations which Henry made in his personal psalter in the 1540s reveal an ongoing pride in his successful efforts to destroy shrines, relics and images.[53] Even so, it is characteristic of inconstant Henry that the King's Book was much more traditionalist on such matters.[54]

This could be seen, together with the destruction of monasteries and the end of pilgrimages, as a shift in Henry's religious stance along Erasmian reform lines. In one other respect, with possible doctrinal implications, Catholic Henry changed his views, and that was in relation to the vernacular scriptures. Although in the 1520s, during the years following the *Assertio*, he was hostile to heresy, he made various promises and predictions that an English translation would be produced at some future date. This was in harmony with the position of both humanists and evangelicals. Their motives, however, differed. Erasmus, Starkey and other humanists pursued Christianity as 'as a way of life', not 'a set of doctrines'.[55] The vernacular Bible would reshape people's lives and so alter the world. The prime evangelical concern was, in contrast, a spiritual one: access to God through the scriptures would bring repentance and redemption.[56] The case for translation was pushed in the 1530s, for example by Robert Wyer's publication of Erasmus's two *Exhortacyons* on the scriptures (1533–4) and Cromwell's letters to bishops and curates (1539). Henry moved in the same direction when he finally authorized the Great Bible in English. When it was published in 1540, Cranmer's prologue stated its value in humanistic terms: that princes would learn how to govern, husbands how to treat their wives and educate their children, and subjects, wives, children and servants how to learn their duty. In brief 'all manner of persons . . . may in this book learn all things'.[57]

The religious king and the middle way

The goals of humanism and evangelicalism were different. In Maria Dowling's words, 'the former was concerned to reform abuses, the latter to refashion dogma'. At the same time evangelicals were equipped by humanists with the necessary 'linguistic skills and biblical studies of the new learning'.[58] Henry's second wife, Anne, favoured access to the Bible and extended her patronage to Cranmer, Edward Crome, Hugh Latimer and other evangelicals. And throughout the thirties Cranmer and Cromwell promoted the evangelical cause. After the latter's fall in 1540, the evangelicals experienced turbulent, even bloody times during Henry's last years. But the fall of the conservatives in 1546–7 set the stage for an evangelical triumph – though whether this was by royal design or accident is a debatable matter.

Although Henry's thinking changed, there is no clear evidence that he became a convert to European reformed religion. The negotiations with the Protestant Schmalkaldic League for a political alliance in the 1530s and early 1540s extended to discussion and even draft of a common confession of faith for England and the Lutheran princes. Despite the act of Six Articles in 1539,[59] negotiations continued intermittently and as late as 1545–6. In the mid-thirties an English delegation was sent to open negotiations with Luther. It did not, however, amount to a formal public rejection of the *Assertio*. Nor can it be determined how serious Henry was about adoption of a Lutheran confession. Diplomatic manoeuvring against his European rivals, especially when he felt under military threat, is the probable explanation for his overtures here, and he remained unpersuaded by the European reformers and their beliefs. Furthermore he was not simply a secular-minded monarch who valued religion only as a political or diplomatic tool. Henry declared that a man's conscience 'is the highest and supreme court for judgement or justice'[60] and his conscience was the engine of direct action against heretics and traitors. He was active in persecution of Protestants: 22 anabaptists, for example, were burnt in June 1535; Robert Barnes, who had served Henry as a diplomat in the 1530s, died in the fire with two other active reformers, Thomas Garret and William Jerome, on 30 July 1540; and two days earlier Thomas Cromwell had been executed for treason and heresy. In June 1546 Anne Askew was convicted of heresy, taken to the Tower 'and their sett on the racke, where she was sore tormented'. On 12 July she was conveyed to Blackfriars, 'from thence carried in a chaire to Newgate' and four days later burned in Smithfield.[61]

Henry was personally involved in the persecution of Protestants. Foxe, the martyrologist, recounted the staging of the trial of John Lambert, on 16 November 1538:

[T]he king himself did come as judge of that great controversy, with a great guard, clothed all in white, as covering, by that colour and dissembling, severity of all bloody judgement.

Cromwell described Henry's role:

[T]he Kings Majestie, for the Reverence of the Holy Sacrament of th'Altar, did sitt openly in his Hall, and there presided at the Disputacion, Processe and Jugement of a myserable Heretick Sacramentary. [I]t was a wonder to see how Princely, withe howe excellent gravite and inestimable Majeste, his Highenes exercised there the very Office of a Supreme Hed of his Churche of Englande; how benigenely his Grace assayed to converte the miserable man: how strong and manifeste Reasons his Highenes alledged against him.

Viscount Lisle's servant, John Husee, added further detail:

The King's Majesty reasoned with [Lambert] in person, sundry times confounding him, so that he alone would have been sufficient to confute a thousand such.

Was this an example of the supreme head's concern for the spiritual welfare of one of his subjects? Or was it merely another exercise in image projection? Husee wrote,

It was not a little rejoicing unto all his commons and to all others that saw how his Grace handled the matter; for it shall be a precedent whilst the world stands.

Cromwell wished that

the Princes and Potentats of Christendom had a meate place for them there, to have seen it. Undoubtedly they shuld have moche merveilled at his Majestyes most highe Wisedome & Jugement, and reputed him none otherwise . . . then (in manner) than the Mirroer and Light of alle other Kings & Princes in Christendome.

This, no doubt, was the image which Henry wished to project.[62]

The king was equally active and brutal, but even more ruthless, in the pursuit of Roman Catholics who would not accept the royal supremacy: not only Sir Thomas More and Bishop Fisher of Rochester, but the Lincolnshire rebels and Pilgrims of Grace, Carthusians and other obstinate monks,[63] and Elizabeth Barton, the Holy Maid of Kent, who was executed in 1534 for prophesying that the king would die within a month of marrying Anne Boleyn. Such people, who adhered to the papal supremacy, were technically traitors, especially after the act of 1534 declaring it to be treason to 'malicyously' deny the king's title.[64] Nevertheless it was a religious issue. So Henry walked his religious 'middle way' as he impartially persecuted and destroyed those papists who denied his supremacy and those Protestant heretics who rejected doctrines of his Church. In a gruesome and cynical manner he publicly exhibited that middle way when, on 30 July 1540, three pairs of papists and Protestants were burned together. The public response, one of disgust and horror, did not deter him.[65]

Henry's religion was a powerful and ongoing force, even if his positions on particular points of doctrine sometimes shifted or fluctuated. He was a pious king who frequently heard masses. He touched for the 'King's Evil' and his recorded privy purse expenses include entries for standard payments of seven shillings and sixpence to two, four or five 'pouer people', 'yong Children' or women. As the entries indicate, he often performed this function, as God's anointed, whilst on his travels, for example at Windsor, the More, Woodstock and, in 1532, at Calais, where money was 'paied to a chielde that the king heled of his sikenes'.[66] Also Henry's love of learning was directed particularly towards theological studies. He may have had an inflated opinion of his personal theological knowledge and skills, and his corrections to the work of others were sometimes 'inept', pedantic or displayed limited understanding.[67] His enthusiasm and dedication, however, cannot be questioned. Although he had help in the production of the *Assertio*, there is no doubt that he was personally involved in the writing. More than once Erasmus attested to this. In 1522 he wrote:

I have never had any doubts that the book by his Majesty . . . was fashioned by the intelligence of the same man whose name it bears, by his own bow and spear as the saying goes.

He reiterated this seven years later:

Although I would not assert that he received no assistance in their composition, as others, even the most learned, do on similar occasions, I am sure that he is both parent and author of those things which go under his name.[68]

As noted earlier, Henry also had a hand in propagandist writings in favour of his divorce in the later 1520s. One of these may have been *Henricus octavus* in 1528; another was *Glasse of the Truthe*. He scrutinized the major works of the later thirties and early forties, such as the Bishops' Book (1537) and the King's Book (1543), and produced a final draft of the Six Articles (1539). Of course Henry had lapses. He could and sometimes did tire quickly, cast down the pen and leave work unfinished. Despite pressure for his approval before the Bishops' Book went to press, he did not scrutinize it until later. Although the statute for Submission of the Clergy (1534) and other acts of 1536 and 1544 provided for revision of the canon law, nothing was done. This may seem predictable, when the Church had a supreme head with a distaste for writing and a preference for passing the printed word on to others. Yet, as Virginia Murphy has shown, much came from his pen in 1527–32, he did annotate and alter the Bishops' Book at length after its publication, and he had a hand in the drafting or extensive 'correction' of other texts in the thirties or forties: a picture of a theological enthusiast rather than of a lazy king.[69]

This was all part of a balancing act, especially during his years as supreme head. He needed to assume, whether sincerely or not, an impartial posture which gratified, or at least placated, the more traditional Catholicism, the humanist desire for improvement and the Protestant desire for doctrinal and other change. This was no mean feat, because he was under pressure, at times influence, of rival religious factions, whilst diplomatic considerations could also have an impact on this inconstant, wayward princely mind. At the same time that balancing act did reveal shifts in his personal religious position. These were evident in the statements of doctrine which were issued during his years as supreme head. The Ten Articles, drafted by Convocation in 1536 and published by Henry's authority, omitted four of the sacraments as Luther had done. They were not, however, meant to be a comprehensive formulary of faith for the English Church, now freed from the papal yoke. The limited purpose was to clarify and resolve points of dispute. So prayers for the dead were approved, implying a continued acceptance of purgatory. It soon became clear that a comprehensive and detailed statement of belief was necessary. When, in 1537, a committee of bishops, archdeacons and university scholars produced the *Institution of a Christian Man* (or Bishops' Book), they made some concessions to Lutheranism. It was structured as a series of homilies, designed to influence the faith of congregations in the 'right' direction. This reveals the hands of Cranmer and Cromwell, not of Henry. The king certainly ordered that portions of the book should be delivered as homilies, but he had read only part of it, and that hastily, when it was released.[70]

The next statement of faith, the Six Articles, was a more accurate indicator of Henry's position. He had been moving towards this settlement for some time, spurred on by the 1538 treaty of Nice between the French and Habsburg Catholic Princes and by the disturbing spread of heresy in England. Henry needed national unity and a European demonstration that he too was an orthodox Catholic. He was helped by conservative councillors in the formulation of the six orthodox articles of 'God's law' – transubstantiation, communion in one kind, clerical celibacy, vows of chastity, private masses and auricular confession. One of the conservatives, the duke of Norfolk, also introduced them to parliament in 1539. Nevertheless in proclamations of 1538–9 Henry had already declared in favour of most of the Six Articles, which were clearly a statement of his innate conservatism.[71] His careful supervision of their affirmation by parliamentary enactment, his detailed editing of the draft bill and the harsh penalties for non-observance – ranging from burning for heresy to execution for felony – attest to that conservatism, even though he did make one concession to evangelicals: that the sacrament of auricular confession was merely 'expedient'. And, as Glyn Redworth concludes, whilst the statute was a victory for conservative councillors, 'as a matter of high policy, it was the king's achievement'.[72]

The Six Articles were the first step towards a comprehensive statement of belief to replace the Bishops' Book. Belatedly, after its public release, Henry worked through the book thoroughly and in the process annotated his copy extensively. Many of his amendments were incorporated in the much more Catholic successor to the Bishops' Book, the *Necessary Doctrine and Erudition for any Christian Man* (or King's Book). The one exception to its conservatism was the way in which it reflected Henry's growing disbelief in purgatory.

In one respect there was no ongoing sense of equilibrium and that was in Henry's relations with the clergy. Great nobles, such as the dukes of Norfolk and Suffolk, whose displacement by Cardinal Wolsey had fuelled their own anti-clericalism, encouraged his increasingly aggressive stance towards them. This manifested itself early in the 1530s, at a time when the clergy were exposed to lay hostility in the Reformation Parliament. In 1531 the king accused them of exercising a separate jurisdiction in the kingdom. Despite a purchased pardon and clerical resistance, it has been earlier noted that in 1534–5 the clergy surrendered and recognized their allegiance only to Henry as king and supreme head. Henry's anti-clericalism also figured in his theological rethinking on the status of the clergy, whilst he remained obdurate about the continuance of clerical celibacy. It was evident too in his willingness to strip down episcopal assets by ostensibly 'voluntary' surrenders of estates, in return for crown lands of lesser value and, increasingly in the 1540s, rectories and spiritual dues. He also condoned the extraction of episcopal estates by peers and gentry, again on the basis of land exchange.[73]

It is ironic that one of the first targets of this acquisitive anti-clerical policy was Archbishop Cranmer,[74] who, in accordance with a statute of 1536, surrendered Mortlake and Wimbledon manors near London in return for monastic property. Cranmer was, after all, Henry's Reformation archbishop, his personal choice, one of his staunchest supporters in the divorce cause from 1529 onwards, defender of the royal supremacy, and one who approved of Henry's policy of balance and compromise, designed to achieve unity. However, the break with Rome and the establishment of the royal supremacy bred religious division, which introduced a new, vicious and bloody element into the competitive norm of Court politics. Even Cranmer was in danger of becoming one of its victims when in 1543, for example, 'the prebendaries and certeyn gentilmen of Kente' complained to Henry of 'the doctrine by hym and his chaplens tawghte in Kente'. The king's response, as he cruised one night in his barge on the Thames, was to call Cranmer aboard, 'saying unto hym merily, "Ah, my chaplen, I have newis for you: I knowe nowe who is the gretest heretique in Kente"'. Thereupon he produced the written accusation, signed by prebendaries and justices, against the archbishop and his chaplains. When Cranmer asked the king to appoint commissioners who would investigate the charges, he replied,

Marye, so will I doo; for I have suche affiaunce and confidence in your fidelitie, that I will committ th'examination herof wholie unto you, and suche as you will appoynt.[75]

When the hardline Catholics on the privy council sought Cranmer's removal to the Tower, Henry once again played political games. He authorized the council to summon the archbishop next day and, if they saw cause, to commit him. But that night, at about 11 p.m., he sent for Cranmer, warning him of what was to come. If the councillors refused to have his accusers brought to face him and they attempted to commit him, 'then appele you frome them to our person, and geve to them this rynge'. On the next day the charade was duly played out. Cranmer was called into the privy council and told that, because the king had received complaints that he and his subordinates 'had infected the hole realme with heresie', he was to be examined in the Tower before trial. When the archbishop produced the king's ring, Lord Russell 'sware a greate othe and saied, "Did not I tell you, my lordes, what wolde come of this matter?"'[76] This was a classic example of Henry the game-player, who took particular pleasure in humiliating or deflating self-important subjects.

Roles, images and iconography

Henry was very conscious of his special relationship with God, not only as king and his anointed lieutenant but also, from 1534, as 'supreme hedd of this his Realme of Englande immediatly under God'.[77] The king's conviction that his supremacy was God-given was expressed in his increasing identification with King David. His Latin psalter, illuminated for him by the Frenchman Jean Mallard, who had been Francis I's Court poet, merged the Old Testament king and the Renaissance monarch, both warriors, into one. When Holbein designed the title page for the Coverdale English Bible (1535), he depicted Henry flanked by David and Paul and holding both sword and scriptures. John King shows how this was designed to create an image of the Tudor monarch 'as a theocratic ruler capable of unifying ecclesiastical and secular authority'. Although the Coverdale Bible was not authorized by Henry, the Great Bible (1539) was published under his patronage. The title page of this first authorized English translation portrays the king in the same unifying role. He is depicted directly receiving 'the word of God' (*Verbum Dei*) and handing it to both his archbishop, Cranmer, and his minister and vicegerent, Cromwell.[78] Although there is no image of David, God is shown choosing Henry as another David, in order to 'govern over England as a new Israel'. So the Old Testament king is 'subsumed' into the Renaissance king.[79]

Conclusion

Hampton Court maze is much easier to negotiate than Henry's conscience. Historians have used a variety of terms to describe his position and policies: for example idiosyncratic, inconstant, unpredictable and impenetrable. Furthermore his mind was on the move. In the 1530s he acknowledged that he had changed since the *Assertio*. The king who heard mass several times daily astounded Cranmer in August 1546, when he announced his intention to reach an agreement with the king of France for changing 'the mass in both the realms into a communion'.[80] When Bishop Tunstal defended the traditional significance of auricular confession, Henry weighed in with an angry and, for him, a very lengthy letter.[81] Not only purgatory but pilgrimages and creeping to the cross were all rejected. It might be argued too that Henry looked to more dramatic change in the future when he entrusted the education of his heir, Prince Edward, to Roger Ascham, John Cheke, Richard Cox and William Grindal, all humanists of evangelical sympathy. Sir Anthony Denny, first gentleman of the privy chamber, increasingly in favour with Henry in his last years and also a reformer, was influential in their choice.

On the other hand, there is no reason to believe that these tutors were advanced by Denny for any reason other than their educational talents. There is no indication that they had, as yet, a strong evangelical commitment. And, if they had, they would not have paraded it before their conservative king. Just as well, because he was not a Protestant. Despite his intermittent negotiations with German Lutheran princes at Wittenberg, during the 1530s and early 1540s, Henry was never a Lutheran and he could never be persuaded to accept Luther's central tenet, justification by faith alone. Scarisbrick neatly summed up his religion as 'a highly personal admixture of new and old. Henry was his own theologian.'[82] There was, however, embedded in this diversity one consistent belief and unswerving aim: unity. Henry's insistence on uniformity and the punishment of nonconformity were directed to that end. So was the speech which he delivered to parliament on its prorogation in 1545. It was a masterful solo performance and swansong, in which he lamented,

I se[e] and he[a]re daily that you of the Clergy preache one against another, teache one contrary to another, inueigh one against another without Charity or discrecion. Some be too styff in their old Mumpsimus, other[s] be too busy and curious in their new Sumpsimus. . . . I am very sorry to knowe and he[a]re how unreuerently that moste precious [jewel], the worde of God, is disputed, r[h]ymed, sung, and [j]angled in every Alehouse and Taverne, contrary to the true meaninge and Doctrine of the same.[83]

As members 'watered their plants', a tearful king and supreme head made a plea for unity in what turned out to be his farewell parliamentary performance.

Notes

1 D. MacCulloch, 'The Religion of Henry VIII', in Starkey, ed., *A European Court*, p. 160.

2 V. Murphy, 'The Literature and Propaganda of Henry VIII's First Divorce', in MacCulloch, ed., *Politics, Policy and Piety*, pp. 147–50.

3 See above, Chap. 2, p. 19 and Chap. 6, p. 108.

4 D. MacCulloch, 'Henry VIII and the Reform of the Church', in idem, ed., *Politics, Policy and Piety*, p. 165; J. Guy, 'Thomas Cromwell and the Intellectual Origins of the Henrician Revolution', in idem, ed., *Tudor Monarchy*, pp. 216–19, 222–4.

5 G. R. Elton, 'King or Minister? The Man behind the Henrician Reformation', in idem, *Studies*, I, pp. 187–8; R. O'Day, *The Debate on the English Reformation*, London, 1986, pp. 106–11, 119; 128–30; Scarisbrick, *Henry VIII*, p. 46.

6 Starkey, *Personalities and Politics*, pp. 107, 125.

7 Murphy, 'Literature and Propaganda', pp. 138–58.

8 Byrne, ed., *Letters of Henry VIII*, p. 82.

9 J. Guy, 'Thomas Cromwell and Intellectual Origins', in idem, ed., *Tudor Monarchy*, pp. 215–16.

10 Murphy, 'Literature and Propaganda', p. 136.

11 Such thinking is evident at a much earlier date. When Henry captured Tournai in 1513, he claimed both spiritual and temporal sovereignty over it 'even against the pope'. T. F. Mayer, 'On the Road to 1534: The Occupation of Tournai and Henry VIII's Theory of Sovereignty', in Hoak, ed., *Tudor Political Culture*, pp. 13–14, 16–19, 22–5.

12 J. Guy, 'Henry VIII and the Praemunire Manoeuvres of 1530–1531', *EHR*, 384 (July 1982), 482–5; J. J. Scarisbrick, 'The Pardon of the Clergy, 1531', *CHJ*, 12 (1956), 25–6.

13 *Praemunire* had been developed in the fourteenth century in order to protect the king's regal power against any encroachment by papal authority.

14 *LP*, 4 (3), 6047 (3); Guy, 'Henry VIII and Praemunire Manoeuvres', 488.

15 For the debate on Henry's motives, see: Guy, 'Henry VIII and Praemunire Manoeuvres'; G. W. Bernard, 'The Pardon of the Clergy Reconsidered'; Guy, 'A Reply'; and Bernard, 'A Comment', *JEH*, 37, 2 (April 1986), 258–87.

16 Guy, 'Henry VIII and Praemunire Manoeuvres', 494–5.

17 Ibid., pp. 495–6; see above, p. 147.

18 Guy, 'Henry VIII and Praemunire Manoeuvres', 498–9.

19 24 Henry VIII, *c.*12, *Stats Realm*, III, pp. 427–9.

20 25 Henry VIII, *c.*20 and 26 Henry VIII, *c.*1, *Stats Realm*, III, pp. 462–4, 492.

21 D. Loades, *Revolution in Religion: The English Reformation, 1530–1570*, Cardiff, 1992, p. 9.

22 Scarisbrick, *Henry VIII*, pp. 404–17.

23 32 Henry VIII, *c.*26; R. Rex, *Henry VIII and the English Reformation*, London, 1993, pp. 156–7; Lehmberg, *Later Parliaments*, pp. 120–1.

24 Ibid., pp. 56–7.

25 Fox and Guy, *Reassessing the Henrician Age*, pp. 174–5

26 Gwyn, *King's Cardinal*, pp. 46–50; *LP*, 2 (1), no. 1313 (pp. 352–3).

27 S. J. Gunn, *Early Tudor Government, 1485–1558*, London, 1995, pp. 170–1.

28 See above, Chap. 2, p. 19, Chap. 6, p. 108 and Chap. 8, p. 147.

29 Ellis, ed., *Orig. Letters*, I (1), pp. 165–8; *LP*, 1, nos 3304, 3497.

30 Ellis, ed., *Orig. Letters*, I (1), pp. 258–9.

31 MacCulloch, 'Henry VIII and Reform', pp. 161, 177.

32 27 Henry VIII, *c.*28, *Stats Realm*, III, pp. 575–8; R. W. Hoyle, 'The Origins of the Dissolution of the Monasteries', *HJ*, 38, 2 (1995), 275–82, 286–9, 291–300; MacCulloch, 'Henry VIII and Reform', p. 174.

33 Williams, ed., *Eng. Hist. Docs*, V, p. 783; E. M. Hallam, 'Henry VIII's Monastic Re-foundations of 1536–7 and the Course of the Dissolution', *BIHR*, 51 (1978), 124–5, 129–31.

34 M. Bateson, ed., 'Aske's Examination', *EHR*, 5 (1890), 558, 561–2; Hoyle, *Pilgrimage of Grace*, pp. 48–50, 455.

35 *LP*, 12 (1), no. 479.

36 Ibid., 12 (2), no. 220; Rex, *Henry VIII and English Reformation*, pp. 62–5.

37 Rex, *Henry VIII and English Reformation*, pp. 65–7; *LP*, 13 (1), no. 1218; *Stats Realm*, III, pp. 733–9.

38 Hoyle, 'Origins of Dissolution', 284–94.

39 B. Bradshaw, *The Dissolution of the Religious Orders in Ireland under Henry VIII*, Cambridge, 1974, pp. 70–4.

40 Hoyle, 'Origins of Dissolution', 290–301; Strype, *Eccles. Mems*, 1 (2), p. 406.

41 Bristol, Chester, Gloucester, Oxford, Peterborough and Westminster.

42 P. Servini, 'Henry VIII: The Reformation', in Lotherington, ed., *Tudor Years*, p. 101; Loades, *Revolution in Religion*, p. 25; G. W. Bernard, 'The Piety of Henry VIII', in N. Scott Amos, A. Pettegree and Henk van Nierop, eds, *The Education of a Christian Society: Humanism and the Reformation in Britain and the Netherlands*, Aldershot, 1999, pp. 66–74.

43 Guy, *Tudor England*, p. 148.

44 Scarisbrick, *Henry VIII*, pp. 516–21.

45 12 Oct. 1546, *LP*, 21 (2), no. 260.

46 Scarisbrick, *Henry VIII*, pp. 519–20.

47 J. J. Scarisbrick, 'Henry VIII and the Dissolution of the Secular Colleges', in Cross et al., eds, *Law and Government*, pp. 58–9.

48 T. Park, ed., Sir John Harington's *Nugae Antiquae*, 2 vols, London, 1804, 1, p. 14.

49 S. Carr, ed., *Early Writings of John Hooper*, Parker Society, Cambridge, 1843, pp. 40–1.

50 See above, Chap. 4, p. 56; Bernard, 'Piety of Henry VIII', pp. 74–6.

51 Guy, *Tudor England*, pp. 178–9; R. Whiting, 'Local Responses to the Henrician Reformation', in MacCulloch, ed., *Politics, Policy and Piety*, pp. 215–20; Douglas, ed., *Eng. Hist. Docs*, V, p. 812; E. Duffy, *The Stripping of the Altars: Traditional Religion in England 1400–1580*, New Haven, 1992, pp. 381, 383–6, 402–4.

52 *LP*, 13 (1), no. 231; Anglo, *Spectacle*, pp. 273–4.

53 MacCulloch, 'Henry VIII and Reform', pp. 177–8.

54 At the same time it was markedly more radical in its hostility to prayers for the dead and purgatory. Duffy, *Stripping of the Altars*, pp. 442–3.

55 Gordon Rupp cit. J. F. McDiarmid, 'Humanism, Protestantism and English Scripture, 1533–40', *Journal of Medieval and Renaissance Studies*, 14 (1984), 124.

56 Ibid., 123–35.

57 Ibid., 123–5,127–9.

58 Dowling, 'Gospel and the Court', p. 38.

59 See below, pp. 162–3.

60 Byrne, ed., *Letters of Henry VIII*, p. 86.

61 Hamilton, ed., Wriothesley, *Chronicle of England*, I, pp. 167–70.

62 Pratt, ed., Foxe, *Acts and Monuments*, V, p. 229; British Library, Harleian MS 282, fol. 217; *LP*, 13 (2) nos 851, 924.

63 L. E. Whatmore, *The Carthusians under King Henry the Eighth*, Salzburg, 1983, pp. 81–6, 94–7, 142–3, 211.

64 26 Henry VIII, *c.*13.

65 Rex, *Henry VIII and Religious Reformation*, p. 165.

66 *Privy Purse Expences*, pp. 16, 20, 37, 40, 46, 156, 160–4, 170, 221, 225, 243, 249, 253, 264, 272, 278; see above, pp. 31–2.

67 Scarisbrick, *Henry VIII*, pp. 405–6.

68 Mynors et al., eds, *Correspondence of Erasmus*, 9, no. 1313, p. 181; *LP*, 4 (3), no. 5412.

69 Scarisbrick, *Henry VIII*, pp. 403–4; Murphy, 'Literature and Propaganda', pp. 138–52.

70 MacCulloch, *Thomas Cranmer*, pp. 185–93, 205–7.

71 P. L. Hughes and J. F. Larkin, eds, *Tudor Royal Proclamations*, 3 vols, New Haven, 1964–9, I, nos 186, 188, 191.

72 G. Redworth, 'A Study in the Formulation of Policy: The Genesis and Evolution of the Act of Six Articles', *JEH*, 37, 1 (Jan. 1986), 45–67; Dowling, 'Gospel and the Court', 58; MacCulloch, 'Henry VIII and Reform', pp. 174–5; idem, *Thomas Cranmer*, pp. 252–3.

73 F. Heal, *Of Prelates and Princes*, Cambridge, 1980, pp. 107–25.

74 The other was the see of Norwich; 27 Henry VIII, *c.*34 and 45.

75 Secretary Ralph Morice's Anecdotes in Nichols, ed., *Narratives*, pp. 251–3.

76 Ibid., pp. 254–7.

77 Act extinguishing the authority of the bishop of Rome, 28 Henry VIII, *c.*10, *Stats Realm*, III, p. 663.

78 See above, Chapter 3, p. 34; J. N. King, 'The Royal Image, 1535–1603', in Hoak, ed., *Tudor Political Culture*, pp. 104–11; idem, 'Henry VIII as David', in Herman, ed., *Rethinking the Henrician Era*, pp. 78–84.

79 King, 'The Royal Image', pp. 110–11; Tudor-Craig, 'Henry VIII and King David', p. 193.

80 MacCulloch, *Thomas Cranmer*, p. 357.

81 Byrne, ed., *Letters of Henry VIII*, pp. 256–9.

82 Scarisbrick, *Henry VIII*, p. 417.

83 Hall, fols 261v–262.

Chapter 9

The Dreams and Costs of Glory

King Henry VIII sought to 'cut a dash' in the early modern political world. A key consideration here is to what extent he did so in pursuit of coherent objectives.[1] One consistent priority was his honour, which, as he told Francis I in 1544, 'we have hitherto guarded and will not have stained in our old age'.[2] Apart from this, however, it is difficult to find anything else consistent in either principle or practice. A. F. Pollard's representation of a coherent policy in pursuit of claims in Ireland, Scotland and France is highly questionable, if not unacceptable.[3] Henry's relations with his British neighbours and Continental powers did not constitute a long-term co-ordinated policy, but consisted rather of expressions of his own ego and *ad hoc* responses to changing political circumstances.

The first of these, ego-fulfilment, is summed up by Scarisbrick, who sees Henry's acquisition of the royal supremacy as an 'addition to his collection of trophies by a man always greedy for new titles'.[4] As a secular Prince he sought diadems rather than dominions, titles rather than territories. He revived the old English claim to the French crown. When Francis I became Emperor Charles V's captive in 1525, Henry attempted to exploit the situation to his advantage. His envoys were instructed to propose to Charles a joint invasion of France and to remind the emperor of his right to the French crown 'by just title of inheritance'. Yet, though he laid specific claim to his Angevin inheritance from the beginning of his reign, they were also to inform Charles that he would even be satisfied with just Normandy *or* Picardy and a few towns, so long as he got the crown.[5] In an age of personal monarchy, foreign policy was about the ego of individual monarchs and relations between them rather than about national interests. The high priority attached to honour, for example, was 'one crucial respect in which high ideals and Henry's sense of his own virtuous self-image fed naturally and directly into politics'. The English king's preference for an alliance with the much more powerful Emperor

Charles, rather than with the French king, exemplifies the personal rival-ries between rulers. The particular rivalry between Henry and Francis provoked what Greg Walker calls the 'heroic posturings behind much of English foreign policy' during Henry's reign.[6] Such posturing was ex-pressed not only in feats of war, but also in peacemaking. Peace required as much justification as war. And the occasion at which peace was achieved had to be one of public magnificence: for example the spectacular cere-monies of the treaty of London, stage-managed by Wolsey in 1518. Its grandiose purpose was to achieve peace by collective responsibility: all the signatories swore to act against any power which broke that peace. Wolsey's achievement brought diplomatic credit and prestige to England and its king, even if only briefly.[7]

Henry VIII's priorities may seem confused and unrealistic to the modern mind. In 1517 Cuthbert Tunstal, the English ambassador at the Imperial Court, wrote to Henry that 'th'emperor [Maximilian] entendeth to resigne the Empire unto your Grace, and to obten your election by his procurement . . . for the avancement of your honor and the love which he berith you'. This renewed an earlier offer in 1513, but there was no positive royal response. When Maximilian died in 1519, however, Henry joined Francis and Charles as an electoral candidate for the vacant office. It is difficult to believe, especially after Tunstal's advice that his election 'cannot be brogth aboute by no means', that he had a real hope or ex-pectation of success.[8] In the same way, in 1521 and 1523 he ineffectively promoted Wolsey as a candidate for the papal office. Reality and royal expectation were often at odds during his reign. On the other hand, the mere fact that an English king strutted the European stage in bids for the imperial crown and the papal tiara for his minister did much for his prestige and reputation.

Diplomatic circumstances frequently and sometimes dramatically changed. The direction of Henrician foreign policy was sometimes dic-tated by such changes, especially in the English king's relations with the two men whom he regarded as his personal rivals, Charles and Francis. At least the growth of permanent embassies meant that monarchs could be better and more regularly informed about political development abroad. Under Wolsey an English network of embassies was developed. It was served by abler, educated and politically skilled though as yet not career diplomats.[9] Royal ministers were better informed than in the past, whilst the extended diplomatic network was valued because it reinforced the desired royal image of a prominent European Prince.

Of course Henry's world did not consist only of fellow Princes, diplo-mats and generals. So, when he resorted to war in pursuit of his foreign policy objectives, did he attempt to justify it to his subjects? Or were his opinions of his power, stature and popularity such that he considered it unnecessary to do so? Although only once did he publicly make a formal declaration of war – against France in 1543 – the proclamation incorporated a justification. More understandably, so did the preambles to the statutes which granted him war subsidies. The arguments which he forwarded were traditional medieval justifications, to which early modern Princes, not just Henry, resorted. One was self-defence against dangerous, aggrandizing monarchs, who threatened his kingdom and his allies (including, in the first half of his reign, the pope). Others were the recovery of lands unjustly seized by them, pursuit of legitimate claims to other kingdoms, and the defence of Christendom. Such wars were 'just' wars.[10] There was general public acceptance of such arguments. After all, 'warlike kings were expected to hide their purposes behind the convention of the just war'.[11] It is ironic that the frankest exposure of the realities of Henry's wars was presented by his future chief minister, Thomas Cromwell. In a speech drafted for delivery in the 1523 parliament, he pointed out the incredible outlay of treasure in order to acquire the 'ungracious doghole' of Thérouanne, the much greater expense which would be required for the seizure of a French province, and, if France could be conquered, the sheer impossibility of holding it. During the 1530s, the years of Cromwell's political ascendancy under Henry, England did not go to war.[12]

France

It can be argued that Henry's revival of the Hundred Years' War, with the twin objectives of regaining his 'inheritance' and asserting his legitimate claim to the French crown – a 'just war' – constituted a long-term, coherent and co-ordinated policy. It needs to be seen, however, rather as a personal expression of a macho-martial king. It was about chivalry, the search for military glory by a warrior Prince, and a transference of personal prowess, honour and courage from the tourney to the battlefield. In the process Henry was able to transform himself from warrior to capable general. When present, he personally determined the order of battle and changes in tactics, both in land and naval battles. In his study of the king's performance during the French assault of 1545, Alexander McKee demonstrated a capable military performance, even though it was 'sometimes thwarted by the weather or the effective tactics of the enemy'. On the basis of his defensive network of coastal forts and batteries (a few in the south-west, but mainly around the Solent, the south-east and the Thames mouth), McKee also concluded, with some justification, that '[a]s a far-sighted war minister, Henry can hardly be faulted'.[13]

War also tickled his intellectual fancy because, in Steven Gunn's words, 'he was fascinated by gadgetry of all kinds and especially by new weapons and developments in fortification'.[14] For public consumption Henry had to express his desire for war in terms of necessity and justified provocation, not mere self-gratification, especially when requesting financial assistance from parliament. In 1523 Wolsey addressed the two houses:

To shew unto you . . . that his highness is commen unto the wars, not by any will and appetite which his grace hath thereunto, but only by extreme constraint, inforce and necessity; as well for the guarding of his honor, and the reputation of this his realm, . . . and for the revenging of such injuries . . . and detaining of his rights from him, by his ancient enemy, the French king.[15]

As France was the traditional enemy, Henry could always count on some support for a cross-Channel assault. Many English detested and despised the French as 'false dogs' and mocked them as faithless peasants.[16] For any self-respecting English king who wanted to embark on war as a pleasure-pursuit, like jousting, tourneying or hunting, the French were a natural first choice, especially as the Valois kingdom was geographically handy and much of it consisted of conquests from the English. Whether Henry's claim to the French crown was a genuine heartfelt priority or simply a diplomatically acceptable justification for war remains uncertain.

At first other European Princes may have attempted to manipulate Henry to serve their particular interests: his father-in-law Ferdinand in 1512 and the Emperor Maximilian in the following year. In particular the destruction of Thérouanne and the capture of Tournai by Henry's army removed French threats to imperial territories.[17] On the other hand, these French conquests, together with his victory in the 'Battle of the Spurs', when the French fled the field of battle, and Wolsey's effective organization of a large, well-armed force, gave the king a military reputation in Europe and made his alliance worth bargaining for. Furthermore, the ongoing rivalry between Francis I and Charles Habsburg, ruler of a vast composite monarchy, also enabled Henry to pick and choose when he would fight and with whom. Honour was therefore tempered by and even subordinated to self-interest. Of course self-interest was not a royal monopoly. The young king was surrounded by militant nobles and gentlemen such as the earl of Surrey, his son Sir Edward Howard, Sir Thomas

Knyvett and Henry's close friend and master of the horse, Charles Brandon. These men, eager for war and the accompanying glory and profit, reinforced the king's own desire to test his warrior skills on the battlefield. It was only in 1512 that he overcame the resistance of older, wiser heads and, in the following year, he launched the first major and seemingly successful invasion of France. At the same time Surrey's army routed a Scottish army, killed King James IV and decimated his nobility at Flodden. Sir Edward Howard and Knyvett were casualties of war, but the warriors who survived were duly rewarded: Surrey became duke of Norfolk; his son, who led the vanguard at Flodden, was created earl of Surrey; and Brandon was raised to the dukedom of Suffolk. Furthermore, Wolsey, the organizer, received the bishopric of Tournai.

In 1514, however, Henry and the French made peace. After a brief revival of hostilities in 1522–4, Henry's shifting priorities, especially hostility toward Charles V and the papacy over the 'divorce question', favoured peace. As he also received a sizeable French pension for many years, it literally paid to remain at peace with France. It is difficult, however, to detect a consistent Henrician policy. During the 1530s Henry was in active diplomatic contact with the German Lutheran Schmalkaldic League – hardly guaranteed to win the sympathy or approval of either Charles V or Francis I. He was certainly influenced by his evangelical advisers, especially Cromwell and Cranmer, but, as Rory McEntegert persuasively argues, he was personally driven by religious as well as political interest. The embassy of Edward Fox, bishop of Hereford, to Germany in 1535–6 opened contact which continued actively for several years. The purpose of Fox's mission was not only political alliance but also to seek the League's advice and counsel on the king's wish 'to procede according to the veray trueth of the gospel'.[18] This policy was resisted by Bishop Gardiner and other conservatives. As theological discussions with the League broke down, Henry turned to parliament for a resolution of certain religious questions. The resultant Six Articles was a defeat for the evangelicals. This did not immediately terminate Henry's contact with the League, for they continued to discuss religion during 1539. However, his unconsummated marriage to the duke of Cleves' daughter, Anne, and Cromwell's fall ended the association with the League for the time being.[19] Henry's interest turned back to European dynastic rivalries. So in his final years, 1543–6, he launched into war again, personally leading his forces and bleeding his kingdom for the acquisition of Boulogne, another 'doghole'. At the same time, however, his fear of a Franco-Imperial alliance and his ongoing desire to gain advantage against the French caused him to resume the Lutheran dalliance in the 1540s.

It is important not to single Henry out as a Prince whose priorities were significantly different from those of his contemporaries.[20] Nevertheless the facts behind the occasional moments of military glory during his reign were harsh ones: war which was 'spectacular but pointless';[21] the costly input of manpower and money; Henry's inflated assessment of the resources available to him; and his pursuit of personal goals regardless of national consequences, such as the dislocation of trade, consequent unemployment and the seizure of the English wine fleet at Bordeaux in 1522.

Scotland

When Henry became king, James IV of Scotland was his brother-in-law. The marriage of the Scottish king and the thirteen-year-old Margaret Tudor in 1503 was seen by many as symbolic of an enduring Anglo-Scottish peace. But the accession of Margaret's brother in England changed all that. The Scottish queen did not receive a valuable legacy of jewels after her father's death in 1509. Then Englishmen killed the Scottish warden of the marches and, at sea, one of James' naval commanders. Henry's anti-French alliance with his father-in-law set off alarm signals for James IV. In 1513 the Scottish king wrote to him in a vain attempt to preserve peace.[22] Henry's resumption of war with France, however, served to trigger the reactivation of the 'auld' Franco-Scottish alliance too. That proved to be an immediate disaster for the Scots, when James, earls, bishops, abbots and many others of the Scottish elite were slaughtered by an English army – under the earl of Surrey, not Henry – at Flodden in 1513. From 1515 John Stuart, duke of Albany, proved to be a frequent source of concern and trouble for Henry. In 1522 an army reputedly of 80,000 men, with many cannons and 'hand gonnes in-numerable', massed on the Anglo-Scottish border under Albany's command. Facing them was Henry's warden of the west marches, Thomas Lord Dacre of Gilsland, with a mere 16,000 reluctant soldiers. Although he had no authority to make a truce, he convinced Albany that he did. In September 1522 a truce was duly signed and the Scottish army disbanded. Northern England was spared invasion and Henry was now free to wage war on France.[23]

Scotland was neutralized until the sixteen-year-old James V seized political control in 1528. Henry's impolitic attempts to control the young king caused him to be very anti-English and loyal to the 'auld' alliance. Deteriorating relations resulted in a border war precipitated by the English king in 1532. In the stressful climate of the divorce proceedings he saw Scotland as a threat. Following his aggressive instincts, his natural impulse was retaliation rather than negotiation.[24] In 1533, however, a truce was signed and under Cromwell a policy of peace and relative reconciliation was pursued. James, however, married French princesses successively in 1537 and 1538. This heightened English insecurity. The English schism heightened tension as the pope and French king explored the possibility of Scottish help against Henry. He in turn sought a *rapprochement* with the Scottish king, who in 1541 indicated his willingness to meet him at York. James' failure to appear, which was a public snub for Henry, was the consequence of pressure from Francis I. Henry's conduct now was based as much on hot emotional response as cool political reasoning. Personal honour, and anger at the way that Scotland harboured his opponents and assisted Gaelic resistance in Ireland, were as motivating as ongoing concerns about border security, the succession and the 'auld' alliance.[25] Thereafter Henry increased English border raids and arson and, in November 1542, he declared 'the trewe and right title that the Kinges most royall majesty hath to the Souerayntie of Scotland'. So, as he intended, he provoked war. Fortunately for Henry, the Scots were defeated at Solway Moss in 1542 and two weeks later James died. His heir, Mary, was only seven days old. Henry seemed to have Scotland at his mercy, but he was not interested in conquest or union, only containment. Furthermore, as Elizabeth Bonner concludes, 'through his own stupidity . . . he was to lose every advantage [and] allow himself to be outwitted and out manoeuvred by the Scots'.[26] The peace and marriage treaties of Greenwich, which approved the marriage of Mary to Henry's heir, Edward, brought English control of Scotland closer on paper. Mary, however, was not to be delivered to England until she was ten. As so often, Henry aggravated hostility by reasserting his claims over Scotland. Anglophobe Scottish politicians repudiated the treaty and the 'auld' alliance was reactivated. Henry's typical reprisal took the form of a military expedition to burn and plunder Edinburgh and to ravage the Scottish Lowlands.

This so-called 'Rough Wooing' did nothing to help his cause, whatever that may have been. His Scottish policy was a characteristic confusion of priorities: sometimes border security, at others peace, conquest, claims to overlordship, and especially an integral part of his French ambitions.[27] It is clear, however, that Henry's treatment of Scotland was not part of a long-term objective, to be *rex et imperator* of a unified British Isles. Cromwell's 1523 speech indicated his wish for Anglo-Scottish union, which would provide security in the north and strike a major blow against

France. As so often, Cromwell's farsightedness was the antithesis of Henry's pursuit of quick success and instant glory.[28]

Effective royal control of the northern borderlands was essential, especially during the wars but also in peacetime. Here too, however, inconsistency ruled. On the one hand, Henry was more interventionist. This was not surprising when the revival of the 'auld' alliance, his divorce and the breach with Rome together created a volatile political climate. The political instability of the northern marches was aggravated by cross-border warfare in 1532–4 over disputed territory (known as the 'Debateable Land') and, from the mid-1520s, by royal attempts to centralize authority, interspersed with periods of neglect. Henry revived the northern council with marcher supervision, removed the experienced, powerful magnate and marcher warden Lord Dacre, and promoted local gentry as deputy wardens. These actions undermined the traditional marcher power structures and simply created political tensions and hostilities.[29] Reducing the power of the great magnates, the traditional crown-backed rulers, 'simply reduced the capacity of royal government in these regions and created more problems than it solved'.[30]

The impact of Henry VIII's activities

Henry's attempts to 'cut a dash' in European affairs had the very limited and ephemeral impact which one might expect. England was, at best, a second-rate power attempting to deal a political hand in a Continent dominated by France and the new Habsburg conglomerate. At the most, therefore, the king's shuffling alliances were expressions of 'opportunism', in which 'the primary objective was to keep options open'.[31] He could hardly hope to compete on equal terms: the French and Spanish kings' subjects were three and over six times as many, respectively, as his; the incomes of Francis I and Charles V were more than three and five times as large, respectively. Furthermore, the national muster of English manpower taken in 1522 revealed that in twenty-eight counties only one-third of the able Englishmen were archers.[32] High desertion levels during campaigns and mutinous demands to end those campaigns were features of English armies in the field. As Gunn concludes, Henry's forces were 'fragile and unreliable weapons for an aspiring conqueror'.[33]

Did Henry have greater impact on Britain than on the European Continent? This depends on the nature and scope of his objectives. These were limited and, as already observed, did not amount to any kind of coherent policy for the unification of the British Isles, at least not until the 1530s:

Wales

The establishment of the Tudor dynasty provided strong bonds of Welsh loyalty to the crown. Furthermore the monarch was by far the largest landowner in Wales, its old feudal elite had declined in strength and numbers, the process of de-feudalization was well underway and, as the executions of the duke of Buckingham (1521) and an angry Welsh magnate, Rhys ap Gruffydd (1531) illustrated, supposed disloyalty was dealt with harshly. But lawlessness and feuding continued and in 1533 Sir Edward Croft, vice-chamberlain of south Wales, wished 'some man to be sent down to use the sword of justice where he shall see cause throughout the principality; otherwise the Welsh will wax so wild it will not be easy to bring them into order again'.[34] Thomas Cromwell appointed, as president of the council in the Welsh marches, Rowland Lee the 'hanging' bishop, who between 1534 and 1540 reputedly executed 5,000 offenders in his campaign against feuding and lawlessness. Far more important in terms of State-building, however, were the statutes of 1534 (strengthening the Welsh penal code and judicial system) and those of 1536 and 1543, which effectively integrated England and Wales under the crown and amounted to an 'Act of Union'. The marcher lordships were shired, the council in the marches of Wales was given statutory authority, English law and local government were introduced throughout Wales, English became the obligatory judicial and local government language and Wales received representation – one member for each county and each shire borough – in the English parliament. Although the process was not completed until after Cromwell's death in 1540, he was the architect and draughtsman. The political crisis triggered by Henry's divorce and break with Rome required 'a more interventionist strategy': one of Cromwell's immediate concerns was to bring more order and control to the borderlands. However, as his wish for Anglo-Scottish union also indicates, his vision encompassed a State which was more efficient, subject to more effective royal control, and British.[35]

Ireland

Henry VIII showed little interest in Irish affairs until the maladministration of the 9th earl of Kildare as governor forced him into action. Kildare was removed from the governorship in 1519. Thereafter he had a chequered career, which included spells in detention in 1519–23 and 1526–30. Henry's experimental replacements included other Anglo-Irish magnates and, in 1520–1, the earl of Surrey, but there seemed no adequate substitute for such a powerful figure as the Fitzgerald earl of Kildare. So he was reappointed in 1524–6 and again in 1532–4. Thus far Henry's under-funded and changeable management had proved muddled and inept. Then in 1534 Thomas succeeded his father as 10th earl and raised a rebellion, but in the following year it was defeated, Thomas surrendered and he was sent to London. Henry was advised that the earl's death might provoke a hostile reaction from the Irish chieftains. In 1537, however, Thomas and his five uncles were executed.

During the 1530s Cromwell successfully effected the change from local magnates with delegated authority to English governors more directly answerable to the royal centre of power. In practice, however, it altered little on the ground. Indeed it magnified problems. English governors were dependent on the goodwill of the Irish political community for any degree of stable royal government. As they were to find, the destruction of the Kildare interest and its widespread support network left a gap in both resources and local loyalties which they could not fill. So the change did nothing to solve the problems involved in governing such a diverse, distant borderland. Steven Ellis touched on a core problem, when he wrote, 'Since the king remained basically uninterested in Ireland and very reluctant to spend money there, the changes of the mid-1530s had a pronounced destabilizing effect on the lordship.' Soldiers were increasingly used to support the civil administration. This required an enlarged military establishment, but Henry's unwillingness to supplement the inadequate Irish revenues led instead to cuts in the military establishment in the 1530s.

The Irish Reformation Parliament (1536–7) provided an opportunity to remedy the financial problem. It granted a parliamentary subsidy for ten years, Church revenues and royal repossession of absentee landowners' property. In 1536 alone, however, Henry had to remit £15,000 to pay the army. That did not last. In 1537–8 royal commissioners halved the military force and reduced soldiers' pay. It signalled Henry's priorities. A king who was prepared to spend extraordinary sums of money on French expeditions underfunded and weakened the government and garrison in Ireland. He was particularly unreceptive to the solution canvassed by some. For example, as early as the 1520s Surrey opined that Gaelic Ireland would 'be brought to no good order unless it be by compulsion'. Cost, if nothing else, was inhibiting. Continental Big Power politics, not borderland management, consumed most of Henry's energy, enthusiasm and money. So, for example, he advised the earl of Surrey to employ 'sober ways, politic drifts and amiable persuasions' – an approach which had the virtue of economy but was hardly a recipe for success in Ireland.[36] Henry literally paid the penalty in the 1540s when both the garrison and financial input had to be increased.

At the same time Anthony St Leger, governor of Ireland from 1540, initiated a programme which held out promise of political stability. It rested upon local support and so did not require heavy military commitment and expense. Furthermore it accorded with Henry's wish for the Gaelic Irish to recognize his sovereignty rather than mere overlordship.[37] St Leger secured the submission of the Gaelic chieftains, who, by a process of surrender of their lands and regrant by the king on terms of perpetual knight service, would bind themselves to Henry as their liege lord. They were to receive peerages, attend parliament and oppose his spiritual rival, the pope. The political restructuring of the medieval lordship was completed when the Irish parliament of 1541 recognized Henry as king of Ireland. The whole process amounted to an inexpensive policy of Anglicization, by way of persuasion, reconciliation and submission. There was, however, one important stumbling block and obstacle to success: the king. He was angry that the scheme had been initiated in Ireland without his consent. He also argued that 'full constitutional status' should be accompanied by 'full payment of taxes'. St Leger and his supporters argued that, especially at this early stage in the liberal programme of reconciliation and transformation, it was both financially unrealistic and politically harmful. Although, after a delay, the submissions and grants of royal charters began to take place at Henry's Court in 1542–3, his involvement in war against France then halted the process. And his death in January 1547 ended it.[38] So the implementation of a long-term, cost friendly programme, which might have united Ireland under Tudor monarchy and achieved political stability, was frustrated.

How did Henry VIII attempt to realize his objectives, ambitions and dreams of glory?

St Leger's aborted initiative in Ireland typifies Henry's inept handling of his borderlands. His replacement of long-serving noble families by others simply antagonized regional magnates, such as Rhys ap Gruffydd in Wales and the Percies and Dacres in the north. Active intervention from the centre, prompted by the divorce crisis and consequent Henrician Reformation, had mixed results. The council of the north was revived in the 1520s, but it lacked noble support, especially in the marches, where it was designed to supersede noble power. As the Pilgrimage of Grace

(1536–7) and renewed Anglo-Scottish hostilities in the 1540s demonstrated, without the Percies, Cliffords, Dacres, Nevilles and other old great families, stability and national defence were very difficult, if not impossible, to achieve. Henry's declaration, that 'we woll not be bounde, of a necessitie, to be served there with lordes', was typically grandiose and pompous. When, however, he acquired the Percy inheritance in 1537 it simply left a power vacuum. And his replacement of Lord Dacre by newly ennobled Lord Wharton in the west marches dramatically escalated Henry's defence expenditure – to little effect.[39]

In contrast, to a large extent stability and order in Wales were successfully achieved. And, unlike the St Leger experiment in Ireland, integration, which started in hesitant fashion, was effectively pursued. Such changes were accomplished by constitutional means, initiated by Thomas Cromwell and culminating in the 'act of union' of 1543.[40] Elsewhere the sword was to be the means whereby Henry pursued his objectives. It can be argued, however, that Henry regarded the sword not merely as the means but as his first priority. In other words, his overriding concern was to lead armies, direct campaigns and strut across France as the Great Warrior King.[41] It was, to some extent, a European projection of a Prince who had a passion for jousting at Court, excelled at it in his early years and continued to participate until his mid-forties. In his pursuit of glory he relied upon several weapons of war: nobility, navy and army.

The nobility

The nobility was also essential as a mainstay of monarchy and political order. Percies, Cliffords, Nevilles and Dacres in the north and especially the marches, Somersets in Wales, Howards in East Anglia and Sussex were vital to good governance. Nobles were also regarded as the crown's natural advisers. For almost two-thirds of his reign, however, Henry VIII depended on two low-born men, Wolsey and Cromwell, elevated respectively to the status of cardinal and earl. This gave rise to much discontent. In 1536 the northern rebels accused the king of taking counsel from 'persons of low birth and small reputation', such as Cromwell. Four years later Cromwell's attainder, in which the duke of Norfolk had a hand, described him as someone raised by the king, 'beyng a man of very baas and lowe degree' who had since been proved by many 'personages of great honour, worship and discretion' to have been 'the moost false and corrupte Traytor, deceyvor and circumventor ageynst yore moost Royall persone and Themperiall Crowne of this youre Realme'.[42] This encapsulated noble resentment. Edward IV and the first two Tudors, however, rejected the nobles' traditional role as natural councillors and chose members of the royal council solely on the basis of loyalty and ability. During the 1530s 'the repository of counsel was exclusively Henry VIII's private *consilium*'. And membership of Cromwell's creation, the new executive privy council which was operative by August 1540, was chosen by Henry 'on the basis of experience, opinion, education or potential . . . not because of birth, blood or landownership'.[43]

The nobles' role as *consiliarii nati* might be defunct, but they were particularly valued by Henry for other purposes, especially jousting and military service: for example Charles Brandon, duke of Suffolk, who served in France and in 1544 captured Boulogne.[44] The Howard family was unmatched in its record of military service. Thomas Howard, earl of Surrey, defeated the Scots at Flodden in 1513. His son Edward, a naval commander, was killed at sea. Edward's brother Thomas, who commanded the vanguard at Flodden, was lord lieutenant of Ireland (1520–2), led forces against the French in 1522 and the Scots in 1542, ended the Pilgrimage of Grace, and served as lieutenant-general in France in 1544 and in East Anglia (1545) as captain-general in anticipation of a French invasion. Such service was richly rewarded by an appreciative king. In 1514 Charles Brandon and the earl of Surrey were elevated to the dukedoms of Suffolk and Norfolk, whilst the latter's son, Thomas, received the earldom of Surrey in his own right. In 1524 Thomas succeeded his father as third duke of Norfolk. He and his son Henry, the poet-earl who shone both in the cultivated Court and on the battlefield, served their king until their joint fall from royal grace in 1546–7.[45] By then others were enjoying the fruits of their martial activity and Henry's appreciation. Amongst them were: John Dudley, who served in Calais, on the Scottish marches and as lord admiral, and was ennobled as Viscount Lisle in 1542; John Russell, who fought in France, was created baron in 1539 and in 1540–2 served as admiral; and the marcher wardens Lords Eure and Wharton (both ennobled in 1544).

The navy

The navy was a crucial instrument of war because of Henry's French ambitions. An island kingdom could not wage successful war without a navy which had the capacity to transport armies, launch assaults and protect it from invasion. The effective fulfilment of these functions required, in turn, control of the seas or at least of the Channel. Henry inherited from his father a small fighting force of only seven vessels, of which two, *Regent* and *Sovereign*, were large built-to-order warships of 600 and 450 tons, respectively. Henry VII understood the importance of artillery and his fleet was far more powerfully armed than that of any previous English king. His legacy to his son included 'a more active and more firmly based naval administration than had existed for many years', as well as a busy shipbuilding programme in progress and a forward-looking plan for growth.[46] This was an obvious benefit to Henry VIII, who had to carry out a radical enlargement and transformation of the navy's fighting capacity if it was to serve his ambitions. So he continued and accelerated his father's policies.

Naval development was an urgent consideration, because Henry embarked on war early in his reign. In 1511 small expeditions were sent to assist the emperor and King Ferdinand and, in response to a petition by London merchants, ships hired by the king defeated and killed the Scottish pirate Andrew Barton. The following year a fleet 'of sixty great ships complete with armament' under Sir Edward Howard escorted an English army to France. Then, with twenty-five of the vessels, Howard also raided the Breton coast and attempted to engage the French navy.[47] In 1513 a fleet of forty-eight ships and 132 victualling vessels ferried the king and his army to France. Howard's task was to 'patrol both the English and the French coasts, so that he might ensure control of the sea'. He was also instructed, however, that if 'he should clash with the French fleet, he was not to avoid a prompt engagement'.[48] Within four years, therefore, Henry had been able to assemble fleets of far greater numbers than the seven warships which he had inherited from his father. Shipbuilding carried over from Henry VII's reign and continued under Henry VIII. In 1509 *Peter Pomegranate* and *Mary Rose* were built and *Sovereign* was rebuilt.[49] Henry also bought a significant number, such as the Genoese carrack *Gabriel Royal*. By the end of 1511 his fleet numbered more than a dozen ships; next year between five and eight were built and six more, including three galleys, were purchased.[50] Others were hired, particularly from Spain. In 1512–13 shipbuilding continued. When the war ended in 1514 Henry owned thirty warships, nine of which had been built in the previous two and a half years.[51] The building style had been changed and the armament was shifting to fewer but more powerful guns. This began in 1509 and continued throughout the reign. In 1515 the *Henry Grace à Dieu* of 1500 tons, 'the most powerful warship the world had ever seen', was launched. The Venetian ambassador, who was invited to dine on board with the king and queen, described it as 'a galeas, of unusual magnitude ... with such a number of heavy guns, that we doubt whether any fortress, however strong, could resist their fire'. It 'seemed to us a fine and excellent engine', but with the proviso, 'provided it can be worked'.[52] As one of Henry's wide-ranging interests was artillery, Oppenheim rightly concludes that it may have been a direct royal initiative, but that, if not, 'he has the merit of recognizing its value and persistently putting it into execution'.[53] In 1511, for example, he established a foundry at Houndsditch, and during his reign he discarded the old iron breech-loading guns in favour of bronze muzzle-loading cannons.[54]

Shipbuilding continued unabated: another eleven vessels were constructed between 1518 and 1524. Henry also continued to hire vessels, not only from London and Bristol but also from smaller centres such as Lynn and Topsham. The demand fell during the years of peace, especially for much of the 1530s. But in the last years of the decade Henry activated a programme to strengthen defences. On 2 April 1539 Ambassador Marillac wrote of Henry's 'marvellous distrust, both of Francis and the Emperor, looking for war as certain'. Approaching Dover he saw an armada which would soon join thirty ships at Portsmouth, 'making in all 150 sail'.[55] Henry resumed war with France in the 1540s. In 1544 he captured Boulogne, after which England was threatened by French invasion. Henry assembled land and sea forces around Portsmouth and the Isle of Wight. Although the French assault of 1545 failed, tragedy struck with the accidental sinking of the English flagship, *Mary Rose*. As she turned with the gunports open she rolled, drowning over 400 men, including her commander, Sir George Carew. His distraught wife, who witnessed this, was comforted by the king. With characteristic sensitivity he reminded her that she had a son to continue the line. When Anglo-French war resumed, the shipbuilding docks, especially at Deptford, became a hive of activity again: as many as nineteen men-of-war in 1544–6.[56] From 1539 the threat of war also accelerated the creation of a complex of coastal defences and fortifications where England faced France across the sea: from the Thames estuary down to St Mawes and Pendennis in Cornwall – and even on the Scilly Isles. The northern fortifications at Berwick and Hull were also updated.[57]

An integral and essential part of the process of naval expansion was the creation of new shipyards and the development of naval administration, as well as supply and other support facilities. Portsmouth dock was enlarged (by 1523), but other, new, dockyards at Limehouse, Erith (by 1512), Deptford (1517) and Woolwich gradually superseded it. Storehouses for rope cables and cannon were constructed at Deptford (1516) and an armourers' forge at Greenwich (by September 1511).[58] Henry's persuasive initiative caused the Trinity House guild of pilots to map the complex navigation of the Thames estuary, Goodwin Sands and English Channel. Meanwhile, much greater naval activity necessitated a more efficient and steadily growing administration. Then, not long before his death, the king established the royal 'council of his marine' – or what amounted to an early version of the future Navy Board under the lieutenant of the admiralty.[59] Little was left untouched: for example Thomas Audley had the task (in about 1530) of devising 'A Booke of Orders for the Warre by Sea and Land'. This provided detailed discipline: any man caught sleeping on watch for a fourth time was to be 'hanged on the bowspritte end of the shippe in a basket with a kanne of bere, a lofe of bread, and a sharpe knife, thus to hang there till he starve or cut him self into the see'; and if a sailor drew a weapon 'or causeth tumulte' in a ship he 'shall lose his ryht hand'.[60] Brutal perhaps, but illustrative of Henry's broad-ranging interest in efficiency.

Henry was not alone amongst European Princes in his attention to the navy. Others had their huge prestige vessels which rivalled *Henry Grace à Dieu*, amongst them Scotland's *Great Michael*, Francis I's *Grand François* and the Swedish *Elefant*.[61] These, however, enhanced the prestige of Princes rather than the efficiency of their navies. Much more important in Henry's case was the arming of the great ships such as *Mary Rose* with the very heavy muzzle-loading guns. These were mounted in lines in the lower decks, from which they fired broadsides through gunports – an English innovation, though Henry's personal role is not known. Such developments signified an important new role for Henry's navy. His ships were not confined to the auxiliary role of army escort or back-up. Now they were used to secure control of the seas, spearhead assaults on foreign coastal sites, seize or sink merchant shipping and destroy enemy warships.

The prime purpose and function of Henry's navy was as a weapon of war, offensive and defensive. But it also fuelled his pretensions and it enabled him to project images and pose upon the public stage. At the launching of the *Henry Grace à Dieu*, he 'dressed galley fashion', but it was a most extravagant sailor-suit: 'a vest of gold brocade [and] breeches of cloth of gold and scarlet hose'. He played the pilot, blowing away on his gold captain's whistle 'nearly as loud as a trumpet'.[62] Such great men-of-war fed his ego and, of course, had a publicity value which promoted loyalty and produced lavish, even obsequious, praise. In c.1540, for example, the earl of Southampton's wife and nine other ladies of the Court visited the king's latest 'Greate Shippe and the rest of your shippes' at Portsmouth. They all signed a letter telling him that they had never seen a more pleasant sight, 'excepting your royall person', and they – his 'most unworthie and humble servaunts and beadwomen' – offered up their 'most humble and entier thanks'.[63] Mock naval warfare could also be a part of celebrations, as occurred after a marriage 'within the Court' in June 1536. A carrack 'well charged with ordnance' battled with another carrack and three other vessels 'made like the Turks' small galleys . . . [O]ne assaulted another marvellously well', though a gunner had both legs broken and, at the end, 'one Gates, a gentleman . . . drowned'. So what! 'Men did not marvel greatly, that knew him, of his misfortune, because he was so great a swearer.'[64]

The redoubtable navy which the king bequeathed in 1547 was a great achievement, summed up by Loades: 'Henry VIII may not have founded the king's navy, but he certainly transformed it.'[65]

The army

In contrast to Henry's navy, relatively little attention or credit is given to his armies. They are generally assumed to have been inefficient, ill trained and increasingly out-of-date in both weapons and organization. England did lag behind France, which had developed a professional army in the fifteenth century. Nevertheless English organization was improved by the newly developed system of indentures: county commissions could now raise troops in relation to the estimated manpower of their counties. Although English infantry were still equipped with bows and bills, it can be argued that, at least during Henry's reign, guns did not yet have the advantages of greater distance and penetration. It seems unlikely that Henry, who was such an enthusiast for gunpowder and guns, would have ignored developments which made handguns more effective than bows on the field of battle. In the Boulogne campaign of 1544–6, for example, he was employing formations of pike men and arquebusiers as well as archers. Growing use of firearms and lack of a domestic arms industry, however, meant growing royal dependence on Antwerp.

The king's enthusiasm for heavy firepower ensured that the army as well as the navy was equipped with heavy guns. The artillery in the 1513 expedition included twelve bombards, pulled by teams of twenty-four Flanders mares. Each took a charge of 80 pounds of gunpowder to fire a 260-pound iron ball, and the maximum firing-rate was five times in a day. Gradually, however, the guns became lighter, more mobile and accurate, although Henry was always attached to great prestige pieces such as the 'twelve guns of unusual magnitude – each cast with the image of an apostle'. When on campaign in 1513, he ordered that the twelve apostles should be fired at Tournai cathedral, 'a building of great beauty', and the canons' houses, 'to wake them up to be more inclined to serve God'.[66] In another way too England was not divorced from European military development: as in Spain and Italy independent light cavalry, recruited from cattle-rustling 'reivers' on the Anglo-Scottish marches, was a feature of Henry's forces. They served as scouts, raiders or part of the army in pitched battle, as in 1513, for example, at Flodden and in the French campaign. One problem which his rivals, Charles and Francis, did not share was the relatively small population of England and Wales. This supposedly caused Henry to employ foreign mercenaries. Yet his use of them has been greatly exaggerated: in 1542 there were 70,000 in French service; in contrast, in Henry's army in 1544 only 10,228 out of 42,500 men were foreign mercenaries.[67] He drew mainly on his English and Welsh subjects for his soldiers.

Gervase Phillips concluded that, whilst Henry's land forces appear to have been less antiquated, inefficient and uninfluenced by European developments than was once thought, any conclusion must be 'speculative'. This is because in Continental Europe 'they fought no pitched battles worthy of the name' – and that is, he argues, 'the ultimate test'. Nevertheless there were undoubted improvements in efficiency, organization and armament, most of which must be attributed to Henry. This was not confined to his knowledgeable and active interest in gunnery and the consequent equipping of army, navy and coastal defences. He established royal armouries at Greenwich, employing Dutch and Germans. He was also the driving force in the development of English cartography, which provided the basis for the coastal fortifications of the 1540s.[68] All of his endeavours bore fruit in 1545, when France mounted a major assault on England's south coast, around the Isle of Wight. A fleet of about eighty English ships mustered at Portsmouth and another of sixty vessels to the west; the coastal fortresses and batteries, many of them new, were fully operational, and four regional armies comprised of county levies provided a third line of defence. The French failure was, to some degree, also a commentary on the improved efficiency, organization and strength of the English war-machine.

The costs of glory

Peace is a modern ideal. It had no place of significance in the priorities, policies or counsels of medieval or early modern Princes. War was a natural weapon in defence of justice or 'true religion'. The warrior-prince was a very important image and military success against one's rivals was significant in terms of prestige as well as power. Therefore Henry should not be criticized or condemned out of hand for the urge to wage war. There was, however, a dark side to the military history of Henry VIII's reign: the financial burden of his military adventures, his reckless waste of resources and, in contrast, his senseless economies, as in Ireland.[69] This does not mean that he was uninterested in matters of income and expenditure. In her study of this subject Sybil Jack summed up the view of his daughter Mary that 'A prince is not brought up to be a book-keeper.' She then demonstrated Henry's involvement in financial operations, operating through a 'multitude of treasuries' and secret cash reserves, frequently exchanging lands aggressively, and especially active in raising levies. All this, however, must be seen in relation to the urgency of his priorities, especially the Court, but above all war. Costs of campaigning and defence soared. Military estimates, especially in the 1540s, bore little if any relation to financial reality.[70]

Henry's costly military pursuits must also be seen in the context of his general financial irresponsibility. His actions were so often driven by greed, ostentation, volatile personal relationships and disregard for others, theatrical ego, assertions of kingship and dreams of glory. His Renaissance Court's magnificence[71] was matched by its expense. In the search for more royal stages he acquired not only Wolsey's palaces and Archbishop Warham's at Knole and Otford, but also many others. Whether acquired by purchase, pressure, acquisition of monasteries or building, their maintenance, staffing and the Court's progress between them added to the running costs of the Court. Henry's wives' children, and their households were an additional, albeit normal and unavoidable item of expense. Typical of this king's inconsistency, however, was the fact that his wives' jointures, ranging from £3,000 to £5,000, generally compared unfavourably with the usual figure of £4,500 for medieval queens, especially when inflation is taken into account.[72] Nevertheless, when the extravagant spectaculars, entertainments and events in the annual courtly calendar were added to the normal running costs of a grand Court, the financial drain was a continuous problem. The large-scale military ventures were additional to the ongoing costs of the Court and also a far greater financial burden.

Henry was not alone. Elton summed up this contemporary European phenomenon:

[T]he most noticeable thing about warfare in this period was the readiness of princes to engage in it who could not, in the simplest sense, afford it.[73]

Henry fits into this category. He had a modest income, perhaps no more than £90,000 in the 1520s. As a limited monarch, he could not supplement it with taxes without parliamentary assent. Whatever was in the treasury when his father died, it was clearly much less than Francis Bacon's later estimate of £1,800,000. In contrast there is no doubt about the hard facts of Henry's first war of 1512–14: campaigning cost and other items, such as payments to the emperor, totalled almost £1,000,000. Clerical and lay taxation account for only a third of that sum. It must be assumed, therefore, that the rest came from Henry VII's accumulated reserve. The wars of the early 1520s not only put further stress on the royal income. They were very unpopular, especially in London, a major victim of forced loans, and in the Suffolk cloth industry, which was especially dependent on overseas markets, but generally throughout the kingdom. Worst and financially most harmful, indeed disastrous, were Henry's simultaneous wars against France and Scotland during the 1540s. The cost of just besieging and then garrisoning and fortifying Boulogne amounted to £1,013,000. His fortification of Calais, the Anglo-Scottish border and the south coast from 1538 onwards cost £375,000, apart from the outlay on 2,250 heavy guns. The total cost of this final lengthy exercise in egomania, by an increasingly bloated warrior whose swollen legs sometimes rendered walking very difficult, was over £2,130,000. In 1545 Wriothesley despaired when he wrote to the privy council that, though there was no money, '[Y]ou write to me still, pay, pay, prepare for this and that.'[74]

The means by which the wars were funded were harmful in a variety of ways. Wolsey introduced a new tax levied upon individual taxpayers, the subsidy, to which parliament assented four times in 1513–15 and again in 1523. This, together with fifteenths and tenths and clerical taxation, amounted to a more realistic supplement to the crown's modest ordinary income. But it could not compensate for Henry's military outlay of more than £1,000,000 between 1509 and 1520. When wars resumed in the 1520s Wolsey resorted to forced loans in 1522–3 (£260,000), another subsidy and an advance payment of the first instalment (1523), and a non-parliamentary, non-refundable levy, the 'Amicable Grant' (1525). The popular responses were evasion, delayed payment or point-blank refusal and, in 1525, tax rebellion in East Anglia. Henry's government became, temporarily, an island in a sea of discontent. Abandonment of the scheme by king and minister was a mark of realism and, as G. W. Bernard observes, 'flexibility: fiscal oppression was not driven too hard'.[75] During the 1530s royal income was dramatically augmented by first fruits and tenths, monastic property and the Statute of Uses, which for a few years guaranteed full royal wardship rights. The defensive and offensive military commitments of the 1540s proved to be the most expensive of the reign. Parliament granted taxes to the value of more than £600,000 and forced loans yielded another £245,000. These were supplemented by £800,000 raised from the sale of most of those Church lands which the crown had acquired by the dissolution of the monasteries. Short-term measures, such as loans on the Antwerp money market, and short-sighted expedients, such as debasement of the currency, were adopted to bridge the financial gap. War funding was also facilitated by the developing importance of the privy coffers, which were housed in palace treasuries and were directly under the king's control. Henry transferred to the coffers annual surpluses from the exchequer or large payments into it. Windfalls were also paid into them, especially the French pension.[76] This was a significant regular addition to Henry's ordinary income, especially after its increase from 1514. Payments stopped in 1533 and so it was not available to Henry in the 1540s. When England and France made peace in 1546, the pension was immediately reactivated, but ceased with the king's death in January 1547.[77]

Henry displayed a consistent disregard for the damaging financial and economic consequences of his showy but unproductive military adventures. The combination of parliamentary and prerogative taxation in the 1540s produced probably the greatest yield from the laity since the fourteenth century. During his reign, the clergy also experienced the heaviest taxation yet. In Ireland during the 1530s and then in England in 1544, 1545 and 1546 the king also resorted to debasement. By reminting the coinage with a lower gold or silver content, the crown produced a surplus of precious metals. It then used this surplus to make more coin for its war-chest. The result was not only a sizeable contribution towards Henry's wars, but also a rapid rise in the price of food, manufactured goods and wages.[78] This in turn increased the costs of the war effort and so quickly cancelled out any immediate benefits to him. Worst of all was his dissipation of the rich assets acquired during the 1530s. It was political common sense for the king to grant or sell some of the monastic lands to nobles and prominent gentry, courtiers and royal officials, lawyers and burgesses.[79] It committed them to the changes of the 1530s and to the ruling house. However, Henry's massive and rapid dissipation of those resources by sale, in order to fund wars in the forties, was a crowning folly. His heirs were amongst the victims of that folly, inheriting a poverty-stricken State, unable to fund foreign wars and even domestic government adequately, often in debt and sometimes driven to further sales of diminishing land resources.[80] As Scarisbrick concludes, although other kings may have been just as 'unaware and irresponsible' as Henry VIII, few if any were as harmful and destructive.[81] But at least his honour was satisfied.

Other victims included economic and social stability. This can be seen in the expressions of public discontent with the government's money-raising activities. The Cornish Rebellion against Henry VII's exactions in 1497 signalled that loyalty had its limits. Polydore Vergil recounted that, as early as 1513, there was 'a sudden new upheaval of the north-country folk caused by the heaviness of the tax imposed. . . . Wherefore they suddenly seized arms and obstinately held to their decision.' In response the king 'freely lifted for the present this burden from the people'.[82] In 1523–5, he was faced with more wide-ranging hostility to the repeated financial burdens of 1522–5: forced loans, parliamentary taxation and the Amicable Grant finally triggered refusals to pay, riots and even armed rising. As we have seen, Henry once again backed down, although in 1529 he obtained parliamentary cancellation of his obligation to repay forced loan contributions – another unpopular action.[83] In contrast to the 'troubles' of 1525, the uprisings of 1536–7 were much more serious, complex and caused by a wider range of problems and grievances.[84] The Pilgrimage of Grace, however, was not fuelled and driven by parliamentary tax grievances; it was, in Hoyle's words, 'England's War of Religion'.[85]

In the 1540s England creaked and groaned under the continuing financial burdens of Henry's military greatness. With a Prince of long-term vision and realistic aims related to resources and feasibility, it would have been otherwise. But not with Henry. When he finally died, in January 1547, he bequeathed to his successor and his people a meagre imperial jewel, Boulogne, and a legacy of financial liabilities.

Notes

1 See Steven Gunn's discussion: 'The French Wars of Henry VIII', in J. Black, ed., *The Origins of War in Early Modern Europe*, Edinburgh, 1987, pp. 28–51.

2 *LP*, 19 (2), no. 19

3 Pollard, *Henry VIII*, pp. 290ff.

4 Scarisbrick, *Henry VIII*, p. 425.

5 Levine, *Tudor Dynastic Problems*, pp. 145–6.

6 Walker, *Persuasive Fictions*, p. 113.

7 G. Richardson, *Renaissance Monarchy: The Reigns of Henry VIII, Francis I and Charles I*, London, 2002, pp. 54–9, 73–4.

8 Ellis, ed., *Orig. Letters*, 1 (1), p. 136.

9 Potter, 'Foreign Policy', pp. 102–5.

10 G. R. Elton, 'War and the English in the Reign of Henry VIII', in L. Freedman, P. Hayes and R. O'Neill, eds, *War, Strategy and International Politics*, Oxford, 1992, pp. 2–5, 7.

11 Ibid., p. 6

12 Ibid., pp. 14–16; Merriman, *Life and Letters of Cromwell*, I, pp. 30–44; see above, Chap. 6, p. 109.

13 A. McKee, 'Henry VIII as Military Commander', *Hist. Today*, 41 (June 1991), 22, 24, 29; B. M. Morley, *Henry VIII and the Development of Coastal Defence*, London, 1976, pp. 7–29, 32–6.

14 Gunn, 'French Wars of Henry VIII', 35.

15 *LP*, 3 (2), no. 2957.

16 Gunn, 'French Wars of Henry VIII', pp. 33–4.

17 C. G. Cruickshank, *Army Royal: Henry VIII's Invasion of France, 1513*, Oxford, 1969, pp. 186, 207.

18 R. McEntegert, *Henry VIII, the League of Schmalkalden and the English Reformation*, Woodbridge, Suffolk, 2002, pp. 6–7, 26–38, 45–7.

19 Ibid., pp. 149–66.

20 Gunn, 'French Wars of Henry VIII', p. 45.

21 D. MacCulloch 'War and Glory under a Young King', in D. Starkey, ed., *Rivals in Power*, London, 1990, p. 30.

22 P. H. Buchanan, *Margaret Tudor Queen of Scots*, Edinburgh, 1985, pp. 39, 60–1, 66–7; Ellis, ed., *Orig., Letters*, 1 (1), pp. 64–5, 76–8.

23 Walker, *Persuasive Fictions*, pp. 54–67.

24 C. Patrick Hotle, *Thorns and Thistles: Diplomacy Between Henry VIII and James V, 1528–1542*, Lanham, Maryland, 1996, pp. 8–28.

25 Ibid., pp. 157–63.

26 *LP*, 17, no. 1033; E. A. Bonner, 'The Genesis of Henry VIII's "Rough Wooing" of the Scots', *Northern History*, 33 (1997), 50–2.

27 Scarisbrick, *Henry VIII*, pp. 424–7.

28 Bonner, 'Henry VIII's "Rough Wooing"', 39, 53.

29 S. G. Ellis, 'Tudor State Formation and the Shaping of the British Isles', in idem and Barber, eds, *Conquest and Union*, pp. 50, 52–5; S. G. Ellis, *Tudor Frontiers and Noble Power: The Making of the British State*, Oxford, 1995, pp. 260–8.

30 Ibid., p. 268.

31 Potter, 'Foreign Policy', p. 118.

32 Ibid., pp. 111–12; J. J. Goring, 'The General Proscription of 1522', *EHR*, 86 (Oct. 1971), 694–5.

33 Gunn, 'French Wars of Henry VIII', pp. 34, 45.

34 *LP*, 6, no. 210.

35 Glanmor Williams, *Wales and the Act of Union*, Bangor, 1992, pp. 8–12, 19–34; Bonner, 'Henry VIII's "Rough Wooing"', 39, 53; Ellis, 'Tudor State Formation', pp. 53, 55;

J. Gwynfor Jones, *Wales and the Tudor State: Government, Religious Change and the Social Order, 1534–1603*, Cardiff, 1989, pp. 6–22, 24–9.

36 S. G. Ellis, *Ireland in the Age of the Tudors, 1447–1603*, London, 1998, pp. 122,143–6; idem, *Tudor Frontiers and Noble Power*, pp. 225–6, 227, 231–2.

37 Ellis, *Ireland, 1447–1603*, pp. 150–2; B. Bradshaw, *The Irish Constitutional Revolution of the Sixteenth Century*, Cambridge, 1979, pp. 194–6.

38 Ibid., pp. 196–219, 254–5, 258–9; Ellis, *Ireland, 1447–1603*, pp. 151–8.

39 Ellis, *Tudor Frontiers and Noble Power*, pp. 246–8; idem, 'Tudor State Formation', pp. 52–5.

40 See above, p. 178; P. R. Roberts, 'Wales and England after the Tudor "Union", 1543–1624', in Cross et al., eds, *Law and Government*, pp. 112–18.

41 His ministers and councillors did not share this enthusiasm: not only Cromwell, but also Paget and others in his last years. Potter, 'Foreign Policy', p. 132.

42 *HLRO, Orig. Acts*, 32 Henry VIII, no. 14; *LP*, 11, no. 705; ibid.,15, no. 498 (p. 216).

43 J. Guy, 'The King's Council and Political Participation', in Fox and Guy, *Reassessing the Henrician Age*, pp. 129–30, 138, 142–3.

44 Gunn, *Duke of Suffolk*, pp. 6–18, 75–6, 183–95.

45 D. Starkey, 'Introduction'; MacCulloch, 'War and Glory'; S. Gunn, 'The King and his Favourite Courtier: The Rise of Charles Brandon, Duke of Suffolk'; S. Gunn, 'The Chief Minister and the Nobles: The Dukes of Norfolk and Suffolk, 1514–1526'; S. Gunn, 'Divorce and Reformation in the Reign of King Henry: The Dukes of Norfolk and Suffolk, 1527–1537'; D. MacCulloch, 'Vain, Proud, Foolish Boy: The Earl of Surrey and the Fall of the Howards', in Starkey, ed., *Rivals in Power*, pp. 9–10, 26–113.

46 D. Loades, *The Tudor Navy*, Aldershot, 1992, pp. 39, 49–50, 53, 55.

47 Ibid., pp. 56,57–60; *Anglica Historia*, pp. 175, 183, 185–9.

48 Ibid., p. 199.

49 The names are significant, denoting monarchy, honouring the king's sister and, in the rose and pomegranate, commemorating the Anglo-Spanish marriage alliance. Similarly the landing barges built in 1511–12 were called *Rose Henry* and *Catherine Pomegranate*. A. Spont, ed., *War with France, 1512–1513*, Navy Records Society, 1897, pp.xiv, xxii, 11, 78.

50 C. S. Knighton and D. M. Loades, eds, *The Anthony Roll of Henry VIII's Navy*, Aldershot, 2000, p. 109; M. Oppenheim, *A History of the Administration of the Royal Navy and of Merchant Shipping, from 1509 to 1660*, London, 1961, p. 49.

51 The 1514 inventory, listed in Knighton and Loades, eds, *The Anthony Roll*, pp. 109–58, consists of thirteen decommissioned ships.

52 *Four Years at the Court of Henry VIII*, 1, p. 138.

53 Oppenheim, pp. 53–6; Loades, *Tudor Navy*, pp. 67–8.

54 D. Loades, 'Henry VIII and the Navy', in Starkey, ed., *A European Court*, pp. 172–3.

55 *LP*, 14 (1), no. 670; W. G. Hoskins, *The Age of Plunder: King Henry's England, 1500–1547*, London, 1976, p. 172.

56 Oppenheim, pp. 50–1; McKee, 'Henry VIII as Military Commander', 24–6. *The Anthony Roll* (pp. 160–67) records thirty-five vessels, including both 'row barges' (or small galleys) and men of war, which, with a tonnage ranging from 20 to 450, were built in 1543–6.

57 J. R. Hale, 'Armies, Navies and the Art of War', in G. R. Elton, ed., *The New Cambridge Modern History*, Vol. 2: *The Reformation, 1520–1559*, Cambridge, 1958, pp. 493–4; Morley, *Henry VIII and Development of Coastal Defence*, pp. 7–19.

58 Loades, *Tudor Navy*, pp. 68, 70; Oppenheim, pp. 68–72.

59 Ibid., pp. 85–7; Loades, *Tudor Navy*, pp. 77–9, 81–8.

60 J. Bald, 'Naval Regulations, c.1530', *Hist. Today*, 41 (1991), 30; Oppenheim, p. 63.

61 Hale, 'Armies, Navies and Art of War', p. 504.

62 *Cal. SP Ven.*, 2, no. 662; Loades, 'Henry VIII and Navy', p. 175.

63 Ellis, ed., *Orig. Letters*, 1 (2), pp. 126–7.

64 Byrne, ed., *Lisle Letters*, 3, p. 440.

65 Loades, 'Henry VIII and Navy', p. 172.

66 Cruickshank, *Army Royal*, pp. 74–6, 145; C. S. L. Davies, 'Henry VIII and Henry V: The Wars in France' in J. L. Watts, ed., *The End of the Middle Ages?*, Stroud, 1998, p. 247.

67 G. Phillips, 'The Army of Henry VIII: A Reassessment', *Journal of the Society for Army Historical Research*, 75 (1997), 11–15, 16; *LP*, 1(2), no. 2391 (p. 1058).

68 Phillips, 'Army of Henry VIII', 22; see above, Chap. 4, p. 67.

69 See above, pp. 179–80.

70 Sybil M. Jack, 'Henry VIII's Attitude towards Royal Finance: Penny Wise and Pound Foolish?', in Giry-Deloison, *Francois 1er et Henri VIII*, pp. 145, 146–8, 149–51, 158–9, 162–3.

71 See above, Chap. 4.

72 D. L. Hamilton, 'The Learned Councils of the Tudor Queens Consort', in C. Carlton, R. L. Woods et al., eds, *State, Sovereigns and Society in Early Modern England: Essays in Honor of A. J. Slavin*, New York, 1998, p. 89.

73 G. R. Elton, 'Introduction', in idem, ed., *New Cambridge Modern History*, 2, p. 13.

74 Guy, *Tudor England*, pp. 190–2; R. Hoyle, 'War and Public Finance', in MacCulloch, ed., *Politics, Policy and Piety*, pp. 77, 85–94; M. Merriman, 'Realm and Castle: Henry VIII as European Builder', *Hist. Today*, 41 (June 1991), 31–7; *LP*, 20 (2), no. 366.

75 Guy, *Tudor England*, pp. 97–102; Bernard, *War, Taxation and Rebellion*, p. 156.

76 Guy, *Tudor England*, pp. 191–2; D. Starkey 'Court and Government' and 'Conclusion: After the Revolution', in Coleman and Starkey, eds, *Revolution Reassessed*, pp. 43–4, 204–5.

77 C. Giry-Deloison, 'Henry VIII pensionnaire de Francois Ier', in idem, ed., *Deux Princes de la Renaissance*, pp. 123–43; Potter, 'Foreign Policy', pp. 125–8.

78 R. Schofield, 'Taxation and the Political Limits of the Tudor State', in Cross et al., eds, *Law and Government*, p. 232; Guy, *Tudor Monarchy*, pp. 228–9; Hoyle, 'War and Public Finance', pp. 92–9; Gunn, *Early Tudor Government*, pp. 129–30; C. E. Challis, 'The

Debasement of the Coinage, 1542–1551', *Econ. HR*, 2nd Ser., 20 (1967), 454–5; J. D. Gould, *The Great Debasement*, Oxford, 1970, pp. 81,151.

79 C. Kitching, 'The Disposal of Monastic and Chantry Lands', in F. Heal and R. O'Day, eds, *Church and Society in England: Henry VIII to James I*, London, 1977, pp. 122–3.

80 Hoyle, 'War and Public Finance', pp. 95–9.

81 Scarisbrick, *Henry VIII*, p. 526.

82 *Anglica Historia*, p. 203.

83 21 Henry VIII *c.*24, *Stats. Realm*, III, pp. 315–16.

84 Hoyle, *Pilgrimage of Grace*, pp. 16–21.

85 Ibid., p. 453.

Chapter 10

Henry's Kingship

Renaissance kingship was characterized by qualities which aroused popular expectations. The monarch supposedly embodied a number of virtues: generosity, expressed in his distribution of favours and his advancement of worthy subjects; his sense of equity, justice, mercy and charity; his defence of the faith; and the prowess and courage of a warrior. In many ways Henry VIII was a characteristic Renaissance Prince. He shone like the sun in a dazzling Court, excelling as musician, scholar and jouster and employing biblical, classical and British imagery to project his virtues.[1] He was even – at least for the first half of the reign – a dutiful son of the Church. But, as the system of government was 'personal monarchy', in other words government by the person of the king, his role was not confined to simple image projection and public performance. It extended far beyond, to personal responsibility for maintenance of law and order, the choice of councillors and ministers, policy-making and administration of the realm. In these, as in all aspects of royal government, the one guaranteed Henrician characteristic was inconsistency.

It is appropriate, therefore, that there has never been anything remotely related to consensus about this king, either amongst historians, or amongst those contemporaries who had the audacity or enjoyed the distant security to speak out. A complicating factor is the way in which Henry's rule and priorities of government changed, especially from the mid-1520s. So A. F. Pollard painted a handsome portrait of a king who 'neither faltered or failed' and who especially cared for his kingdom's 'peace and material comfort'. In contrast the Catholic Philip Hughes, writing specifically on 'the divorce', described Henry's 'active, aggressive, bitter, revengeful blood-thirstiness, the craft, the cruelty, the lies, the royal affectation of piety, the personal resentment that borders on mania'.[2] Should we dismiss such an indictment out of hand? After all, historians have become more critical of Henry since Pollard,[3] although David Starkey has more recently put on the scales 'what the King broke down and what he built up', without handing down a judgement.[4]

Contemporary assessments were diverse. Was he an effective, popular monarch, who used his skills in the effective, beneficial management of his kingdom and people? The problem is that Henry was like a large gold coin, rich and dazzling, but with two faces. He was the versatile, God-fearing, cultivated, benevolent, self-confident and martial king, whom the arch-conservative Bishop Gardiner later remembered as a 'trewe Christen man' and 'wise prince', who would 'neither hurt or inwardly disfavor him that had bene bold with him'.[5] Reformers were naturally ambivalent towards Henry. Nevertheless one notable reformer, John Foxe, presented him as 'a model of virtue for [Queen] Elizabeth to emulate'. Two others, Thomas Becon and Nicholas Udall, praised him variously as a king of 'unmeasurable kindness' and 'singular prudence, . . . a very rare spectacle of humanity . . . [and] a special pattern of clemency and moderation'.[6] Events of the 1530s, however, polarized opinions and caused mounting criticism and condemnation, hostility and resistance, even hatred. Here was a king who slaughtered opponents great and small,[7] whose parliaments enacted forty-four penal statutes in the years 1529–39,[8] who expelled the gypsies and authorized the execution of those who remained,[9] made free use of the 1534 treason law, which allowed conviction on the death of only one witness, and caused monks and friars to suffer the fate of heretics or traitors at Norwich, Glastonbury and elsewhere. Londoners in particular had to suffer repeatedly the smell of fires at Smithfields fuelled by heretics (including John Lambert, who was tormented by the guards with hideous cruelty),[10] and also to witness 'traitors' being drawn on hurdles to Tyburn and then their 'qwarteres with their heddes set up abowte the citte'.[11] Between 1535 and 1547 the Grey Friars Chronicle recorded not only many burnings in London but also more than eighty deaths for treason and twenty-nine for felonies, including 'a mayde boyllyd in Smythfelde for poysonyng'.[12] Under its king 'of clemency and moderation', London lived with the frequent stink of death.

On the other hand, Henry enjoyed a considerable and ongoing reputation amongst many of his subjects. He was an effective public communicator, often visible and accessible, though only within a limited range of the London metropolis and his Home Counties circuit of palaces and hunting lodges – just once, in 1541, did he progress as far north as York. 'Great' achievements also contributed to his reputation. He was the Roman Catholic champion and *Defensor Fidei* who then repudiated the pope. He also 'cut a dash' with great European Princes, notably Charles V and

Francis I, whom he met publicly on what were seen as equal terms. The Venetian ambassador's secretary wrote in 1515 that 'the like of ... two such kings as those of France and of England have, I fancy, not been witnessed by any ambassadors' from Venice for fifty years.'[13] War with the French king for territory was, for Henry, a matter of honour. At the same time, his relationship with Francis fluctuated dramatically 'from undying brotherhood to deadly feud as though they were two knights in a romance'.[14] He also won the occasional battle honour and made a few conquests, such as Tournai and Boulogne. Peace-making too was a matter of honour.[15] The two kings were engaged in a constant competition for Europe's admiration, whilst Henry was also a frequent recipient of a French pension. In such ways did he add to his reputation.[16]

Henry emerged as the dominant ruler in the British Isles. The Franchises Act of 1536 removed private jurisdictions and made them as subject to royal authority as the rest of England. Wales was incorporated into England by statutes in 1536 and 1543. Under Wolsey, regional councils, of fifteenth-century origins, became effective administrative and judicial bodies which governed the north, Wales and the Welsh marches – the more distant parts – for the king. When, in 1541, Henry altered his title from 'lord of Ireland' to 'king', he rejected the Irish claim that his lordship was subordinate to Rome. Now he claimed constitutional authority throughout the British Isles, except for Scotland. A consistent problem, however, for those whom he appointed to advise and govern in his name, was his erratic pattern of conduct. Henry was so often distracted by other pressures, pleasures or priorities. Therefore, for the sake of 'good governance', it was fortunate and important that the king had a keen eye for talent. He displayed a consistent ability to advance men of ability, energy and loyalty: especially his great ministers, Wolsey and Cromwell, but also William Paget, Thomas Wriothesley, Richard Rich and others. In some cases they were groomed by politicians to catch the king's eye, but he had a good eye and so he was well served.

Nevertheless, there were major debits as well as credits. For example, 'He raised talented people to high office', but 'he destroyed them too'. Glenn Richardson puts it succinctly: 'He built much and he destroyed much.'[17] In the process of governing, Henry inflicted great damage upon his dominions, on English society and the economy, and on the future prospects of the Tudor monarchy. Although he was concerned about religious uniformity, especially in his later years, his own inconsistency, fuelled by the influence of Anne Boleyn, Cranmer and Cromwell, Gardiner and the Howards, contributed to continuing religious division. Henry bequeathed a decidedly divided Church to his son. He also destroyed its medieval heritage and plundered it to the advantage of the crown and favoured members of the social elite. The supreme head then wasted his enormous gains on palaces, patronage and especially the offensive and defensive needs of war. According to Gunn, it can be argued that war served important domestic needs. It responded to the Court culture of chivalry and it satisfied the influential men around Henry by rewarding them with military commands (and therefore patronage) and, as with the Howards, titles. Gunn points out, however, that Henry's military commanders were also his amply rewarded peacetime advisers. '[T]hey had no overwhelming interest in urging Henry into war', which was, above all, his costly pathway to glory.[18] It solved nothing and, close to home, it left an Anglo-Scottish legacy of hostility and more war. The fixation with expansion in Britain and Europe also caused Henry to ignore the New World, apart from an early passing interest in the Cabots' North American voyages.

In one other and particularly important respect Henry was not a success, though whether this was a physical, rather than a personal or political, shortcoming cannot be known. It was essential for political stability that a personal monarch should provide a guaranteed succession, preferably male. One young son and two bastardized daughters were a lean harvest after twenty years of matrimonial adventures and the accompanying trail of carnage.

The perpetuation of Henry VIII's public image over the centuries often serves to obscure the harsh realities and harmful effects of his kingship. At the time, however, the successfully projected image of the mighty, majestic, great and glorious, seemingly invincible Tudor had great value. It probably contributed to the remarkable public loyalty both to Henry and, afterwards, through reverential folk memory, to the dynasty in its often difficult, even critical times. There is no doubt about one very positive feature of his kingship: Henry had a remarkable flair for winning and retaining loyalty.

Notes

1 But Scarisbrick regards him rather as 'the last of the troubadors and the heir of Burgundian chivalry'. Idem, *Henry VIII*, p. 16.

2 Pollard, *Henry VIII*, p. 353; P. Hughes, *The Reformation in England*, 3 vols, London, 1952–4, I, p. 156.

3 See above, Chapter 3, p. 28.

4 D. Starkey, 'The Legacy of Henry VIII', in idem, ed., *A European Court*, pp. 8–12.

5 Muller, ed., *Gardiner's Letters*, pp. 287, 374.

6 King, *Tudor Royal Iconography*, pp. 158–60; E. H. Hageman, 'John Foxe's Henry VIII as *Justitia*', *Sixteenth Century Journal*, X, 1 (1979), 42; Strype, *Eccles. Mems*, 1 (1), pp. 602, 604.

7 E.g. Robinson, ed., *Orig. Letters*, I, pp. 219–20.

8 G. R. Elton, 'State Planning in Early Tudor England', *Econ. HR*, 2nd Ser., 13, 3 (1961), 436.

9 Ellis, ed., *Orig. Letters*, I (2), pp. 100–3.

10 Pratt, ed., Foxe, *Acts and Monuments*, V, p. 236.

11 Nichols, ed., *Grey Friars Chronicle*, pp. 38–9.

12 Ibid., pp. 38–53; also Hamilton, ed., Wriothesley, *Chronicle of England*, I, pp. 123–6.

13 *Four Years at the Court of Henry VIII*, 1, p. 79.

14 S. J. Gunn, 'Henry VIII's Foreign Policy and the Tudor Cult of Chivalry', in C. Giry-Deloison, ed., *Deux Princes de la Renaissance*, p. 32

15 Richardson, *Renaissance Monarchy*, pp. 53–9; see Chap. 9, p. 171.

16 S. Beguin, "Henri VIII et François Ier, une rivalité artistique et diplomatique', and Giry-Deloison, 'Henri VIII pensionnaire de François Ier', in idem, ed., *Deux Princes de la Renaissance*, pp. 63–75, 121–43.

17 Richardson, *Renaissance Monarchy*, p. 196.

18 Gunn, 'Henry VIII's Foreign Policy', pp. 28–32.

Further Reading

As explained in Chapter 1, this book is neither a biography nor regnal history, but, as the sub-title indicates, a study of kingship as practised by one Renaissance Prince. Its particular concerns include Henry's conception of his authority, his image projection, ambition and the techniques which he employed in order to exercise effective government. It also examines the changes which, on his own initiative or at the prompting of others, he carried through. Such changes were designed to sustain and reinforce a Prince's power. He remained, nonetheless, a limited monarch. The existing biographical literature and regnal histories constitute a vital critical source for such a study of kingship. A number of major biographical studies and histories of early modern England, in which historians have offered their critical assessments of Henry VIII, have been discussed in Chapter 3 (pp. 26–8 above). There is, however, a formidable library of such works, because Henry has always had – and continues to have – a seemingly irresistible fascination for both historians and the general reading public.

Once the Tudors had gone, with the death of Henry's daughter Queen Elizabeth I and the accession of the Scottish King James VI as James I of England, biographies and English histories in which he figured began to appear in print. Doubtless it was safer then to publish critical evaluations, unfavourable assessments and harsh words about controversial 'Great Harry'. The published works of William Camden, Sir Walter Ralegh and Edward Lord Herbert of Cherbury have already been considered above. Others include the *Annals of England: containing the reigns of Henry the Seventh, Henry the Eighth, Edward the Sixth, and Queen Mary,* written by Francis Godwin, bishop of Hereford (1676), and *Modal [= Model] for the French king* (1682). Sometimes authors looked back nostalgically to Henry as an heroic and godly Prince: for example, the sub-title of *Modal* was *The memorable acts of Henry the Eight: extirpating popery and introducing the Protestant religion.* In a more secular age, however, the 'extirpation of popery' was no longer seen as the mark of a virtuous king. (And, it should be added, the anonymous author above misread Henry and his reign when he attributed to him the founding of a Protestant

Church.) Although some historians of the nineteenth and twentieth centuries, most notably J. A. Froude and A. F. Pollard, remained favourably inclined towards Henry, others, such as G. R. Elton and J. J. Scarisbrick, were harshly critical, even condemnatory.

Perhaps more significant, the king's role was reassessed to his disadvantage. Central, indeed dominant, in this re-assessment was Elton, who re-shaped our understanding of the nature, meaning and purpose of the changes which occurred in the crucial decade of the 1530s. According to Elton, during those years, when the Church broke with Rome, the State also underwent a bureaucratic revolution. Furthermore, the architect and driving force of these dramatic changes was not the king but his chief minister, Thomas Cromwell. In *The Tudor Revolution in Government* (Cambridge, 1953), *England under the Tudors* (London, 1955), 'King or Minister? The Man behind the Henrician Reformation', *History*, new series, 39 (1954), 216–32, 'The Political Creed of Thomas Cromwell', *TRHS*, 5th series, 6 (1956), 69–92 and other works, Elton developed, expounded and rounded out this interpretation. But it was clearly unacceptable to some historians. In a rather inconclusive set-piece debate in the journal *Past and Present*, Geoffrey Elton was challenged by Penry Williams and G. L. Harriss (*PP*, 25 (1963), 3–58), he replied (*PP*, 29 (1964), 26–49), and further responses followed (*PP*, 31 (1965), 87–96 and 32 (1965), 103–9). During the 1980s there were much sharper exchanges between former teacher and ex-student, Elton and David Starkey (Elton, 'A New Age of Reform?', *HJ*, 30 (1987), 709–16 and Starkey, 'A Reply: Tudor Government: the Facts?', *HJ*, 31 (1988), 921–31). Starkey's criticism was also central to *Revolution Reassessed. Revisions in the History of Tudor Government and Administration*, published in Oxford in 1986 and co-edited by Christopher Coleman and Starkey. At the end of the book Starkey concluded, 'Tudor re-adjustment in government indeed, but no revolution.'

Starkey's own research work was on an important development in Henry VIII's Court. The subject of his Cambridge PhD (1973) was 'The King's Privy Chamber, 1485–1547' and it is regrettable that it has not been published. The reconstructed privy chamber and the creation of the office of gentleman of the privy chamber transformed it into an important and very influential political institution. Fortunately Starkey has utilized his thesis in his essay 'Intimacy and Innovation: The Rise of the Privy Chamber, 1485–1547' in *The English Court from the Wars of the Roses to the Civil War* (London, 1987), a collection of essays which he also edited. This work is symptomatic of a very important literature which has been generated in the past twenty years by historians' recognition of the significant place of the Court in government and politics. As early as 1976 Elton signalled the way ahead in his three published lectures on 'Points of Contact: I. Parliament; II. The Council; and III. The Court' (*TRHS*, 5th series, 24 (1974), 183–200; 25 (1975), 195–211; 26 (1976), 211–28). Since then, works ranging from A. G. Dickens, ed., *The Courts of Europe: Politics, Patronage and Royalty, 1400–1800* (London, 1977) to D. M. Loades, *The Tudor Court* (London, 1986 and Bangor 1992) and A. Weir, *Henry VIII: The King and His Court* (London, 2001) illustrate a fascination with the Renaissance Court. Two works in particular mine and put on display the artifacts of Henrician kingship and the Court:

1 D. Starkey, ed., *Henry VIII: A European Court in England*, London, 1991. This was produced for the Greenwich exhibition which, in 1991, commemorated the 500th anniversary of King Henry's birth.
2 Idem, ed., *The Inventory of King Henry VIII: The Transcript: Society of Antiquaries MS 129 and British Library MS Harley 1419*, London, 1998. In 1547 commissioners were ordered to 'list the contents of the King's houses and to note where and in whose charge the goods were deposited' (p. xix). The volume is a cornucopia of crucifixes, images, pots, cups, bowls, 'saltes' and 'juelles' of gold, 'rich hanginges of clothe', arras and tapestries, furniture and cushions, armouries, 'ordenaunce artillery' and 'cloth of silver checked with silke [and] damaske worke'.

Other works deal with the culture, artistic reputation and iconography of king and Court, the role and significance of ceremonies – and, in some cases, their relation with contemporary politics. For example: (1) S. Anglo, *Images of Tudor Kingship*, London, 1992; (2) John N. King, *Tudor Royal Iconography: Literature and Art in an Age of Religious Crisis*, Princeton, 1989; (3) J. Loach, 'The Function of Ceremonial in the Reign of Henry VIII', *Past and Present*, 142 (1994), 43–68; (4) R. Strong, *The Tudor and Stuart Monarchy: Pageantry, Painting, Iconography: I. Tudor*, Woodbridge, Suffolk, 1995, especially pp. 1–85; (5) S. Thurley and C. Lloyd, *Henry VIII: Images of a Tudor King*, Oxford, 1990; (6) G. Walker, *Persuasive Fictions: Faction, Faith and Political Culture in the Reign of Henry VIII*, Aldershot, 1996, especially Chapter 3; (7) idem, *Plays of Persuasion: Drama and Politics at the Court of Henry VIII*, Cambridge, 1991.

Those interested in the naval history of Henry VIII's reign should read C. S. Knighton and David Loades, *Letters from the Mary Rose*, Stroud, 2002. Two-thirds of the book are devoted to the history of the vessel from its building to its sinking. This also provides a vehicle for the story of the naval campaigns in which the Mary Rose took part. The volume is handsomely illustrated.

In the near future there will be a very important addition to the secondary literature on Henry VIII. The *New Dictionary of National Biography* is a University of Oxford project funded by the British Academy and Oxford University Press. It replaces the original *D[ictionary of] N[ational] B[iography]*, which was published at the end of the nineteenth century. The biographies in the original *DNB* have either been revised or completely re-written and other names have been added. In addition to Henry, his wives, ministers, prominent nobles and clergy, there are, amongst the 50,100 entries in the *New* edition, many revised, rewritten or additional biographies of those who were significant and/or important in his reign. The publication date of the new DNB is 2004.

Index